The King of Romance
A Portrait of Alexandre Dumas

The King of Romance

A Portrait of
ALEXANDRE DUMAS

F. W. J. HEMMINGS

Hamish Hamilton
London

First published in Great Britain 1979
by Hamish Hamilton Limited
Garden House, 57/59 Long Acre, London WC2E 9JZ

Copyright © 1979 by F. W. J. Hemmings

British Library Cataloguing in Publication Data
Hemmings, Frederic William John
    The king of romance.
    1. Dumas, Alexandre, b.1802—Biography
    2. Authors, French—19th century—Biography
    I. Title
    843'.7   PQ2230
    ISBN 0-241-10264-2

Printed in Great Britain by
Ebenezer Baylis & Son Ltd
The Trinity Press, Worcester, and London.

Contents

Contents

List of Illustrations

1 Roots

Alexandre Dumas inherited a surname already made famous by his father, a general in the armies of the First Republic, but not borne by his father's father, who was called Alexandre-Antoine Davy de la Pailleterie. The question how the name Dumas came into the family leads straight to the heart of an obscure and tangled imbroglio with all the elements of sibling rivalry and long-lost heirs that the novelist himself, had he had any inkling of it, would have recognized as a heaven-sent plot for one of his own best-selling romances.

The Davys were an old but undistinguished and not very well connected family of Norman squires, who had held the manor of La Pailleterie uninterruptedly since about the middle of the sixteenth century; the first Sieur de la Pailleterie, a certain Pierre Davy, died around 1575. It was his great-grandson in direct line of descent, one Alexandre Davy, who became lord of the manor in 1709 and, marrying shortly after, founded a family of three sons and three daughters, the eldest being the aforementioned Alexandre-Antoine, the novelist's grandfather, born in 1714. The rules of primogeniture as applied in eighteenth-century France meant that it was this boy who could be expected to inherit the greater part of the estate at the death of his father; but there is little doubt that the fortunes of the family would have been better entrusted to his brother Charles, born two years later. Alexandre-Antoine was a feckless voluptuary, though not devoid of acumen where his private interests were concerned. Charles, on the other hand, was an energetic, enterprising man, extremely ambitious and prepared to work hard to see his ambitions fulfilled.

Both boys, as soon as they were of age, joined the army. Neither had any inclination to enter the Church, and to take the king's commission was, under the *ancien régime*, about the only respectable alternative for the sons of the minor nobility. Alexandre-Antoine became an officer of artillery; Charles joined a brigade of marines destined for service in the French colony of San-Domingo. This was tantamount to a decision to emigrate. Although barely turned sixteen, Charles felt he could never stand the tedious and narrow life of a regimental officer stationed at home; he had visions of settling overseas as a gentleman farmer or merchant venturer, and eventually building up a fortune.

The island of San-Domingo, today divided between the Dominican

Republic and Haiti, had originally been discovered by Columbus, who named it Hispaniola or Little Spain in honour of the land of his adoption. Ceded to France under the terms of the Treaty of Ryswick, it remained one of the most valued overseas possessions of the French crown down to the Revolution. The land was highly fertile, for it was only at a later period that deforestation of the interior brought about the soil impoverishment which today makes Haiti one of the poorest countries in the Western hemisphere. At the beginning of the century a variety of tropical crops had been planted: tobacco, cotton, sugar, cocoa and, after 1730, coffee. But disease wiped out the cocoa-trees and competition from Virginia and Maryland ruined the market for tobacco. There remained cotton and, even more important, sugar and coffee; the continent of Europe depended on San-Domingo for the bulk of its supplies of these two commodities. Sixty per cent of French overseas trade was with this one colony, and before the Revolution a fleet of 600 merchantmen crossed and recrossed the Atlantic, their holds stuffed with the bales of island produce.[1]

Charles Davy spent his first six years on the island eating his heart out as a penniless subaltern; without capital, he saw no possibility of starting any of the business enterprises of which he dreamed. Then his opportunity came: he proposed marriage to a young woman with title-deeds to a sound property, and was accepted. Marie Tuffé, born in San-Domingo, was an orphan; the sugar plantation she owned was situated at a spot called Le Trou de Jacquezy, in the north of the island. By the strangest of chances, the nearest township bore—and bears to this day—the name of Monte Cristo which a century later his grand-nephew was to make famous throughout the world when he incorporated it in the title of one of his most widely read novels. Alexandre Dumas, however, was not thinking of this remote spot in the Dominican Republic, of which he quite possibly had never heard, but of a tiny Mediterranean island just south of Elba.

The same year that Charles got married his elder brother, Alexandre-Antoine, having resigned the service, arrived in San-Domingo ostensibly to help the younger run his estate. The newly married couple made him heartily welcome at first. The life led by the white planters was a harsh and often lonely one. They were obliged to spend most of the year on their estates, since the raising, harvesting, and processing of the crops needed constant attention. With the horse-drawn cart the only method of transport, visits to any of the larger towns involved several days' travel, and were in consequence only undertaken for pressing reasons of business, to arrange the sale of produce or to purchase a fresh batch of slaves in place of those that had died under the overseers' whips. Journeys were, in any case, never lightly to be embarked on, since anywhere along the road the traveller risked being ambushed by bands of marauding maroons, escaped slaves who had taken to the hills and resisted all the attempts of the militiamen to ferret them out and exterminate them. Whether working in gangs on the plantations or hiding in the jungle, the blacks outnumbered the whites ten to one, and the latter were able to stay in control only by the use of intimidation and systematic brutality.

As a general rule they kept strictly aloof from the slaves who worked in the fields or performed domestic duties indoors. Racial segregation was official policy, and had indeed been enshrined in the Code Noir, the French law regulating conditions of work and life in the colony. But there must always have been some Europeans who disregarded its provisions, since otherwise there would be no explaining the presence on the island of a sizeable population of mulattoes, hated by the blacks because they were widely employed as slave-drivers, and looked down on by the white landowners, the *grands blancs*, because of their mixed origins.

Over the ten years during which the brothers Davy lived and worked side by side in San-Domingo, the younger, Charles, grew steadily richer and more respected, patiently adding one piece of land to another until his plantation became one of the most important in that part of the island; while the elder fell into habits of indolence and, worse, started fraternizing with the blacks on the estate. Dissension between the two brothers flared into a sudden, violent quarrel in 1748. If they did not actually come to blows, enough was said to cause Alexandre, the weaker character, to take fright. Secretly, he made off into the hinterland, taking with him three of his brother's slaves, two negroes and a woman who went under the offensive name of Catin (whore).

Charles alerted the authorities, and an official inquiry was set afoot; but in this ill-policed colony a man who wanted to disappear had no real difficulty in doing so. Up to a point he felt relieved at being rid of his lazy, good-for-nothing brother; but the fact remained that Alexandre was the elder, and Charles could not help worrying about what was likely to happen at their father's death if the rightful heir were still absent.

Meanwhile, he continued as before, extending his holdings by careful purchase until, in 1752, an inventory shows him to have owned no fewer than 191 slaves (114 male, 59 female, and 18 children under age).[2] Shortly afterwards, however, he developed gout. The medical advice was that he could only mend in a more temperate climate, and accordingly he returned to France with his family, leaving a steward in charge of his sugar plantation. He bought an estate near Montargis, just south of Paris, established his right to the title of marquis, and when, five years later, in 1758, his father died at the ripe age of eighty-four it was Charles who, his brother being now presumed dead, entered into possession of the ancestral title and lands.

Materially, however, his fortunes had passed their zenith. Since his arrival in France, the profits from the sugar plantation had steadily fallen off; other business ventures turned out badly, while the purchase of the Montargis estate and a town-house in Paris ate deeply into his savings. He had one final triumph: his only child, a daughter born in San-Domingo, was asked for in marriage by a man belonging to the highest aristocracy, Comte de Léon Maulde. The marriage contract was signed at Versailles in the presence of the royal family. None of the Davys had ever risen to such dizzy social heights before. But Charles's satisfaction was short-lived. Financial disasters continued to beset him until, regretfully, he decided to return to his neglected estate at Le Trou and try to use it as a basis for restoring his fortunes. It was in 1771 that he returned to the colony; two years later, a final attack of his old illness carried him off.

The lawyers in France were still trying to sort out the complicated tangle of the family inheritance when a traveller from San-Domingo disembarked at Le Havre and announced himself as none other than the long-lost elder son, Alexandre-Antoine. His credentials proved unassailable, and on December 23rd, 1775, he was ceremoniously welcomed back at the Château de la Pailleterie as the rightful heir. His reappearance, after an absence of twenty-seven years during which he had never given a sign of life to any of his relatives, was a nine days' wonder, which his reticence about his past activities did nothing to dispel. Such few facts as became known derived from the inquiries which his niece's husband, Léon de Maulde, made privately of various administrative officers in the colony after the prodigal's return.

When in 1748 Alexandre-Antoine disappeared into the interior, taking with him his black concubine Catin and two male slaves belonging to his brother, he appears to have worked his way over to the west of the island, eventually arriving at the coastal settlement of Jérémie, situated on the extreme end of the promontory in modern Haiti which points like a finger across the sea to Jamaica. It was a well-watered spot, covered with luxuriant vegetation, where the mountains marched down almost to the coast; the harbour was usually busy, there being considerable maritime traffic to Port-au-Prince and Cap-Haïtien. Here the fugitive, who to avoid discovery and apprehension had taken the name of Antoine Delisle, rented a small allotment and settled down to till it with his stolen labour force.

For a while he prospered; then his fecklessness and dissolute habits forced him to give up his smallholding. He raised some cash by selling off his brother's slaves, and spent most of it in the acquisition of another black girl who must have been of unusual beauty, since Léon de Maulde's informant mentions that he paid 'an exorbitant price' for her.[3] She was called Marie-Cessette Dumas. Although slaves were still being transported in shiploads from the Guinea coast—the appallingly high death-rate in the plantations kept up the demand for new labour, which could only come from Africa—it is likely that Cessette had been born in Haiti, and that her surname Dumas was that of her or her father's original owner, some hard-faced French colonist who could never have dreamed that it would be through this despised piece of chattel-flesh that his name would be perpetuated and achieve world-wide fame in the following century.

Over the next twenty years or so the heir to the name and estate of La Pailleterie eked out a poor livelihood by one or other of half a dozen trades, as ship's chandler, broker's clerk, bailiff or overseer, a 'poor white' despised by his fellow countrymen for having 'gone native'. Marie-Cessette bore him one child after another: first a son, Adolphe, then two girls, christened Jeannette and Marie-Rose, and finally, on March 25th, 1762, another boy, Thomas-Alexandre. It was this last who was to father in his turn the novelist Alexandre Dumas.

Ten years after the birth of this second son, Marie-Cessette died. About the same time Alexandre-Antoine Davy, alias M. Delisle, got word of his brother's death the year before at Le Trou and, taking one thing with another, decided it was safe for him to come out of hiding, return to France and claim his inheritance. There was no question of taking his illegitimate half-caste family with him; nor could they be left to fend for themselves, being too young and besides, as mulattoes born in slavery, enjoying no civil rights in the colony. So he left them, all except the youngest, in Jérémie, entrusting them to a certain Caron, a native of Nantes, on whom he could rely to treat them well. In order to make the transaction legal, a fictitious sale was arranged. So Adolphe Dumas and the two girls remained in Haiti where it is not impossible that their distant descendants are living to this day, though in the absence of records and registers on that troubled island, one can only speculate about this. What seems certain is that Alexandre Dumas never realized he had an uncle and aunts, and possibly coloured cousins, living in the West Indies, his father never having chosen to mention the fact.

Thomas-Alexandre might well have been left behind too, were it not that his sixty-year-old father seems to have developed a special liking for the boy, his Benjamin. He took him as far as Port-au-Prince and there sold him to a ship's captain in return for his own passage-money, but with the express proviso that the man would keep the fifteen-year-old mulatto with him and put him on a ship to France as soon as his father had sent the necessary money. This happened, of course, once Alexandre-Antoine had succeeded in establishing his identity and entering into possession of the ancestral estates.

It soon became apparent that the new Marquis de La Pailleterie had no plans to end his days in edifying retirement; encroaching old age had no power to diminish his appetite for pleasure, any more than it would his grandson's, as we shall see in the last chapter of this book. He plunged straight into a life of wild dissipation, firstly at Lisieux and then, when his debts there became too troublesome, at Saint-Germain-en-Laye, a town where a number of retired colonials had settled. He did not neglect his son's education, however, and when Thomas-Alexandre, now generally known as Thomas de La Pailleterie, was of age he agreed to set him up in a modest establishment in Paris. The son whom, in course of time, Thomas-Alexandre was to father in his turn describes him as having, at this period, 'that bronzed complexion, those velvety brown eyes and straight nose which are met with only in those of mingled West Indian and Caucasian blood. His teeth were white, his lips curled attractively, his head sat well on powerful shoulders; further, although full five feet nine inches tall,[4] he had hands and feet as small as a woman's. It was his foot in particular that damned his mistresses, for it seldom happened that their slippers would not fit him.'[5]

His conquests were, no doubt, numerous; he was moving in the same society as Choderlos de Laclos wrote about in his *Liaisons dangereuses*, that bland exposure of the elegant immorality practised by the young bloods of Louis XVI's reign. Though no malignant Valmont—there was nothing diabolical about Thomas who was, now as at all times of his life, a generous-hearted, uncomplicated man—he had been taken straight from a semi-barbarous tropical island and plunged with scarcely any transition into the *fêtes galantes* of the most debauched capital city in Europe; he would have needed to possess a veritable vocation for the ascetic life not to have wanted to taste to the full the pleasures it offered. However, his ambiguous status as a nobleman's bastard son, of mixed race and moreover slave-born, meant that the fops of the town were not prepared to do more than tolerate him in their society. One incident in particular, which happens to be well documented, illustrates the point.

On September 15th, 1784, Thomas took his current mistress, a creole beauty, with him to one of the more disreputable Paris theatres, an establishment on the Boulevard du Temple run by a certain Jean-Baptiste Nicolet and specializing in low farce. During the interval a member of the audience swaggered up to his lady-companion and started making insulting proposals to her. The young woman replied with some indignation that she had not come unescorted to the theatre; hearing this, the man grinned and, quizzing Thomas, exclaimed in mock-apology: 'The mistake is mine; I took the fellow to be your lackey.' This was more than the young mulatto could stand; he protested hotly, whereupon the ruffian, who as it subsequently emerged

was an infantry major attached to a regiment in Martinique, turned on
him threateningly, shouting: 'My friend, I know a half-breed when I
see one. In our country, you would be fettered hand and foot. If you
dare add another word, I'll have you arrested and put in a cell.' Thomas
defied him to do his worst, but at this juncture another man in the
major's party raised his cane shouting: 'Arrest him!' and, gripping him
by the wrist, told him to kneel and ask forgiveness in the presence of
the lady. She, however, left the theatre without waiting to see the outcome and Thomas returned to his box, trembling with rage.[6]

The episode must have impressed on him how insecure his situation
was, labouring as he did under the double disadvantage of illegitimate
birth and membership of a despised race. Trained to no particular
profession, with no friends to help him embark on a career, he depended
entirely on his father's good will, and even that was placed in jeopardy
when the old marquis, to his horrified amazement, announced that he
was going to get married. His bride, Marie-Françoise-Elisabeth Retou,
was aged thirty-three; he had just turned seventy. The offspring of
humble villagers, she and her sister had come to Saint-Germain looking
for work as domestic servants and the marquis had engaged her as
housekeeper. Thomas-Alexandre was seriously put out; he refused to
attend the wedding, after an unpleasant scene with his father who told
him flatly he would no longer support him in idleness. The young man
took the only course open to him: he declared he would join the army
and secure his independence that way; and, rather than allow his
father to purchase him a commission, he would enlist as a private
soldier. The marquis, remembering that he had served in his youth as
an artillery officer, made no attempt to dissuade his headstrong son
from joining up; but he did insist that, if he was to serve in the ranks,
he should not use the aristocratic family name. So, as a subtle reproach
to the stiff old man, he adopted the surname of the poor black slave-
girl who had borne him, and proceeded to cover it with glory in the
ensuing wars. The name Davy de la Pailleterie died when his father
died, on June 15th, 1786, a bare fortnight after the son enlisted in the
Queen's Dragoons.

Three years later the fall of the Bastille marked the beginning of the
French Revolution. Cavalryman Dumas, at that time, was stationed at
Soissons, and one day in August 1789 his squadron received orders to
ride over to the nearby town of Villers-Cotterêts, the local detachment
of the National Guard having sent a request for reinforcements. This
was the summer of the Great Fear, when bands of starving peasants
were roaming the countryside, pillaging food-stores and sacking un-
defended manor-houses. Villers-Cotterêts boasted a handsome renaissance château, the property of the Orléans family, and a very likely
target for one of these attacks. Earlier in the century, during the regency

of Philippe d'Orléans, it had been the scene of disgraceful orgies: Saint-Simon, in his memoirs, tells of riotous supper-parties at which the guests, men and women alike, all caroused stark naked. But in 1789 all this was no more than a memory conserved by the older inhabitants of Villers-Cotterêts. It was a prosperous little town, situated at a distance of some fifty miles by road from Paris, in lovely forest country. Normally, in summertime, the court aristocracy flocked there, the favoured few staying at the château, the others at any of the thirty-odd hostelries in the town.

The proprietor of one of these inns, L'Ecu, was also the local defence commander, and it was he who had sent off the request for army reinforcements. In his younger days this man, Claude Labouret, had served as majordomo in the household of the Duc d'Orléans; now he was the father of a grown-up family, a man of substance, much respected by his fellow citizens, and it naturally fell to him to arrange the billeting of the dragoons on their arrival. His daughter, Marie-Louise-Elisabeth, then aged twenty, described the occasion in a letter to a girl-friend written two days later. 'The men have been made welcome in this house and that. My father made his choice of a coloured man in the detachment. He is very nice. He is called Dumas. His comrades say that is not his real name. According to them, he is the son of a lord in San-Domingo or thereabouts. He is as tall as cousin Prévost but has finer manners. You see, my dear, kind Julie, that he is a handsome young man.'[7] What Julie could chiefly see, reading between the lines of this school-girlish letter, was that her friend was already more than a little in love with this 'coloured man' with his refined manners and exotic origins. As for Dumas, he had by now sown his wild oats; banishing memories of the fashionable light-o'-loves in Paris and the coarser camp-followers who had succeeded them, he decided that this simple, rosy-cheeked innkeeper's daughter would give him just the sheet-anchor he needed in the roving life he was leading. Within a few weeks, the two had reached an understanding. Claude Labouret was content, asking only that they should wait until his future son-in-law had won his corporal's stripe.

Two and a half years elapsed before this condition was fulfilled but then, war having broken out, several more months passed before the soldier could return to Villers-Cotterêts and claim his bride. By this time he had already attained commissioned rank and thereafter promotion, so slow in peace-time, proceeded at a dizzy pace. He was married on November 28th, 1792, spending a seventeen-day honeymoon at the Hôtel de l'Ecu; by January 10th, 1793, he was already in command of a regiment and six months later he achieved the rank of brigadier-general. The emigration of so many royalist officers, depleting the higher echelons of the army, partly accounts for the phenomenal transformation in Dumas's fortunes; but his reputation as an intrepid leader in battle, first demonstrated during the French invasion of the Netherlands, was the main reason for his rapid progress up the ladder of promotion. One of the relics of this period, preserved by his son long after his death, was an Austrian musket split down the middle of the barrel and only held together by two bent fragments of iron. Dumas had been leading his men across a field of tall rye in which, unknown to them, a force of Dutch infantry had taken cover. Suddenly, at no more than fifteen yards' distance, he saw one of the enemy taking aim at his chest. Quicker on the draw than anyone, Dumas pulled his cavalry pistol from its holster and fired, with such deadly accuracy that his bullet went straight up the muzzle of the Dutchman's gun.

His first assignment as army commander was to take charge of the French forces in the south-west, the Convention having declared war on Spain in March 1793. But down on the Pyrenean frontier he was given only a lukewarm reception; the local politicos would have preferred a man of more extreme revolutionary views, for although no one could doubt the purity of his republican convictions, Dumas's reputation was that of a moderate. The building allocated to him as headquarters in Bayonne overlooked the city square where the guillotine had been set up; it was observed, however, that on the days appointed for the execution of enemies of the Republic, the general ordered all the shutters to be closed on that side of the building from which the scaffold could be seen. For this he earned the dangerous nickname 'Monsieur l'Humanité'.

The following year he displayed his disapproval of unnecessary bloodshed in an even more incautious manner; this time, the incident resulted in his being denounced and charged under the *loi des suspects*. Fortunately it took place a long way from Paris, in the little town of Saint-Maurice just south of the Lake of Geneva, and news travelled slowly in those days. Dumas had been on his way to take command of the Army of the Alps. Seeing a scaffold freshly erected on the market-place, he inquired about the pending execution, and was told that four men had been sentenced to death for attempting to stop the local church bells from being melted down; the Convention had made this a capital offence, both because it betrayed criminal sympathies for the old and now proscribed religion and because, in any case, the metal in the bells was badly needed for founding cannon for the armies of the Revolution. It was mid-winter and Dumas, on the pretence that he needed fuel for his camp-fire, ordered his men to break up the scaffold; worse, he cut the bonds of the convicted felons and told them to make themselves scarce.

Information was laid with the Committee of Public Safety and six months later General Dumas was handed an order, signed by Collot d'Herbois, requiring him to return immediately to Paris and stand trial. But in the meantime he had won a resounding victory over the Piedmontese in the Alps. The enemy had established a redoubt on Mount Cenis from which it was essential to dislodge them if the eastern frontier was to remain sealed. Dumas had had no earlier experience of mountain warfare; he started by making friends with the local chamois hunters and accompanying them on their expeditions. In this way he was able personally to reconnoitre the terrain around Mount Cenis and draw up his plan. This involved carrying out feints up the three most accessible approaches while, having engaged the enemy's attention in this way, he would personally lead a picked detachment up a sheer slope, deemed impregnable by the Piedmontese and left unguarded apart from a stout wooden palissade round the cliff top.

Before launching the assault, he got each of his men to camouflage himself by donning a white cotton nightcap and pulling a nightshirt over his uniform. Then he issued a warning that if anyone lost his footing on the precipice, it would be impossible to come to his rescue; there would therefore be no point in his shouting out, since this would not save him and would only betray the presence of the rest of them to the defending garrison on the summit. In the event, three of the climbers slipped and fell during the ascent; the others could hear the dull thud of their bodies rebounding from boulder to boulder, but not one of the three let out a cry.

Thus the force was able to reach the top undetected; they were then confronted with the tall fence the Piedmontese had erected. Fearing that, if they were to climb over, the shaking of the posts might alert some guard, Dumas grabbed each of his men by the collar and the seat of his breeches and threw him over bodily; the soft snow on the other side cushioned his fall. This feat of strength was nothing to a man of whom it was related that, reining in his heavy cavalry horse under the beam of a barn, he was capable of gripping it with his two arms interlocked and, by twisting his legs under the horse's belly, raise the animal clear from the ground.

The surprise attack was completely successful: taken by the rear, the Piedmontese put up only a half-hearted resistance, and within the hour the tricolour was flying over Mount Cenis. News of this exploit preceded Dumas to Paris and in any case, by the time he arrived—for he responded with no over-zealous alacrity to Collot d'Herbois's summons—Robespierre had fallen and the case against Dumas was dropped.

At the end of 1794 he was granted a much overdue furlough which he spent at Villers-Cotterêts. He now had an infant daughter, Marie-Alexandrine-Aimée, born on September 10th, 1793, some ten months after his marriage. The reunion with his wife was to result in the birth of another daughter who, however, died before she was a year old, in February 1797. The funeral took place in the absence of the infant's father who at that time was far away fighting under Bonaparte in the brilliant campaign waged in North Italy that winter.

He first met the new commander-in-chief, with whom his relations were to pass through such disastrous vicissitudes, at his headquarters in Milan on October 19th, 1796. Bonaparte gave him a cordial welcome, and his consort Joséphine an affectionate one. Having been born and brought up in Martinique, she took great delight in exchanging reminiscences with this good-looking officer about life in the Caribbean settlements. But Bonaparte's business was war, not social dalliance. His orders from the Directors in Paris were to consolidate his conquests in North Italy by invading Tuscany and forcing the Pope to acknowledge French supremacy. This meant crossing the River Po, and an essential step in the operation was to take Mantua, where there was a strong Austrian garrison which it would have been foolhardy to leave in the rear of the French army moving south.

In December General Dumas found himself stationed at Marmirolo, in command of one of the divisions investing Mantua. On Christmas Eve a detachment brought in a civilian whom they had caught trying to enter the besieged city. The fellow had a plausible story: he was living in Mantua, had slipped out to spend the night with his sweetheart in one of the neighbouring villages, and had been apprehended as he was trying to return. Nothing was found in his pockets to suggest that he might be an Austrian agent, but to satisfy himself, Dumas had him stripped. When it was obvious the man was concealing nothing on his person, he was about to give him leave to put on his clothes when a smirk on the prisoner's face made him change his mind. Throwing him across the table, he shouted to his aide to fetch the regimental butchers who arrived straight from their work of cutting up carcasses, with their aprons all bloody and their knives and hack-saws stuck in their belts. 'Either he'll tell us where his dispatches are, or we'll open him up and see for ourselves,' he thundered. The threat, which one can be sure would never actually have been carried out, was uttered with enough conviction to break the prisoner's nerve. He confessed he was carrying a message for Wurmser, the commander of the Mantuan garrison, which had been written on a scrap of paper and sealed in a small box coated with wax. His orders had been to swallow it if there were any danger the French might intercept it.

A powerful purgative was administered, and the wretched man spent the early hours squatting on a chamber-pot under the watchful eyes of the sergeant of the guard. The tiny box, when retrieved, was found to contain a letter informing Wurmser when he might expect the relief force to arrive; the message even indicated the route they would follow. Dumas sent his second-in-command, Dermoncourt,[8] to ride hell for leather back to Milan with the captured document. Bonaparte, once Dermoncourt had told him how it had been procured, let out a guffaw and shouted for his aide. 'Take a good sniff at that, Berthier,' he said, handing him the paper, 'and tell me what it smells of.' 'Why, General,' Berthier replied, 'it smells of shit.' 'Right first time,' Napoleon answered, and burst out laughing again.

But the future Emperor had a short memory for help received, and a long one for acts that displeased him. Only a few weeks later, a terse letter of protest Dumas sent him brought about his fall from favour. The Austrian forces in Mantua finally capitulated on February 4th, 1797, but before this happened, Marshal Wurmser led his men on a desperate sortie to try and break the ring of iron. Dumas's troops, outnumbered three to one, bore the brunt of this attack and stood their ground; but in the official report on the engagement he was given no credit for his steadiness, and complained about this bitterly in a message to the commander-in-chief remarkable for the soldierly crudeness of its language. After this he was attached in a subordinate capacity to Joubert, who had his headquarters at Trent, in the Tyrol mountains. It was a demotion, though whether inflicted by reason of his blunt manner in addressing his superiors, or whether because Bonaparte judged him to be lacking the qualities needed for high command, it is hard to say.

Certainly there is nothing in Dumas's army career to suggest that he had a strategist's gifts, though the manner of his capture of the Mount Cenis redoubt shows that he possessed to the full the skills of the military tactician. But he was above all a fearless fighter, achieving prodigies in hand-to-hand combat; something demonstrated time and again in the march on Bolzano, undertaken in the spring of 1797. The manoeuvre was part of a general advance on Vienna ordered by Bonaparte in defiance of the instructions of the timorous Directors in Paris. Dumas rode like a demon up the hilly road, always in hot pursuit of the retreating Austrians, among whom he was already a dread legend; they called him the Black Devil (*der schwarze Teufel*) with reference to the darkness of his complexion by which he could always be recognized. He was for ever at the head of his troops, spurring his horse to catch up with the enemy, more like one of Charlemagne's doughty champions falling on the fleeing Moors than a cavalry officer carrying out his field commander's orders in a modern European army. On one occasion, being well mounted, and a long way ahead of the French vanguard, he was brought to a halt at a bridge from which all the planks had been removed. The Tyrolese, seeing the Black Devil all alone, rallied and directed their fire on him, hitting and killing his horse in the first burst. Dumas flung himself into a ditch, where he found a quantity of loaded muskets discarded by the panic-stricken soldiers. Posting himself behind a fir-tree, he opened a deadly fusillade, keeping the enemy at bay until his own men could rejoin him.

Finally he rode into Brixen (Bressanone) on a captured Austrian horse and Dermoncourt, seeing him stagger into his quarters as pale as a ghost, thought he must be wounded. 'No,' replied Dumas, 'but I have killed so many, so many of them . . .' and he slumped on to the floor in a dead faint caused by extreme exhaustion. He had not eaten since six in the morning, had ridden and fought all day, and it was then four in the afternoon. His sabre was so chipped and warped that it protruded four inches out of the scabbard.

Hostilities with the Austrian Empire ended with the signing of the treaty of Campo-Formio later that year, and Bonaparte, having crushed all France's enemies on the Continent, could now turn his attention to the only power left which might raise up a future coalition against her. To cross the Channel and invade England was too risky an undertaking, but there was much to be said for re-establishing French power in the Mediterranean and denying the British merchant navy access to the ports of the inner sea. So a plan was hatched to transport an army across the water to Alexandria, seize Egypt, and bring the British to their knees by cutting the trade route to the Levant and India.

The energy Dumas had displayed in the last Italian campaign had restored him to Bonaparte's good graces, and he was told to report to the headquarters of the expeditionary army at Toulon. Accompanied by the faithful Dermoncourt, he was shown into Bonaparte's room early in the morning while he was still in bed with Joséphine. The night had been warm, and the couple were covered by nothing more than a thin sheet through which their bodies could be clearly discerned. Joséphine was in tears, her husband in high spirits, wiping her eyes with a handkerchief held in one hand while with the other he beat a military tattoo on her rump. The poor woman was inconsolable at the thought of being left behind, and her husband was trying to cheer her up by promising she should sail with the first contingent of reinforcements—accompanied, he added in an afterthought, by Mme Dumas. 'And when we are all together there, my sweet Joséphine, Dumas, who can only father girls, and I who can't even manage that, we'll both do our damnedest to get a son, each of us. And if you and I have a boy,' he went on, giving Joséphine an extra hard smack, 'he and his wife will be the godparents, and we'll be the godparents if he has a son.' The promise, whether or not seriously meant, was never carried out, for many years of privation and suffering were to pass before Dumas saw his wife again; and by the time she was able to give him the son whose career is the principal subject of this book, Bonaparte had turned finally and irrevocably against his former friend, whose name he refused even to allow to be mentioned in his hearing.

The rift between them opened up in Egypt. The French fleet, evading Nelson's squadrons, had sailed unimpeded to Alexandria. But instead of the splendid city of antiquity, they found nothing but a huddle of mud huts and an abject population who offered the invader no serious resistance. Cairo was reached after a gruelling march across barren desert. The troops suffered not just from the heat, but from hunger and thirst as well, for, accustomed in their earlier campaigns to live off the land, they carried no provisions with them; and Egypt, which had been the granary of the ancient world, was now little better than a fly-ridden dust-bowl.

The native troops were worsted after a fierce battle outside Cairo, and Bonaparte was able to enter the capital and to set about putting the country's government on a modern footing, reforming the law-courts and reorganizing the tax system. Once the natives had been brought to realize the benefits of civilization, the hope was that Egypt would become, like the new states set up in North Italy, a dependable ally of France; Bonaparte could then sail back with his army, leaving a token garrison in Cairo, or else march on to fresh conquests in the East. But what had all this to do with safeguarding the integrity of French territory, or even with promoting republican idealism? was the driving force behind the strategy not rather the private ambition of the commander-in-chief, Bonaparte? Was he acting merely as an obedient servant of the people of France or was he not, potentially if not yet in fact, another Alexander, another Caesar?

These questions were asked, and debated, by a few of the 'old republicans' among the generals of the Army of Egypt; and reports of their treasonous talk reached the commander's ears. He sent for Dumas, either because he had been told Dumas's tongue wagged most, or because he regarded him as the easiest to break. As to what passed between them, we have two accounts: the first, contained in his son's memoirs, according to which Dumas spoke his mind boldly, saying among other things: 'I believe that the interests of France must take precedence over the interests of one man, however great he may be'; the other, recorded by Desgenettes, surgeon-general, who reported Napoleon's own version of the events. Having roundly charged Dumas with spreading disaffection, for which he threatened to have him shot out of hand as a traitor, he watched him sardonically as he faltered out some defence and then fell to weeping. 'I saw that he was a harmless fellow who had been put up to it,' commented Bonaparte. 'He has, in any case, not much sense.'

Shortly afterwards Dumas recovered, briefly, the good opinion of his chief, when he displayed his customary reckless courage in helping to put down a serious local revolt in Cairo. Although at the time ill of a fever, Dumas, on hearing the shouts and the firing, staggered out of bed, pulled on breeches and riding-boots, and leaped on his horse without waiting for it to be saddled. Bare from the waist up, waving his sabre over his head, and roaring horribly as he charged the rebels, Dumas appeared to them not so much a 'black devil' as the Angel of Death, and they scattered in dismay wherever he appeared on his charger. By the following day the revolt was all but crushed; only the leaders of the jihad held out, having barricaded themselves inside a mosque. French cannon smashed down the doors, and Dumas was the first to cross the threshold, mounted on his fierce stallion. Halfway down the dimly lit hall the animal, confronted by a marble tomb, reared up whinnying and planted its forehooves on the top of the obstacle. The Arabs, terrified, shrank back, crying 'the Angel! the Angel!'

Bonaparte, at his headquarters in Gizeh, sent for Dumas and on his arrival hailed him as the Hercules who had crushed the many-headed hydra. Probably he would have preferred to keep this stalwart fighter by his side, if he had shown the unswerving devotion to his person that he required of all his followers and found in most of them; but Dumas was moody, volatile, and insubordinate. He was, as his son later wrote in one of the rare pieces of character analysis he ventured on, 'a creole, that is, a mixture of nonchalance, impetuosity, and inconstancy. However ardently he desired something, a profound disgust of what he had achieved overcame him as soon as his desires were gratified. The energy he had displayed to accomplish his ends subsided forthwith and was replaced by his customary casualness and bored melancholy. Then, at the slightest setback, he would talk longingly of the delights of country life . . .'[9] Dermoncourt, who knew him, perhaps, better than anyone else during his period of active service, relates how, more than once, Dumas handed him a letter of resignation with instructions to forward it to the authorities in Paris; Dermoncourt would take it, say nothing, and quietly tuck it away in a drawer.

But after the crushing of the Cairo insurrection the mood of black discouragement into which Dumas relapsed was too profound to be conjured by Dermoncourt's tactful exhortations. His homesickness was aggravated by the dearth of news from France for, after Nelson's annihilation of the French fleet at the Battle of the Nile and his subsequent blockade of the coast, communications between the expeditionary force and the mother country were all but cut off. Bonaparte did not try to argue with him when Dumas applied to return to France, but told him he would have to make his own arrangements for the sea-journey. Accordingly he chartered a vessel, took on board as cargo 4,000 lbs. of coffee and eleven Arab horses, and with a few adventurous companions set sail.

La Belle Maltaise was, however, less seaworthy than she should have been, and at the first storm they started shipping water. The captain declared they would have to lighten their load if they were not to founder; the bales of coffee, which Dumas was counting on selling for a good price in France, were jettisoned and then all but two of the noble horses had to be slaughtered and their carcasses flung into the heaving seas. Finally they made port at Taranto.

When Dumas had set sail the year before from Toulon, the Kingdom of Sicily had been linked to France by a treaty of friendship. But the alliance had lasted only a short while; once the British victory at Aboukir Bay had given the Royal Navy absolute control of the Mediterranean, Ferdinand of Naples, imagining that with their best general marooned in Egypt the French were no longer to be feared, had declared war on the Republic. Thus, when Dumas and his fellow officers landed on the Italian coast, they found themselves on enemy territory. They were arrested, conducted to a nearby fortress and kept there in close confinement for two years (from March 17th, 1799, to April 5th, 1801).

For a man as active as Dumas, this long imprisonment constituted the worst of mental tortures, and led to serious impairment of his health. He was convinced he was being deliberately poisoned. The doctor attending him treated his symptoms by bleeding him in the foot; the foot then became infected. He suffered from incessant migraines, became deaf in one ear and almost lost the sight of his right eye.

He was liberated on an exchange of high-ranking prisoners of war and returned, a shadow of his former self, to Villers-Cotterêts. Almost as hard to bear as his physical infirmities was the fierce grudge Napoleon nurtured against him for having, as he saw it, deserted him in Egypt. Dumas was allowed no portion of the 500,000 francs indemnity which the Neapolitan government had been forced to disgorge as compensation to the French prisoners it had kept locked up. He was taken off the active list, and a humble petition he sent to the First Consul, requesting settlement of arrears of pay, went unanswered. Officers whose length of service was shorter than his were now Marshals of France, but declined to use their influence on his behalf for fear of sharing the odium he had incurred. There were no means by which he could soften Napoleon's relentless hostility, and the unfortunate general remained under the deep shadow of this disgrace, living at Villers-Cotterêts in near poverty, broken in health and shunned by his former comrades, for the few remaining years of his life. His only solace was the tender affection of his wife and the pride he took in the little son born to them a year after his return to the bosom of his family.

II Mother and Son

Villers-Cotterêts, which in later years exerted over Alexandre Dumas a nostalgic spell similar to that which Illiers cast over Marcel Proust, was at the beginning of the nineteenth century a small market town numbering perhaps 2,500 souls. It was a staging-post on the highroad from Paris to the east, and for the local inhabitants the day centred round the arrival of the mail-coach from the capital, bringing with it the latest information about the stirring or disturbing events which marked the first thirteen years of Dumas's life.

Every year, at Whitsuntide, there was a fair which enjoyed a reputation extending far beyond the confines of the little town. For three days people walked, rode, or drove in from far and wide, from Ferté-Milon and Crépy, from Soissons, Château-Thierry and Compiègne, even from Paris. They thronged the fine park, bordered by magnificent beeches, chestnut- and lime-trees, where there was dancing every evening and, in the daytime, shooting-galleries and other side-shows to coax the small change out of the holiday-makers' pockets.

In Whitsun 1802 General Dumas's wife, now far gone in her third pregnancy, went along with a woman friend to visit the fairground. They decided to pay a few pence to see a traditional enactment of the Faust legend, done by puppets. The showman had taken a lot of trouble with his devil who for some obscure reason bore the name of Berlick. This puppet was coal-black, with a scarlet tongue and tail, and spoke with a harsh, grating grunt. Mme Dumas was strongly affected by the performance and, as she left the booth on her friend's arm, she murmured to her: 'I'm lost, I'm going to give birth to a Berlick!'

There was more to this dread than a pregnant woman's morbid fancy. Her husband would have told her, naturally, of the nickname the Austrians had given him, the Black Devil; and however rudimentary popular understanding of human genetics was at the time, every good wife knew that there was always a chance, when a white woman was cohabiting with a mulatto, that she could give birth to a black child, a 'throw-back'. Remembering again that at this time the negro race was superstitiously regarded almost everywhere in Europe as an inferior species, degraded in habits, lazy and untrustworthy, one can begin to appreciate Mme Dumas's apprehensions.

These increased as the date set for her delivery approached. The child's movements became very troublesome; only a little demon could twist and turn so; she imagined she could feel the creature's hooves and claws tearing at her vitals. And indeed, the unborn Alexandre does appear to have displayed unusual activity inside the womb, as the result of which the umbilical cord got twisted round his neck; he emerged black in the face, half-strangled. The midwife uttered a terrified scream. 'Mother of God,' cried the patient, 'he's black, isn't he?' Instead of a wail, the new-born child could only grunt until his neck had been freed; his mother, hearing this ominous sound, fainted away, convinced that her worst fears had been realized, and that she had given birth to the devil Berlick.

Possibly the father too had not been without his misgivings, and remembering an old specific he had heard recommended in the Isles, had insisted on his wife taking regular nips of brandy during her pregnancy. This was supposed to whiten the skin of the unborn child. The prescription had seemed to work for, as a small boy, Alexandre had as rosy-white a complexion as any of the other children of Villers-Cotterêts; his eyes were light blue, and his head was covered with a tangle of soft fair hair, curling loosely. Only later, after puberty, did his skin darken and his hair develop the crisp curls seen in all the portraits.

The General was, of course, delighted that he had a son at last. His excitement comes through in the letter he sent to an old comrade-in-arms, Guillaume Brune, to invite him to act as godfather. 'I am writing to give you the joyful news,' the letter starts, 'that my wife was delivered yesterday morning [July 24th, 1802] of a big boy, weighing 9 lbs and measuring 18 inches. No need to tell you that if he goes on growing in the outside world as he did inside, he promises to reach a pretty good height.' There was a postscript, of the kind one old army man could permit himself when writing to another: 'I have reopened my letter to inform you the young fellow has just peed over the top of his head. That augurs well, eh?'[1] When one remembers, as no doubt the proud father did, how at Toulon, before they sailed for Egypt, Bonaparte had promised to be at the christening if ever he had a son, this letter, for all its cheerful coarseness, takes on a certain pathos. By interesting Brune in his young family, General Dumas may have thought to use him to help patch matters up with the First Consul. If so, he was disappointed; Brune invented a plausible excuse to decline the invitation to stand sponsor for young Alexandre Dumas.

Three years later, as his health continued to deteriorate, the General resolved on a visit to Paris, partly to get specialist advice from a good doctor, partly in the hope of obtaining an audience with Napoleon. The master of France had now crowned himself Emperor; Brune and another old friend, Joachim Murat, had been promoted to the rank of

marshal; and Dumas persuaded them both to come to lunch, trusting
at least to interest them in the fine young son he had brought with
him to Paris. The little boy, ignorant of the issues at stake, paid no
attention to their talk. Almost his only memory of the occasion in
later years was the view from the window of the restaurant which
overlooked Montmartre, in those days a green hill dotted with wind-
mills; in the sky above them he watched, fascinated, a huge kite darting
and floating, obedient to the tug of an invisible cord.

The trip to Paris brought the elder Dumas no comfort, since the
Emperor refused to see him and the doctors could only confirm that
his days were numbered. Even so, depressed and worried though he
must have felt when he thought of what little provision he could make
for his widow and two young children after his death, he still gave the
impression of a fit and active man, never happier than when he had
bagged a few brace of partridges on the wing. Nor was he so ostracized
as to be compelled to forgo the pleasures of social life; he was on calling
terms with all his neighbours, some of whom were relations of his wife
who, if the bad days came, would see to it that she did not starve.
Occasionally, too, there were clandestine visits from highly placed
friends he had made during his earlier years of active service in Italy
and Egypt.

Thus it happened one morning that he told his small son to put on
his best clothes and then set off with him to drive over to a handsome
château the child had never been to before. They were shown into a
richly furnished boudoir where he saw, lying on a sofa, a dazzlingly
beautiful woman in her mid-twenties wearing a bright négligé who,
instead of rising when they entered, simply stretched out one bare
arm for the General to kiss her hand. He made to draw up a chair, but
she waved it away and motioned him to sit on the rug beside her, so
that she could put her slippered feet on his knees and flick the buttons
of his coat with her toes. Little Alexandre stood beside them, looking
on in wonderment, until she reached for a tortoiseshell comfit-box
encrusted with gold and, after emptying out the sweets it contained,
handed it to him. His father asked her why the boy was to have the
box without the sweets, and she leaned forward to whisper her reply
in his ear. Alexandre could not hear what she said, but his memory
always preserved the vision of the princess's delicate pink and white
cheek almost pressed against his father's lean brown cheek, and both
of them laughing at the joke they would not share with him.

For this mysterious young woman was a real princess, Pauline
Bonaparte, a younger sister of Napoleon, married to Prince Camillo
Borghese; one of the most notorious society beauties of the day, she
was to model for Canova, two or three years later, as 'Venere vincitrice',
that is, the goddess of love reclining in triumph after being awarded

the apple that was the prize 'for the most beautiful'; the statue in the Palazzo Borghese in Rome preserves the grace and the shapeliness that the boy saw, even though he was not of an age to appreciate it. How did his father contrive this secret rendezvous with her, chaperoned only by a puzzled three-year-old? It was obviously not their first meeting, if the lady was prepared to flirt so outrageously with him; later that morning, when Alexandre was attracted to the window by the sight of a stag, pursued by hounds, running across the courtyard, she pretended she was too tired to walk and he watched his father raise her in his arms, carry her over to the window and hold her up to wave to the huntsmen below.

The probability is that the two first met at the Palazzo Montebello (Mombello), near Milan, where Bonaparte had set up his headquarters after the brilliant campaign of 1797 in which, it will be remembered, Dumas played no small part. The commander-in-chief had invited various members of his family living in France to stay with him, his brothers Joseph, Louis, and Jérôme, and his sisters, including his favourite Pauline, or Paulette as she was commonly called in the family circle. At seventeen, already man-mad, she was giving considerable trouble, and Napoleon was hoping to marry her off to Charles-Victor Leclerc, one of his most trusted staff-officers, a competent, ambitious soldier whom Paulette was quite ready to accept, more for the sake of being married than of being married to him in particular.

This, at any rate, was the view taken by the playwright Antoine-Vincent Arnault, a man whom Alexandre Dumas got to know well many years later, when he settled in Paris in his twenties, for Arnault was a close friend of the Leuvens and the Leuvens were, as we shall see, about the only family with whom he was on visiting terms when he first moved to the capital. Arnault was once invited to Montebello and found himself seated next to Paulette at dinner. She was, he later recorded, 'though quite the prettiest person one could imagine, undoubtedly also the most linnet-brained. She had no more idea of how to behave than as if she were still at boarding-school. She chattered incessantly, laughed at nothing and everything, mimicked the most stately people, put out her tongue at her sister-in-law [Joséphine] when she was not looking, nudged me with her knee when I was not paying enough attention to her monkey-tricks, and drew on herself from time to time one of those terrifying glances with which her brother could reduce the boldest men to silence. But that scarcely bothered her; a minute later, she started all over again, and the authority of the general officer commanding the Army of Italy was set at naught by a little girl's wilfulness. She was good-hearted, however, though more out of natural disposition than by deliberate intention, for she had absolutely no principles and was even capable of doing someone a good turn by pure whim.'[2]

It was perhaps this last trait that General Dumas was gambling on when he paid her this visit, for Napoleon had always been fond of her, however infuriated he was at times by her lack of decorum, and he might have been prepared to listen to her if she could be prevailed on to plead his cause. We have, of course, no possible way of knowing what the two talked about, in that quiet drawing-room in the Château de Montgobert, but there would have been at least one topic of common interest. Shortly after her first marriage, Pauline had accompanied her husband to Dumas's native island of San-Domingo, which had had a chequered history since he left it at the age of eighteen. The black population had been emancipated by edict of the Convention in 1794. In the ensuing wars, they had joined with their former masters in beating off the British who had attempted a landing and then, under their leader Toussaint-Louverture, had proclaimed the island's independence. This development did not suit Napoleon who, as soon as British neutrality had been ensured by the Peace of Amiens, fitted out an invasion fleet and sent his brother-in-law General Leclerc, at the head of an army made up largely of Polish volunteers, to re-establish colonial government and reimpose slavery of the black population. Leclerc defeated the islanders after a short campaign, and Toussaint-Louverture was sent back in chains to France. But the victors' triumph was short-lived: an epidemic of yellow fever spread through the camp, and Leclerc was one of the victims. Pauline caught the fever too, but, unlike her husband, recovered and was able to return to France. Indeed, scarcely had she properly convalesced when she married again, with what her all-powerful brother considered unseemly haste, though as her choice had fallen on a Roman prince, reputed the wealthiest man in Italy, he forgave her.

Whatever promises the pretty Paulette may have given to General Dumas, she seems to have had no more success in interceding with Napoleon on his behalf, if indeed she remembered to try and do so, than any of the field-marshals whose good services he had tried to enlist. Only a few weeks later (on February 26th, 1806) the honest soldier lay on his death-bed. His son was not there to see him die, having been taken to spend the night with a cousin. It may have been this cousin who broke the news to the little boy, telling him he would not be seeing his father again 'because God has taken him from you'. He slipped away, found his way home, entered the house unobserved, and his mother was aghast to see him climbing the stairs, trailing behind him his father's fowling-piece which he had taken from its stand. She asked him where he was going. 'I am going to the sky to shoot God dead, because God's taken papa away.' The story is reminiscent of Stendhal's account of his own reactions at his mother's death, which occurred when he was not much older than Dumas when his father died. He overheard the family confessor offering consolation to the bereaved widower: 'My son, this is sent by God'; and Stendhal dated his own loss of religious faith from that moment. He had a reflective nature, Dumas an active one, and the two reacted differently to very similar catastrophes. But perhaps one should beware of regarding the child as father to the man; as Stendhal went on to observe in the same passage of his autobiography: 'I have no faith in the clever remarks of children presaging the superiority of the men they will grow up to be.'[3]

As the unfortunate general had foreseen, his death left his little family practically penniless. All he had had to live on was his retirement pension of 4,000 francs, 1,200 of which had gone to pay his daughter's boarding-school fees in Paris. Now she had to return home, and there was no alternative but for the widow—to whom Napoleon obstinately refused to grant a pension—and the two orphan children to go and live with old Claude Labouret who had, some time before, decided to retire from the hotel business and had taken the lease on a house big enough, fortunately, to accommodate his daughter and his two grandchildren.

Whatever Mme Dumas may have thought of the move from a large house, where she had a staff of servants at her beck and call, to one where the domestic work had to be managed with little or no assistance, the boy Alexandre suffered scarcely at all from the change. If instead of an extensive garden there was only a small backyard, what did it matter when he had the endless forest on his doorstep, with all the woodland creatures to watch and, if he was quick enough, to catch? Beasts, large and small, four-legged, winged, or legless, always fascinated him and, as we shall see, when he became rich enough to indulge his fancies this interest led him to assemble an extraordinary menagerie of pets. One of his earliest friends, when he was still a toddler, was his father's gardener, Pierre, who knew everything a countryman could know about the ways of birds and animals. Alexandre never forgot the day when Pierre called him to see a grass-snake he had just found. Alexandre had seen grass-snakes before, but this one had a great swelling in its belly. 'Now watch,' said Pierre, and taking up his spade, very neatly sliced the reptile in two just below the swelling. Out of the cavity tumbled a small frog which lay for a moment in the sunshine, then stretched its legs gingerly, opened its mouth wide to take in air, and after a moment hopped slowly off, praising the god of frogs for this miraculous delivery.

His interest in the habits and peculiarities of living creatures had one unexpected result: it led to his learning to read at an earlier age than he otherwise might, and almost without needing to be taught his letters. A good lady with whom his mother used to spend her evenings happened to possess a set of Buffon's *Natural History*, with coloured engravings, and it was enough to place a volume of this work in the boy's hands to be sure he would sit still and not fidget until the time came to go home. To understand the pictures he was forced to puzzle out the text. That his first introduction to French literature should have been through the writings of so pure a stylist as Buffon was a stroke of good fortune. Of course he did not stop there; other books considered suitable for his age, such as a children's adaptation of *The Thousand and One Nights* and a couple of popular works retelling the Greek myths, helped to stimulate his powers of imagination and to cultivate his sense of wonder.

Still, no one could call him a precociously studious boy. Most of his time was spent out of doors, playing with children of his age and in particular with the younger members of the Deviolaine family. The father of this numerous brood was a man who, on first encounter, could terrify a child out of his wits, until it was realized that, for all his booming voice and hectoring manner, M. Deviolaine was in reality a kindly, even soft-hearted man. He held an important position in the neighbourhood, that of chief verderer, *inspecteur des forêts de Villers-Cotterêts*, and was regarded as a relative by Mme Dumas, in those days when even the remotest ties of kinship counted. Jean-Michel Deviolaine had married one of her father's nieces, so his children were spoken of as Alexandre's cousins, and two of them, Cécile, a regular tomboy, and her brother Félix, were his constant playfellows. Their favourite spot for romps was the old convent of Saint-Rémy, which M. Deviolaine had purchased during the early years of the Republic, when church property, confiscated by the revolutionaries, was being sold off at knock-down prices in order to replenish the depleted national treasury. He appears to have left it just as it was, with its cloisters, huge staircase with iron balustrades, and empty apartments, the refuge now of stray cats and the rats and mice on which they preyed. The abandoned nunnery was an ideal playground for the children on Sundays, and Alexandre chased around with the others, though staying for preference on the ground floor. His one weakness was a fear of heights, something that remained with him all his life and caused him agonies of sick terror on certain mountain paths, later, when he went exploring Switzerland. His cousins soon discovered his Achilles' heel and, after the fashion of children, made a point of teasing him about it; they would decoy him into an upstairs room, a hayloft for instance, and lock the door behind him, so that his only means of egress was out of the window and down a long ladder; eventually, pale and trembling, he would clamber out clumsily and descend, clutching the rungs feverishly, while Cécile danced around below, shrieking with delight and calling him a stupid ninny.

She did, however, do him one good turn, this irrepressible girl-cousin, though quite unintentionally. He was ten years old; his mother had been anxiously wondering for some time how she could afford to send him to school. In those days there was no state provision for the education of the children of the poor, and Mme Dumas's means were slender. The attempts she had made to obtain him a free place at one of the schools for officers' sons had all been rebuffed, and she was at her wits' end to know what to do when, providentially it seemed, another distant relative, a priest, died bequeathing Alexandre a bursary tenable at the seminary of Soissons. Now Mme Dumas had never specially wanted her son to train for the priesthood; the idea appealed even less to the ten-year-old; but at least he would get an education, so after much argument he gave way. The news spread swiftly, as news tended to in Villers-Cotterêts, and the evening before he was due to leave he was accosted by the mischievous Cécile, who started complimenting him ironically on his new-found vocation, and assuring him of her custom as soon as he had qualified—that is, she promised she would have no other confessor, once he was a tonsured priest. This was more than Alexandre could stand. Declaring hotly that nothing would persuade him to set foot in the seminary, bursary or no bursary, he ran off, and neither his mother nor any of the other townspeople saw him for three days.

Alexandre, who was never in his life very particular about the company he kept, had made friends with a certain ill-favoured, pock-marked poacher called Boudoux. Boudoux had a reputation second to none for imitating the whistling of birds and attracting them in this manner on to limed twigs. With this companion, the boy disappeared into the woods, where they lived on their catch, making savoury stews over a camp-fire, until Alexandre's conscience began to trouble him and he returned, a little sheepishly, to confront his mother, now almost out of her mind with worry. She was, however, so relieved to see him that there was no further question of the seminary. Instead, she managed somehow to scrape together the wherewithal to send him to the local school, run single-handed by the parish priest, the Abbé Grégoire who, though an honest man and a conscientious teacher, had his limitations: Latin was the only subject on the school syllabus. Dumas later drew an affectionate portrait of him in *Ange Pitou*, a novel partly set in Villers-Cotterêts.

Meanwhile, the face of Europe was changing. However little the outside world may have impinged on the child's sheltered life, his elders could not fail to take note of the cataclysmic events of these years, portending the fall of the First Empire. After the disastrous

Russian campaign of 1812, there followed the bloody battles of Bautzen, Dresden, and Leipzig. Napoleon was forced out of Central Europe, and the armies of the Allies moved steadily nearer the eastern frontier.

Dumas's birthplace was plumb in the path of the invader and the alarm of the inhabitants was, in the circumstances, fully understandable. It was the Russians they chiefly feared; the Cossacks had a frightening reputation, and were depicted in French propaganda sheets as clad in animal skins, riding fierce little ponies, and carrying lances and bows and arrows—exactly like the hordes of Attila the Hun. There were constant false alarms; the sight of horsemen approaching was enough to start a panic, even before they had been identified. Once, on a misty morning in February, a stray detachment of Cossacks actually did gallop through the little town; one of them pulled his pistol, let fly at a hatter who, out of curiosity, had incautiously opened his door, shot him dead, and then they were gone.

The restoration of the Bourbon monarchy, which followed swiftly on Napoleon's abdication and banishment to Elba, posed a dilemma for Alexandre, as his mother explained. Either he could assume the old aristocratic family name, which his father had renounced, and as Alexandre Davy de la Pailleterie, whose grandfather had served in the royal army before the revolution, he stood a chance of obtaining a scholarship to a Paris *lycée* and, later, a position in the new administration; or alternatively he could keep the name Dumas, but that would brand him as the son of one of Napoleon's generals and effectively bar him from employment under the Bourbons. The twelve-year-old boy, to his mother's quiet satisfaction, refused to consider relinquishing his father's name, which was also, of course, that of his Haitian grandmother. In the event, the removal of Napoleon actually served their interests, for it became possible for their friends to solicit a small favour which the vindictive Emperor would never have granted, and Mme Dumas was awarded one of the coveted licences to retail tobacco, a commodity which has always been a state monopoly in France. Though this was not the most lucrative of trades, it did offer a welcome supplementation of her minute income. The shop was opened on the ground floor of an ironmonger's establishment in the Place de la Fontaine.

The good Abbé Grégoire was less fortunate; he was compelled to close his school, and this might have brought about a serious interruption in Alexandre's studies were it not that his mother, out of the modest profits of the snuff and pipe-tobacco business, was able to pay for the priest to visit the house and continue the Latin lessons privately. She also found the money for her son to be given tuition in arithmetic, a branch of learning for which Alexandre showed no great aptitude, remaining quite incapable, to the end of his life, of doing long division

2

sums. But his teacher, a certain M. Oblet, happened also to be an expert penman and, seeing how impressed his pupil was with his pothooks and hangers, offered to throw in a few lessons in calligraphy. It was an art in which Dumas rapidly excelled his master and indeed, as we shall presently see, the fineness of his penmanship stood him in better stead, when it came to earning a living, than all the Latin the Abbé Grégoire had so painfully drilled into him.

But the lessons he followed with the greatest assiduity were those that he took, surreptitiously, from Boudoux's successor, the poacher Hanniquet, nicknamed Biche. He was a mine of information about the ways of animals and birds and was so cunning a tracker that he normally used nothing but a stout stick to knock down his prey. For shyer game he held in reserve an ancient flintlock of a type long since obsolete and which he alone had the knack of firing. Alexandre, who had plenty of free time now that the school was closed, spent it mostly with Hanniquet in the woods and after a while became almost as skilled as his master in trapping rabbits and shooting game-birds, and in the even more difficult art of avoiding brushes with the gamekeeper while pursuing these illicit activities. Long impunity, however, made him over-confident and one bright, snowy February morning in 1815, creeping from tree to tree in pursuit of a thrush, he failed to notice that someone was creeping up behind him. At last the elusive bird found a patch of mistletoe to settle on; Alexandre, holding his breath, raised his gun and aligned the sights unerringly. But he had scarcely pulled the trigger and seen the dead bird tumble to the ground when a heavy hand fell on his shoulder and an angry voice shouted: 'Ah, you little rascal, I've caught you at it!' Ducking, he managed to twist himself out of the gamekeeper's grasp and, putting his long legs to good use, had soon outdistanced his pursuer. But his escape did him little good, for the man had recognized the delinquent and reported him to M. Deviolaine who, relation or not, would certainly have let the law take its course if, providentially, news had not arrived of Napoleon's landing at Antibes on March 1st. This startling intelligence threw everything in turmoil, and in the agitated speculation that ensued the illegal slaughter of a thrush was quite forgotten.

Since Villers-Cotterêts was a predominantly royalist town, the news of Napoleon's return from Elba caused more dismay than delight among the inhabitants. Those Frenchmen who rallied to his flag were regarded as black traitors, as was graphically demonstrated by an ugly incident later that month when two high-ranking officers, Gen. François-Antoine Lallemand and his brother, were driven under close guard through the streets of Villers-Cotterêts on their way to Soissons, to stand trial for having attempted to subvert a brigade of artillery stationed at La Fère. Recognizing them, the bystanders booed and shook their fists; one woman, shrieking insults, jumped on to the dash-board, spat in the general's face, and reached out to tear his epaulettes from his shoulder. Alexandre's mother, who had witnessed the scene, returned home in pensive mood. It was true that she had no cause to be grateful to the ex-Emperor and could expect no betterment in her situation if his bid to regain power proved successful. Still, she was the widow of one of his generals. Their fellow townsmen assumed that the Dumas were Bonapartists, and Alexandre had fought many a battle with the local boys who called him names on this account. Taking what was perhaps the boldest initiative in her life, she set out with her thirteen-year-old son for Soissons, and once there, she handed him a couple of pistols, with ammunition, and a roll of fifty *louis-d'or*. It happened that she knew the keeper of the prison at Soissons, who had a son of Alexandre's age with whom he had played on previous visits. She told him she was taking him there to see his friend again and that, if he could find out where the Lallemand brothers were being held, he was to do his best to smuggle the firearms and the gold into their cell.[4] The boy discharged the commission admirably, and managed to have a few words of hurried conversation with the prisoners. The general thanked him but refused to accept the package, being confident that Napoleon would have reached Paris and made himself master of France before he and his brother could be brought to trial. This was, indeed, what happened, and the Lallemands were freed without needing to bribe their jailers to let them escape.

In the summer of that year Napoleon passed through Dumas's native town on his way to meet the combined Prussian and British armies in Belgium. Half the population of Villers-Cotterêts, fore-warned by the bulletin published in *Le Moniteur*, flocked out to line the Paris road and cheer him as he passed. Alexandre, with a crowd of schoolmates, made for a hillock giving a good view up the road, and remained there from early morning till three in the afternoon. A courier on horseback was sighted preceding the two carriages, each drawn by a team of six, which appeared in a cloud of dust on the horizon; without waiting, the boys tore back to the inn-yard, where the ostlers were already bringing out fresh horses. In the few minutes needed to harness them, Alexandre caught a brief glimpse through the carriage-window of the man about whom he had heard so much ever since he was of an age to understand what his elders were talking about. All he could make out through the glass was Napoleon's head and the top of his famous green coat; his face was expressionless, his complexion the colour of yellow wax, his eyes seemingly lost in visions of the future.

No more than a week later, rumours of a huge military disaster began to trickle back, and the boy and his mother spent a whole day hanging around the posting inn, hoping to pick up fuller details from travellers as they stopped for refreshment. There certainly had been a battle, fought at a place called Waterloo, for which Alexandre searched in vain on the map. When darkness fell they were still there, mother and son, still uncertain what had happened. At ten o'clock a coach halted in front of the inn. The postmaster, holding a blazing torch over his head, ran out and started questioning the travellers through the window; but as soon as he saw them he took a step back, exclaiming in astonishment: 'It's the Emperor!' Alexandre climbed up on a stone bench to get a better view over his mother's shoulder. Napoleon was sitting there, in the same seat as before, with his head bent forward, and exactly the same abstracted look in his eyes. On hearing the postmaster's words he looked round and spoke, in his usual clipped, harsh accents. 'Where are we?' 'At Villers-Cotterêts, sire.' 'How many leagues to Paris?' 'Nineteen, sire.' 'Tell the postillions to make haste.' After giving this order, promptly obeyed, he leaned back in his seat, his chin falling once more on his chest. And that was all. A fresh team of horses whirled him away through the night, to Paris . . . and to St. Helena.[5]

III Buds of May

Dumas's formal education ended just before, or just after, his fourteenth birthday when, with no great enthusiasm, he took a job as under-clerk in the office of a local notary. What little useful knowledge he had acquired at this stage had been learned out of school: he had a good seat on a horse, could shoot straight, and had shown enough aptitude in repairing broken firearms for the gunsmith at Villers-Cotterêts to have offered to take him on as apprentice. But, having always preferred outdoor sports to indoor study, he was almost totally ignorant of those branches of knowledge essential to the writer of historical plays and novels that he was to become. French history was not a subject taught at the parish school; nor, for that matter, was French literature, with which the boy had only the scrappiest acquaintance. Only the smattering of Latin he had acquired saved him from appearing a complete ignoramus. On one occasion, indeed, and quite unexpectedly, the endless translation exercises done for the Abbé Grégoire did turn out to have some practical value. During the Allied occupation of France it happened that a British regiment was stationed in the vicinity, and Mme Dumas had a couple of English officers billeted on her. They spoke not a word of French, which did not stop one of them from addressing Alexandre earnestly and persistently in a language which struck him as vaguely familiar. It dawned on him that the officer was speaking to him in Latin, a Latin very oddly accented to his ears, and was in fact pressing him to join them in a glass of wine. Waterloo having been won on the playing-fields of Eton, subsequent fraternization with the defeated enemy was facilitated by what had gone on in the class-rooms of the same college.

The law, to which he now found himself indentured, held no great attraction for Dumas, though he dreamed optimistically of the day when he would have a practice of his own and money enough for his mother and him to live in comfort. But in fact the amount of legal knowledge he picked up was even less than did Balzac, who at precisely the same time was working unwillingly as a solicitor's clerk in Paris. Mostly his days were spent engrossing deeds in a back office; but occasionally the notary, Mennesson, would give him the job of calling on some small farmer in the neighbourhood whose signature was needed on a document. These excursions made a welcome break in routine; on the way there and back, there was the opportunity to engage in his favourite pastime, setting snares for thrushes, jays or blackbirds, or, if he was carrying his gun, trying for a hare or a rabbit and trusting that the noise of the discharge would not reach the ears of yet another officious gamekeeper.

When the client to be visited did not live within walking distance, a friendly baker would lend him one of his horses. He was jogging back on a moonless night from one of these extended trips, carrying a sum of money collected for M. Mennesson in his satchel, when suddenly, on a lonely stretch of the road, his horse shied violently, threw him, and cantered off. What had frightened the animal, as Alexandre discovered when he got to his feet and made a full investigation, was the body of a man lying across the road; not, however, as he first thought, a peasant sleeping off his wine, but a corpse already cold, stripped and robbed. Fearfully, he looked around him, and fancied he saw the shape of another man skulking in the ditch. This was quite enough; panic-stricken, he took to his heels and ran the rest of the way home. He found his mother in a state of acute alarm, the baker having already visited her with the information that his horse had returned to its stable riderless. Having heard his story, she told him to say nothing about his discovery of the crime, terrified of the expense she would be put to if he had to appear as a witness at the assizes when the murderer was apprehended and brought to trial.

Nothing more eventful came to disturb the even tenor of their lives until in 1818, a little before the Whitsun holiday, Alexandre had an unexpected visit from his old teacher Grégoire who had a favour to ask him though, after the fashion of schoolmasters dealing with ex-pupils, he framed the request rather as a directive. Faced with the awkward problem of devising entertainment for a young niece and her schoolfriend who were arriving from Paris to stay with him, he had decided that Dumas, just coming up to his sixteenth birthday, was of about the right age to squire the two girls; accordingly he was told he would be expected for lunch the following Sunday to make their acquaintance.

To do his old master honour and make a favourable impression on the young ladies Dumas must, he told himself, look his best. However, a careful inspection of his wardrobe led to the melancholy conclusion that he had really no clothes fit for the occasion. Not a jacket but had a patch in at least one elbow, not a single pair of trousers but was darned. Finally his anxious search brought to light the suit that had been made for him two years earlier for his confirmation. It was rather splendid: nankeen breeches, a cornflower blue coat with gold buttons, and a white piqué waistcoat to wear underneath. Admittedly it was a little tight in places, Dumas having shot up in the interval.

Thus arrayed, he presented himself at the priest's house and was introduced to the two girls whom he was to look after during the three days of the summer *fête*. Grégoire's niece Laurence turned out to be a tall, willowy, fair-haired damsel. Her companion Vittoria, a señorita from Spain no less, was a complete contrast, with her olive complexion, black eyes, well developed bust and broad hips. She seemed amused, Laurence on the other hand appalled, at the sight of the dandified hobbledehoy Laurence's uncle had unearthed for them, while his own uneasiness increased at every observation they made. The stroll he took after the meal, arm in arm with Laurence, while Vittoria and Grégoire's hunchback sister walked behind, was pure torment. The looks cast at the quartet by passers-by were charged with irony for which, as Dumas realized, his costume alone was responsible. Knee-breeches, *de rigueur* in polite society before the Revolution, were in this age worn only by old men who refused to move with the times; added to this, the length of his legs, the thinness of his calves, his knobbly knees and the exiguity of the knickerbockers made him look more like a melancholy heron than the smart man-about-town he should have appeared in this company. His embarrassment and humiliation were complete when the party passed a young man of his acquaintance called Miaud, dressed according to the latest fashion in a pair of tight fitting fawn trousers tucked into soft leather boots, and above, a buff waistcoat and sober brown jacket with a high collar. Miaud quizzed him through his eyeglass as he approached and drawled: 'Aha! here's Dumas going to his first communion for the second time; only he's holding a different sort of taper now.'

Unwisely, he thought to efface the impression that Miaud's elegance had made on the two young ladies by a piece of boyish showing off; he announced he would leap across the fourteen-foot ditch which bordered the park, a feat he had accomplished before then, to the admiration of every other young athlete in Villers-Cotterêts. 'You wouldn't catch Miaud trying that,' he boasted. 'He'd be a fool if he did,' retorted Laurence. 'What good would it do him?' Somewhat dashed by this chilling observation, Dumas none the less took a run, flew over the ditch,—but as he landed on the other side, the ominous sound of rending material brought it home to him that a tight-fitting confirmation suit was not the ideal gear for impromptu displays of gymnastics. Realizing in a twinkling he could not possibly take the girls to the dance with split breeches, he continued running like one possessed, and reached home a few minutes later in a state of near-collapse.

It took no longer for him to recover his breath than for his mother to repair the damage with a needle and thread; even so, Laurence and Vittoria had reached the dance-hall before him and the detested Miaud had already invited Laurence to join him in a quadrille. 'That's what comes of wearing knee-breeches,' he murmured as he passed, thus proving that he, at least, was well aware of the reason for Dumas's sudden flight from the scene of action. Laurence waited icily for his explanations and apology. He stammered something about having forgotten . . . forgotten . . . 'Forgotten your gloves,' she replied coolly. 'Yes of course, you were quite right, you couldn't possibly think of dancing without gloves.'

He managed to find a dancer who consented to lend him a spare pair to cover the indecent nudity of his hands, and once he was on the floor his self-confidence gradually returned. Dancing happened to be one of the few social accomplishments Dumas possessed; he could even waltz, at a time when, this dance having been only newly introduced, those who had mastered its mysteries in a country town like Villers-Cotterêts were conspicuously few. Vittoria, who waltzed with all the abandon of an Andalusian, complimented him on his proficiency. Her appreciation, he replied gravely, meant all the more to him because hitherto he had waltzed only with chairs, his confessor having agreed to his learning this lascivious dance only on condition he practised with an inanimate and sexless partner. This artless admission sent Vittoria into a paroxysm of stifled laughter, but his next remark delighted her even more. Not only was it the first time he had waltzed properly, it was also the first time he had held a young woman close to him, close enough to smell her perfume, feel her hair brush his cheek, caress her smooth shoulders with admiring eyes. He breathed a shuddering sigh of pure rapture, and when Vittoria asked him what was the matter, he replied, as they revolved ritually round the room: 'What's the matter? Only that I find it's so much better waltzing with a woman than a chair.'

But his exaltation was abruptly dispelled a moment later when he overheard, or divined, a whispered conversation between the two girls, the one laughingly reproaching the other for 'stealing her schoolboy from her', the other saying she only wanted to 'borrow him for the waltzes'. Dumas never forgot the acute anguish that this light-hearted exchange gave him, proving as it did that in the eyes of these two heartless beauties he was no more than 'a kind of shuttlecock, which they felt no compunction in sending to and fro, from one battledore to the other, never minding if a careless hit dislodged some of the feathers. I had aged considerably in ten minutes; for this discovery no longer filled me with shame, but with a deep depression . . . All my earlier life vanished in a twinkling, as do in an earthquake towns and villages, valleys and mountains, rivers and lakes.'[1]

The following day he managed to wheedle enough money from his mother to pay for a pair of boots and a proper suit, but by the time they were ready and he felt he could face Laurence and Vittoria again, they had returned to Paris, leaving him a mocking farewell letter. Possibly this experience, though he could smile over it when, at the age of fifty, he consigned it to his memoirs, left a deeper and more permanent impression on him than anything else that happened during his adolescence; it is not difficult to suppose that this precocious sexual humiliation lay at the root of the aversion he felt all his life for women of wit and refinement belonging to the more elegant circles of society. With such, he was careful to have no truck except in so far as, like Princess Mathilde Bonaparte, they were hostesses at dinner parties to which he was invited. For the feminine company which was, all his life, as necessary to him as breath itself, he turned to women who had no pretensions whatsoever to superiority, whether social or intellectual; women of a kind who could never, whatever happened, disdain him.

This was the result of no conscious decision, but of an instinctive need to cauterize a wounding experience. Fortunately he was able to satisfy this need almost immediately, and without having to seek far. The small town where he lived was not short of girls of his age of much humbler social origins than his, among whom he felt at ease and who gave him a ready welcome. There were Joséphine and Manette Thierry, the two charming daughters of a bald-headed tailor; Louise Brézette, the niece of an ex-army corporal—the very man, in fact, who had given Alexandre those dancing lessons that he had turned to such account; and two apprentice dressmakers, one a brunette, the other golden-haired, with pink cheeks that dimpled charmingly whenever she smiled, which was often; she was called Adèle Dalvin.

They all had their sweethearts, but it so happened that Adèle had just lost hers; his parents had insisted that he break off relations with her and pay court instead to a young woman with more substantial expectations. Plump, cheerful, diminutive, Adèle was the daughter of honest smallholders with whom she was still living. For no other reason, at the beginning, than that she was the only unattached member of the little band, Alexandre started 'going out' with her, which meant meeting her every evening after each of them had finished work and then, in summer, walking in the park or sitting under the trees or, in winter, joining the circle of her friends and their 'young men' in Louise Brézette's house. At ten, the couples would disperse; each of the girls would be escorted home, there would be low-toned conversations on the door-step interspersed with intervals of silence until finally, hot-cheeked, the maiden would slip indoors and the street-door would be firmly shut.

Dumas performed this courtship ritual faithfully for a full year before Adèle's door, after closing inexorably as usual at eleven o'clock, was gently reopened a few minutes later; a soft hand took his, led him

2*

down an open passageway into a little garden, then up a flight of stairs to her bedroom, which was on the first floor of a wing built on to the farmhouse. At three in the morning, well before the lark, 'that herald of the morn', made her song heard, this village Juliet led her lover back the same way, across the garden, down the dark passage and out through the street-door. He got home to find his mother waiting up for him, tearfully indignant but also greatly puzzled, for although she had a strong suspicion in whose bed he had spent the better part of the night, she had seen him arrive from quite the wrong direction. In fact, for a seventeen-year-old, he had been remarkably discreet. Instead of returning by the quickest way, he had taken a long, circuitous route across open fields and over brooks, so as to enter the town from the opposite side.

He continued this laborious deception for the two years during which he and Adèle held nightly tryst in her parents' house, so that their secret was kept in spite of the lively curiosity of the gossips in the little town. In fact, a rumour got around—and Dumas, to his shame, did nothing to scotch it—that his intrigue was with Eléonore Lebègue, one of the married daughters of M. Deviolaine. She was something of a coquette, but did not deserve this slur on her reputation, and was so indignant when the story came to her ears that she refused to see Mme Dumas or her nuisance of a son from that time on.

The affair with the little dressmaker was ended, if not by mutual consent, at least for reasons he could not in all honesty combat. As a nineteen-year-old with poor employment prospects and no capital, he was in no position to marry her; she, on the other hand, having already turned down two or three offers, decided as a sensible French girl that she could not refuse the latest suitor to come courting, a man who had made a mint of money in Spain, was twice her age, and could provide her with a good home. Between jobs, Alexandre was invited to spend a couple of months with his married sister at Dreux, and left not knowing what his mistress was planning. Within an hour of his return from Normandy, he heard all the details of the forthcoming wedding. Determined to avoid the heart-ache of witnessing it, he went off into the woods and spent as happy a day as he could engaged in his old pursuit of snaring birds. The evening shadows found him perched high up in a tree in a coppice not far from Haramont, a picturesque little hamlet he was later to use as the setting for some of the scenes in his novels *Ange Pitou* and *Conscience l'innocent*. The stillness was broken by the distant sound of laughter and the strains of a fiddler playing a jaunty tune. Then, along the woodland path, he saw a troop of merry-makers approach with, at their head, Adèle in her white bridal dress, with the traditional bouquet of orange-blossom in her hand, and the bridegroom's arm round her waist. What Dumas had not been told was that the wedding-feast h̶ ̶ ̶arranged to take place at Haramont, in the house of one of Adè ̶ ̶s; the newly married couple, with their friends, were now w̶ ̶ ̶ack to Villers-Cotterêts, and passed directly beneath the tree ̶ ̶ he sat unobserved and from which he watched them gradu̶ ̶ ̶pear into the darkness of the forest, the white dresses of ̶ ̶smaids making them appear like a procession of bucolic

This was not quite ̶ ̶e saw of Adèle; in real life there are no tidy endings. Some ̶ ̶r, when he was settled in Paris with a new mistress and ̶ ̶ning to make his name as a dramatist, he was walking back ̶ ̶dgings one wet November night, his head full of plans for ̶ ̶y *Christine* of which the idea had come to him only that ̶ ̶just as he was turning off the boulevard, at the Porte-Sain̶ ̶e heard shouts and through the murk saw a scuffle in prog̶ ̶e pavement behind him. A man and a woman were being ̶ ̶y a couple of footpads; one of the robbers was trying to w̶ ̶gentleman's stick from him while the other had tumbled th̶ ̶ to the ground and was struggling to wrench off her neckl̶ ̶s, having run back, leapt on him from behind and bore him̶ ̶round in his turn, seeing which the other villain ran off. A d̶ ̶t of soldiers, coming up to investigate the disturbance, took a̶ ̶ them off to the guard-room. Only then did Dumas recog̶ ̶victims of the attack as Adèle and her husband. They had spen̶ ̶ening at the theatre and were returning to their hotel afte̶ ̶ight supper when the thieves waylaid them.

̶ ̶iers, unwilling to take the responsibility of deciding who w̶ ̶aggressors in the affray, insisted that guilty and innocent s̶ ̶e locked up together until the inspector of police, arriving ̶ ̶owing morning, could have a chance of examining them. So ̶ ̶s spent a wakeful night watching his one-time mistress sleeping ̶ ̶y, propped up against her husband's shoulder. She had, as he ̶ ̶ed, two children now, and was a happily married woman who ̶ ̶ put the past behind her. Eventually his thoughts reverted to the ̶ ̶w play he was planning; as he observed sententiously, recording his thoughts at this point in his memoirs: 'by this time I had given my imagination, if not my heart, to a mistress who was to make things very hard for my past and future mistresses'[2]—that is, Melpomene, the muse of the dramatic art.

Dumas's interest in the theatre can properly be called life-long. As a boy he used to attend productions put on from time to time by strolling players passing through Villers-Cotterêts, and even acted a part in one of them, a melodrama based on the life of the notorious Mediterranean pirate Hariadan, when the company, probably in order to attract larger audiences, advertised for local talent to take a few

juvenile leads. None of the other children in the town could cajole
their parents into allowing them to appear on the boards, for acting
was still considered a highly disreputable profession. But Mme Dumas,
for some reason, proved more broad-minded than her neighbours, and
rigged up a splendid costume for him to make his stage début as a
Spanish cavalier.

Later, he organized amateur theatricals among his friends, assigning
the women's parts to Adèle Dalvin and Louise Brézette. Performances
took place in the upper storey of a long hangar, the ground floor of
which was used by a master carpenter as a workshop. Dumas chose
and cast the plays and directed the rehearsals, advised by two
experienced friends who had the advantage of an intimate knowledge
of the theatrical world of Paris: Adolphe de Leuven and Amédée de
la Ponce.

Both were young men of good family, enviably free of the obligation
to earn their own living. Adolphe was the son of a Swedish nobleman
who in his youth had served as captain in one of the foreign regiments
employed by Louis XVI. Thus he had known Versailles in the palmy
days before the Revolution and had been presented to Marie-Antoinette.
Returning to Sweden in 1791, he had been implicated in a plot to
assassinate Gustavus III and sentenced to perpetual banishment. He
settled first in Switzerland, where he joined the cosmopolitan circle
gathered at Coppet round Mme de Staël, then later returned to France,
purchased an estate and lived on it quietly until the fall of Napoleon,
refusing all offers of employment in the imperial army for fear of being
obliged, one day, to bear arms against his native country. At some
stage in this adventurous, wandering life he had married; his son
Adolphe was a somewhat lackadaisical but good-natured youth of
about Dumas's age. The chief bond between the two was their common
interest in the theatre and the ambition they shared to make their mark
as dramatists.

De la Ponce was six or seven years older, an officer of hussars with
such rounded features and so delicate a complexion as to risk appearing
effeminate, were it not for a huge sabre cut running vertically down his
left cheek which, without actually disfiguring him, gave him an
indisputably martial air. Whether this was a battle-scar or the relic of
a duel he never said; but at all events his fighting days were behind
him now; he had married a friend of Dumas's sister and was living
the life of a country gentleman. Earlier travels had turned him into
something of a linguist, and it was from him that Dumas learned
Italian, the only foreign language he ever mastered. They started by
working through Ugo Foscolo's *Ultime lettere di Jacopo Ortis*, the first
specimen of romantic literature Dumas had as yet come across. The
second was Bürger's ballad *Lenore*. De la Ponce's efforts to teach him

German as well as Italian were unavailing, but he took the trouble to write out for his young friend a French prose translation of this eerie poem. Dumas was spell-bound by both these works, but the real revelation came with *Hamlet* which, even in the pedestrian and unfaithful version due to Shakespeare's eighteenth-century translator Ducis, excited him almost to the point of delirium when he saw it produced in the theatre at Soissons. On his return he hastily sent off to Paris for a copy of the text, and within three days of receiving it he knew the part of Hamlet by heart. No other dramatic work had left him with such an impression, 'profound, full of inexplicable sensations, of vague yearnings and mysterious gleams which disclosed, as yet, nothing but chaos to my eyes.'[3]

That he might himself win fame and even, perhaps, make a living as a writer of plays was an idea that took hold of him in the course of eager conversations with Adolphe de Leuven, after his friend returned from a six-month visit to Paris. During this stay, Adolphe had had the opportunity of meeting a few of the leading actors, theatre-managers, and dramatists of the time. Foremost among them was his father's old friend Antoine-Vincent Arnault, the climax of whose literary career had been the tumultuous production, in 1817, of *Germanicus*; opinions about the merits of this play were so divided on the first night that fighting broke out in the pit, and thereafter, for a while at least, it was fashionable to refer to gentlemen's canes, the principal arguments used in this dispute, as 'des germanicus'. But there were other playwrights about whom Adolphe was able now to talk knowledgeably: Casimir Delavigne, the author of the much adulated *Vêpres siciliennes* of 1819; Lebrun, whose adaptation of Schiller's *Maria Stuart* was the great theatrical success of 1820; and Amédée Pichat, shortly to come to the fore with his Spartan tragedy *Léonidas* which, banned by the censor in 1822, had a sensational first night in 1825. All these and others too—Alexandre Soumet, Népomucène Lemercier, Etienne de Jouy—were names to conjure with in the early days of the Restoration; but today, relegated as they are to the footnotes of literary history, the celebrity they enjoyed seems almost incredible. A few of them sensed that something else was required than everlasting imitations of the masterpieces of Corneille and Voltaire but, hamstrung by a suspicious theatre censorship and an ultra-conservative theatre public, they scarcely dared risk the mildest of innovations. Dumas himself, and then Vigny and Hugo, were to sweep their unreal, unpoetic, bloodless tragedies into the limbo of forgotten things; romanticism, when it dawned, banished them as daybreak banishes the pallid ghosts of the night.

Not that it occurred to Dumas, at this point, to set out to rival the masters of neoclassical drama. To select an episode from the histories

of Livy, Quintus Curtius, Tacitus or Suetonius and spin it out into
five ponderous acts, faithfully observing the unities of time and place
and all the other 'rules', was something quite beyond his powers,
luckily. But there were other kinds of play currently attracting audiences
in Paris. The melodrama, popularized by Pixerécourt twenty years
earlier, was enjoying a new lease of life thanks to the elaborate sets and
stage-machinery introduced at the Ambigu-Comique by Daguerre (this
was before he turned his attention to photography). Then there was
the vaudeville, an art-form entirely refurbished by one of the most
successful playwrights of the day, Eugène Scribe. In its simplest form,
the vaudeville was a short, humorous sketch, with unexpected twists
and farcical situations, further enlivened by sentimental or satirical
songs. Scribe poured out his vaudevilles untiringly; they were shown
in the Théâtre du Gymnase, a sparkling new playhouse which catered
chiefly for half-pay officers and small shopkeepers who brought their
wives and families along, for Scribe could always be relied on never
to write anything in the least *risqué*. Fashionable society contributed the
rather thin audiences at the Théâtre-Français, while artisans and the
like crowded into the Porte-Saint-Martin and other boulevard theatres
which fed them on a stimulating diet of melodramas.

Seeing Dumas so anxious to break into this magic world, Leuven
suggested they might collaborate in devising a few plays which he
would try and get accepted on his next visit. The writing of these far
from imperishable masterpieces—we know of them today only by
their titles—kept the two friends busy for a whole twelvemonth (in
1820 and 1821) for, if Leuven had as much spare time as he needed,
Dumas's, what with his daytime job at the notary's and his nightly
assignations with Adèle Dalvin, was strictly limited. In the end,
however, their joint efforts bore fruit, in the shape of a couple of
vaudevilles and a melodrama drawn from the chronicles of the
Moorish kingdom of Granada. Leuven set off in euphoric mood and
Dumas remained behind, impatiently awaiting his letters. The news
they contained, when they arrived after an ominous delay, could not
have been more discouraging. On one pretext or another—either
because the plots were too thin, or the subjects too hackneyed—every
theatre Leuven tried had declined their offerings.

Dumas, however, was not the man to give up easily. What he needed,
as he told himself, was to make direct, personal contact with these
blinkered theatre-managers. As a go-between, Adolphe, with his
polished, languid manners, lacked push. Moreover, Dumas had another
play in reserve, which he had written entirely by himself, basing it on
an episode in Scott's *Ivanhoe*, a newly published novel which Leuven
had sent him from Paris on his first visit.[4] The difficulties, however, in
arranging even a short stay in the capital were formidable. He was no

longer living at Villers-Cotterêts but at Crépy, a new job having been found him at another notary's office; it had the advantage that board and lodging were provided but, on the other hand, the salary attached afforded him little more than pocket-money. Then, one morning in November 1822, he glimpsed his opportunity. An old acquaintance called Paillet, formerly head clerk at Mennesson's office when Dumas was working there, dropped in to pay him an unexpected social call, and Dumas, learning that Paillet had a horse, and knowing that M. Lefèvre, his employer at Crépy, would be away for a few days, decided that this was the moment to make a surreptitious trip to Paris and spy out the land for himself. True, he and Paillet between them had no more than 35 francs, but Dumas, resourceful as ever, convinced his friend that they could manage very well by, as it were, living off the land. Their road lay through country well stocked with game. He had his gun, and at this time of the year he was confident he could bag any number of fat birds. Paillet, on horseback, would keep watch for irate gamekeepers. If any such were seen approaching, Dumas, with the gun and the *corpus delicti*, would change places with him and canter off, leaving Paillet, an inoffensive wayfarer, to confront the man and purchase his silence with a modest tip.

This strategy worked wonders; they arrived in Paris the following evening with four hares, six brace of partridge and a couple of quails strung from the saddle. An obliging hotelier agreed to give them free board and lodging in return for these provisions. Early the following morning Dumas burst into Leuven's room to drag him off to visit Talma. He had already seen the street placards advertising Talma's appearance that evening in Jouy's tragedy *Sylla*; nothing would satisfy him but that they should go and see it, and the only way to do this without paying was to persuade the star actor to let them have a couple of complimentary tickets.

Talma, the grand old man of the Paris stage, was a living legend. The son of a French dentist practising in London, he had, as a boy, watched Macklin and John Philip Kemble at Drury Lane and when, in 1787, he joined the Comédie-Française, his great ambition was to introduce a measure of historical realism into the highly artificial acting traditions of the old royal theatre. He became a firm friend of David and, with the artist's help, started the fashion for authentic costumes in plays set in ancient Rome, so that, for instance, as Proculus in Voltaire's *Brutus* he appeared on stage, to the amazement of the audience and the scandalized disgust of the rest of the cast, wearing toga and sandals and, instead of a wig, his own hair cut short. Napoleon, who appreciated his naturalistic style of acting, became another close personal friend at a rather later date. As the Roman dictator in *Sylla*, the play Dumas wanted to see, he deliberately imitated Napoleon's mannerisms and even appearance, in order to underscore the topicality of Jouy's otherwise rather dull play. Talma was no true devotee of the neoclassical French tragedies in which he was obliged to play the leading parts at the Théâtre-Français; he always retained his early love of Shakespeare, and down to the very end of his life he was constantly hoping for some kind of theatrical revolution to shatter the rigid conventions governing the form and content of serious plays in his day. He was to die, however, in his early sixties, before he had the opportunity of witnessing the sweeping changes that romanticism was to introduce in the French theatre at the end of the decade.

The two young men found Talma at his ablutions, stripped to the waist, so they made their call a brief one. Dumas, however, was touched that the great actor remembered having met his father in happier days; and he signed them their tickets of admission without demur. The evening's performance amply fulfilled Dumas's expectations; then, after the curtain had fallen, Adolphe took him backstage, where there was a huge press in the antechamber to Talma's dressing-room. The actor, who was short-sighted, recognized Dumas by his height and his tousled hair and called him over. He asked him if he was intending to come and see Lucien Arnault's *Régulus* which was to replace *Sylla* in a couple of days' time. Dumas had to explain that he could not stay in Paris, and mentioned his humble job in a notary's office. 'Don't despair,' cried Talma. 'Corneille worked as an attorney's clerk! Gentlemen!' he added, looking round. 'I present to you a future Corneille!' Dumas blushed, and asked Talma to touch him on the forehead, to bring him luck. Talma did better; laying his hand on his head, he declaimed: 'Alexandre Dumas, I baptize you poet in the name of Shakespeare, Corneille, and Schiller! Return to the provinces, go back to your office, and if you truly have a vocation, the Angel of Poetry will seek you out and snatch you up by the hair, like the prophet Habakkuk, and bring you wheresoever you need to be.'[5]

Outside in the corridor, Dumas could hardly refrain from throwing his arms round Leuven's neck. 'Never fear,' he said. 'I will be back in Paris, depend on it!' He found time to leave the manuscript of *Ivanhoe* with a member of the company of the Ambigu-Comique (she returned it later, with a brief note saying they were 'flooded out with plays'), and then he and Paillet took the road back to Crépy. Unfortunately M. Lefèvre had returned before him and the clerk had to confront a displeased employer. Lefèvre would have been content to let the truant off with a wigging; but Dumas had already decided to throw up the job, and without further ado packed his belongings and set out for Villers-Cotterêts. His mother, naturally, was full of misgivings, but Alexandre's confidence and high spirits cut her remonstrances short. There were, however, sundry debts to pay off before he left home; in particular he was being dunned rather persistently by a troublesome tailor. The necessary cash was raised by two fortunate strokes of business. Firstly, he found a purchaser for a set of Piranesi engravings his father had brought back from Italy; then, by great good fortune, he was told of an eccentric Englishman needing a hunting dog, who was prepared to go to ten napoleons for his pointer. Dumas, unwilling to take advantage even of an Englishman, refused to accept more than five gold pieces for the animal, a sum which sufficed to pacify the tailor. After that he said his farewells, boarded the coach, and sped away to Paris, this time for good, with a light purse and a light heart.

IV Bureaucracy versus the Theatre

In the early nineteenth century, before paper qualifications and success in competitive examinations had taken on the importance they have today, protection and patronage were all that counted when it came to seeking employment in the public service. What Dumas was relying on, when he rashly decided to move to Paris without any post to take up, was the helping hand he expected would be extended to him by one or other of his father's old army friends. Even though the restored monarchical régime had to take account of the claims of émigré nobles for well remunerated posts as the due reward for their past loyalty, it was not possible to dispense entirely with the services of the experienced men who had occupied high administrative office under the previous régime. Thus, Louis XVIII's Minister for War was Victor, Duc de Bellune, whom Napoleon had promoted to the rank of marshal after the battle of Friedland. Alexandre had in his portfolio a letter from Marshal Victor to his father, thanking him for some service General Dumas had done him in Italy, and promising to repay his kindness at the first opportunity; well, the opportunity had come, but it would be the son who would be the beneficiary, or so he thought, as he composed a respectfully worded petition to the minister. He had similar letters from two other high-ranking officers, Jourdan and Sébastiani, both of whom had sworn allegiance to their new royal master and were well placed to help him. He called on each of them in turn. The one professed to be unconvinced that Alexandre was really General Dumas's son, the other dismissed him with a few benevolent but non-committal words. He returned, disconsolate, to the modest hotel where he had taken a room.

Here, flicking through a directory, he chanced on the name of General Verdier, and remembered hearing his mother talking about this man who had served under his father in Egypt. Nothing venture, nothing gain. Dumas set off for the address indicated, and found it to be a very modest dwelling-house in an unfashionable quarter. The door was answered by a hale man in his sixties, wearing an artist's smock and holding a palette in his left hand. After some initial confusion, it emerged that this was indeed the general, who had taken to painting battle-scenes as a means of beguiling his enforced retirement. Dumas realized at once that the man had no influence and was therefore in no position to help him, but at least Verdier did not regard him as an interloper. The advice he offered, if chilling, was realistic. As the son of a republican general, Alexandre had less chance of entering the civil administration than if his father had fought for the Russians or the Austrians. The men currently in charge of affairs in France were more reactionary than any who had held power since the return of the Bourbons; the assassination in 1820 of the Duc de Berry, the only male member of the royal family still young and vigorous enough to beget an heir to the throne, had brought about the replacement of the conciliatory cabinet of Decazes by one headed by the ultra-royalist Villèle. In these circumstances, no one who might be suspected of republican or Bonapartist sympathies could hope for preferment. Marshal Victor owed his portfolio solely to the fact that, when Napoleon returned from Elba, he had refused to join him and had followed Louis XVIII into temporary exile at Ghent.

But Dumas had one other letter of recommendation, of which he had not so far made use, addressed to none of the men in power but to General Foy, one of the leaders of the liberal opposition. In the last elections Foy had only managed to retain his seat thanks to the efforts of an energetic party manager, a small landowner called Danré; and Danré, who had been on friendly terms with Mme Dumas ever since she had nursed him after a hunting accident, had given her son this letter of introduction to Foy. Verdier urged his visitor to make use of it without further delay, and Dumas did as he advised.

Foy, respected even by his political opponents as an incorruptible and fearless parliamentarian, was at this time a man verging on fifty, with a beaked nose and a lofty brow, brusque in speech, unbending in manner. Altogether a daunting person for the young man to confront, and the relentless questioning he submitted him to made the unfortunate applicant wish the earth would open and swallow him. What were his qualifications? In mathematics? algebra? geometry? physics? 'He paused after each word, and at each word I felt my face redden and the perspiration start on my forehead.' Foy asked him if he had taken a law degree.

'No.'

'You know Latin and Greek?'

'A little.'

'Can you speak any foreign languages?'

'Italian quite well, German rather badly.'

'Perhaps I can find you a job in Laffitte's bank, then. Do you understand bookkeeping?'

'Not the first thing about it.'[1]

Finally Foy, who genuinely wanted to help him and was perhaps
just as embarrassed as Dumas at this recital of the gaps in his education,
told him to write down his address. Then he clapped his hands. 'We're
saved!' he exclaimed. Dumas's handwriting, thanks to the lessons he
had taken with Oblet in Villers-Cotterêts, was his one asset; in the
days before the typewriter made the accomplishment obsolete, to be
able to write rapidly, legibly, and stylishly did at least qualify one for
employment as a copy-clerk. Foy got him to compose a letter of
application on the spot, which he promised to pass on to the Duc
d'Orléans with whom he was, by a fortunate chance, dining that very
evening; and he invited Dumas to come back and have lunch with him
the following day. When he did so, Foy greeted him with a broad
smile; he was to be taken on as a probationary clerk in the Duke's
secretariat, at 1,200 francs a year.[2] Dumas showed himself properly
grateful and, growing expansive over lunch, confided to Foy the plans
he had for carving himself a literary career. 'Yes, General, my handwriting will earn me a living now, but one day, I assure you, I shall
make my living by writing.'[3]

One of the first hints he was given, by a friendly fellow clerk the
day he reported for work, was to keep quiet about these literary
ambitions of his. Career bureaucrats did not like to think that their
juniors had only entered the service as a temporary expedient to keep
the wolf from the door until the royalties started rolling in. Even
though it was generally understood that the salaries paid were barely
adequate to support life, and that some supplementation by moon-
lighting was almost essential, they much preferred to think that their
clerks were doubling as head-waiters in the evenings or had contracted
a sensible marriage with the proprietress of a laundry than that they
were earning money on the side by writing for magazines or collaborat-
ing in the confection of some flimsy theatrical sketch.[4] Dumas's
immediate chief, a man called Oudard, was proud of having risen
from his originally humble station in life—he was the son of poor
peasants—to his present position as private secretary to the Duchesse
d'Orléans, and he made no secret of his belief that Dumas's hopes of
writing for the stage were totally illusory and might, if persisted in,
jeopardize the steady and honourable career which, thanks to Foy and
the royal duke, he was now embarked on.

The same message was conveyed to him, much more brutally, by
another department head, none other than Deviolaine, with whom
Dumas had had far from easy relations in the past; we have seen how,
nine years previously, he had been hauled up before him to answer
charges of poaching and resisting arrest by a gamekeeper. As a relative,
Deviolaine had naturally been consulted when the question of giving
his young cousin a job in the office was mooted, and had at least

acquiesced in the appointment; so Dumas felt it was only proper to visit him and tender his thanks. He found him as gruff and coarsely spoken as ever, but Dumas knew him better than to take his outbursts too seriously. When Deviolaine threatened him with all kinds of dire but unspecified consequences if he persisted in writing his 'filthy plays and beggarly verses', Dumas answered imperturbably that the only reason he had come to Paris was to make a name for himself doing precisely that.

'No, but seriously,' asked Deviolaine, 'do you really mean to tell me that, with an education at three francs a month, you can become a Corneille, a Racine, a Voltaire?'

'If I became one of these three men, I should merely be what another had been, and it wouldn't be worth it.'

'So you're going to do better than they, you mean?'

'I'll do something different.'

'D'ye mind coming a little closer, so I can give you a good kick up the arse?'[5]

Whereupon, Deviolaine sent him about his business, though not before pressing him most cordially to come and dine *en famille* whenever he had a free evening.

With his rude comments on the deficiencies of Dumas's education Deviolaine had, of course, struck home; the would-be author was already painfully aware how little he really knew and painfully anxious to fill in the gaps in his knowledge; but where to start? Lassagne, the same friendly clerk who had put him on his guard against talking too freely about his literary ambitions in the office, gave him some excellent advice about the programme of reading he ought to undertake before he should even think of writing. As far as the drama was concerned, there were only four authors he needed to study: Aeschylus, Shakespeare, Molière, and Schiller. The neoclassical tragedians of the day, whom Dumas had naïvely supposed represented the *nec plus ultra* of the dramatic art, men like Arnault, Lemercier, Jouy, were idols with feet of clay; if it were not for Talma, nobody would bother to go and see their plays. The younger generation of playwrights, Alexandre Soumet, Casimir Delavigne, etc. were talented enough, but should be regarded as no more than transitional writers. It would require a man of more revolutionary genius than any of them to invent the new drama and give it substance; the mass of playgoers were not clear what they wanted, only that it should be something radically different from what the Comédie-Française had been showing ever since the reign of Louis XIV. Perhaps tragedy was in any case on its way out; perhaps the future lay with that much despised literary *genre*, prose fiction. The astonishing success of the translations of Scott that had been pouring from the presses over the last few years suggested there might be a great untapped demand for historical novels in France, and Lassagne told Dumas he could not do better than to spend his spare time studying the old chroniclers and memoir-writers, from Joinville and Froissart to Retz and Saint-Simon.

If Dumas does not appear to have acted with any great alacrity on this advice, it was not through laziness or because he lacked the leisure to embark on a course of reading such as Lassagne had sketched out for him. His office hours were not unreasonably long: from 10.30 to 5, though on certain days he was required to return and put in a couple of hours in the evening. Also, the work made no great demands on his concentration, consisting as it did for the most part in copying out letters for Oudard or someone higher up the official hierarchy to sign. This almost totally mechanical occupation should have left his mind fresh enough, on his free evenings, to sample all those authors Lassagne had told him about. But Dumas had another call on his time.

As soon as his job had been settled, he had moved into a small apartment on the Place des Italiens, at no great distance from the Palais-Royal which was his place of work. The occupant of the flat across the landing was, he discovered, a young woman living on her own. Although not strikingly beautiful, nor even pretty in the usual sense, she had a winsome little face and her skin had that special pale-ness that always seems to have attracted Dumas; possibly the childhood memory of his father's swarthy cheek pressed against the pink-and-white cheek of Pauline Borghese had left a deeper impression than he realized. He seized the next opportunity to pump the concierge about his neighbour. She had come from Rouen, he was told; her name was Mme Labay and she was working as a sempstress. Married, then? Yes, but separated; it seemed they hadn't hit it off, the two of them. This information reassured Dumas. There was no fear of a jealous husband turning up at an awkward moment but, on the other hand, divorce having been legally abolished in 1816, there was no risk either that he would be expected, in certain circumstances, to marry her. In fact, this story of her brief married life was pure invention on the part of Catherine Labay who was certainly a spinster, even if she were not a virgin, when she became Alexandre Dumas's mistress.

It needed no very consummate strategy to overcome her resistance: a suggestion they should pick the next fine Sunday to make an excursion to the woods at Meudon, a few ardent protestations as they sat on the grass, and she was ready to follow him docilely into one of the mossy grottoes nearby. Dumas, whose two-year liaison with Adèle Dalvin had had no untoward consequences, may have been a little taken aback when, so soon after the seduction, Catherine told him she was with child. It was an uncomplicated pregnancy and, on July 27th, 1824, a boy was born and duly registered under the name of Alexandre.[6] In later years the father came to regret this choice of name, for his son turned out to have inherited his literary gifts and it then became necessary to distinguish between the two writers by calling the elder Alexandre Dumas *père*. The word, he thought, was altogether too dignified; and it made him sound older than he felt.

Although the couple were now living together and consequently could economize on the rent, with two extra mouths to feed Dumas found it hard to make ends meet on his meagre salary. Fortunately he was given a rise, from 1,200 to 1,500 francs, at the beginning of the year, but this small increase of income had the effect, paradoxically, of adding disproportionately to his commitments. For his mother decided that, since Alexandre was obviously making good, she would join him in Paris; she disposed of the tobacconist's business, realized her few assets in Villers-Cotterêts, and arrived with the remnants of her life-savings, 2,000 francs in cash. As a dutiful son, he took another two-bedroom apartment where they could be together, at the rather high annual rent of 350 francs. Naturally, he did not dare explain to his mother that he now had a mistress and child to support.

Eighteen months later the 2,000 francs had melted away; if he were not to fall into debt, it was imperative to find some way of supplementing his inadequate salary, and the only course he was prepared to consider was to turn to good account the dramatic talent which he was sure he possessed. He persuaded Leuven that, since no theatre was prepared to put on any of the sketches they had written together, they had best associate themselves with a professional dramatist, one who knew the ropes and could tell them where they were going wrong. The man they settled on was a notoriously dissolute writer called Pierre-Joseph Rousseau. Tippler he may have been, but his plays were at least acted and made him enough money to keep going. So one Sunday, after treating him to a good lunch in town, they took him back to Leuven's rooms, settled him in a comfortable armchair and read him their collected—but unpublished, unplayed and apparently unplayable—works: two melodramas and three vaudevilles. Long before the reading was over, the two authors noticed that their guest had fallen fast asleep; roused, he explained apologetically that he had been on a binge the previous evening and had spent the night sleeping off his wine in the street, just outside a fruiterer's, his fellow revellers having made him as comfortable as they could on an improvised bed of cabbage-leaves and carrot-tops.

Rubbing his eyes, he said he would take their manuscripts away, read them at his leisure, and let them know the verdict in a week's time. The two friends found they could only hold him to this promise by standing him another lunch; and all he could tell them then was that no amount of rewriting could turn their plays into viable propositions; the subjects were altogether too flat and trite. The conversation sheered off on to other topics, and Dumas started telling one or two amusing stories he remembered from his hunting days in the Forest of Fontainebleau. Suddenly Rousseau smote the table: why not turn that anecdote into a vaudeville? it had all the makings of an excellent farce. So, over a third bottle of champagne, they drew up the plan of *La Chasse et l'Amour*; it was agreed that Dumas should write the opening scenes, Leuven the middle, and Rousseau the conclusion. Predictably, Rousseau had not written a word when they met again, but the three of them put their heads together and the missing scenes were all composed between nine in the evening and one in the morning.

Rousseau took the play first to Poirson, the director of the Théâtre du Gymnase, who pronounced it far too vulgar for the choice clientèle he catered for; he objected most strongly to a fairly inoffensive pun about hares and rabbits which Dumas had introduced into one of the songs. So the sketch was offered instead to the Ambigu-Comique, where it had its first performance on September 22nd, 1825. Dumas's name did not appear on the playbills, but he had his 33 per cent share of the royalties, 6 francs an evening, and in addition was able to negotiate the outright sale of his complimentary tickets for 50 francs. The man who paid him this princely sum, a former hairdresser called Porcher, was the providence of all struggling playwrights of the time; he made his living from this traffic, but had a flair for budding talent, and once it was clear that *La Chasse et l'Amour* was set for a longish run, made no difficulty about advancing Dumas a further 300 francs to enable him to publish a slim volume of army tales which appeared under the lack-lustre title, *Nouvelles contemporaines*, in 1826.

It was a disastrous speculation from all points of view. The first—and only—printing was of 1,000 copies of which precisely four were sold; Dumas lost the whole of his investment. But a first work of fiction, by an unknown and above all unbefriended writer, was almost bound to fail spectacularly. The episode, besides demonstrating a pathetic ignorance about the way the book market operated in his day, highlights a constant feature in Dumas's career as a writer, not just in his beginnings but throughout his life. Although far from being a natural solitary, and always willing—perhaps too willing—to enter into partnership with lesser writers whether for the confection of plays or novels, Dumas never attached himself to any of the numerous literary coteries which, by judicious advertisement of their members' past achievements and future potential, succeeded in getting their works published or produced on the stage and talked about in the newspapers and monthly periodicals. Victor Hugo, who was pretty nearly the same age as Dumas, had, with his two brothers, launched a magazine, *Le Conservateur littéraire*, as early as December 1819. It served as a forum for a small nucleus of unknown poets, including Alfred de Vigny and Alexandre Soumet, who before long had a literary *salon* of their own with a recognized meeting-place in the home of one of their number, Emile Deschamps. *Le Conservateur littéraire* faded out in 1821 but in 1823 its place was taken by *La Muse française*, another literary journal sustained by the same group, more or less: Hugo and Vigny, Soumet, Deschamps, Alexandre Guiraud, and half a dozen others. They constituted the first *cénacle*, meeting in Hugo's home—the precocious poet was now a respectable married man. Nor was this the only literary *salon* in Paris. The art critic Etienne Delécluze held regular weekly conversazioni attended notably by Stendhal, Mérimée, and Victor Jacquemont; and there was the better-known group which foregathered in Charles Nodier's chambers in the Bibliothèque de l'Arsenal. In 1824 *Le Globe*, another literary journal, of a different political complexion from *La Muse française*, started to appear; founded by an ex-schoolmaster, it acted as an organ for the so-called *doctrinaires*, or liberal intelligentsia, and published articles by Sainte-Beuve, Victor Cousin, and Charles de Rémusat, among others.

Anyone hoping for a career as a professional writer in the 1820s was practically obliged to frequent one or other of these *salons* and get himself known by his contributions to the particular literary periodical published under its aegis. But it had never occurred to Dumas to seek entry to one of these clubs. He had met Nodier almost as soon as he arrived in Paris but had never troubled to cultivate his acquaintance. The only *salon* which afforded him any contacts at all with writers was Arnault's, and Arnault belonged to the least progressive wing of the contemporary literary movement. His weekly dinner parties, at which Dumas was a fairly regular guest, were attended by older men, most of them Bonapartists or at any rate hostile to the Restoration régime; whereas the young Romantics were, at the time, loyal supporters of throne and altar. Through a certain Colonel Bro, a friend of Arnault's, Dumas got to know, superficially, Benjamin Constant and, rather more intimately, the poet Béranger, whose subversive ballads landed him in prison twice at this time, once during the reign of Louis XVIII and once during that of Charles X. But neither of these writers was of his generation, being men already in their fifties, and the future was certainly not in their hands; whatever their prestige, they lacked the kind of influence that might have smoothed Dumas's difficult path.

So he continued his apprenticeship as a vaudevillist. After *La Chasse et l'Amour* came *La Noce et l'Enterrement*, a sprightly comedy with an oriental setting, based on one of the stories in that favourite book of his childhood, *The Thousand and One Nights*. It was written in collaboration, this time, not with Leuven but with Lassagne, the colleague who had previously given him such sensible if scantly regarded advice on the reading he would need to undertake to complete his education. *La Noce et l'Enterrement* was under consideration by the management of one of the boulevard theatres when Oudard got wind of what his two juniors were up to and, greatly shocked, demanded they should withdraw the play. Lassagne was inclined to submit, but not Dumas, who went and had the matter out with Oudard. What right had he to forbid them, he asked hotly, to engage in this harmless out-of-office activity? Oudard tried to explain: it was not the fact of writing for the theatre that he objected to, but of discrediting the service by putting their names to such trivial rubbish. 'Follow in the footsteps of Casimir Delavigne and instead of blaming you, we will encourage you.' Dumas made a defiant answer and left the room; but privately he had to admit that, however preposterous the notion of taking Delavigne as a model, there was a certain justice in Oudard's reproaches. At the first night of *La Noce et l'Enterrement*, which he attended incognito (for he had asked not to be named as one of the authors) he overheard the gentleman sitting next to him mutter, as the final applause broke out: 'It's all very well, but that's not the kind of stuff that will save the theatre!' Maybe not, but for all that the comedy went down well enough with the rest of the audience and, since there were some two score performances for each of which Dumas was paid eight francs, he and his mother—not to mention Catherine Labay and her son—were able to weather the winter of 1826–7 in relative comfort.

The event which, more than anything else, gave Dumas's dramatic career a new direction and a new impetus at this point was the visit of a star company of British actors whose repertoire, though it included works by Sheridan, Otway, and Nicholas Rowe, was chiefly devoted to the Shakespearian masterpieces. There had been an earlier opportunity, in 1822, for Parisian audiences to see Shakespeare acted in his own language, but the visiting players had been second-rate and the violent anglophobia of the time had made it literally impossible for them to gain a hearing. But the booking of the Odéon in the autumn of 1827 for a season of plays by a company which could command the services of Macready, Edmund Kean, and Charles Kemble was recognized from the start as a major attraction. The impact not just of the tragedies, *Hamlet* and *Romeo and Juliet* in particular, but of the totally different style of tragic acting practised in Regency England, was ultimately decisive for the victory of romanticism on the Paris stage and had, besides, considerable repercussions on the development of French art and even music during the next decade; for among the audience were Delacroix, who had a good command of English, and young Berlioz who could not understand a word of what was being said but was ravished by the sight of Harriet Smithson impersonating Ophelia,

Juliet, and Desdemona. Both Hugo and Vigny saw the performances, and so too did many of the senior actors and actresses of the Comédie-Française, Mlle Mars among them, as well as boulevard players such as Frédérick Lemaître, Marie Dorval and Bocage who were to incarnate the heroes and heroines of the great romantic dramas produced after the July Revolution. The transformation of acting style on the Paris stage was as significant a result of the visiting company's performances as was the catalytic effect on the younger generation of dramatists of seeing and hearing Shakespeare no longer through the muddy medium of imperfect translations but in versions which accorded, more or less, with the Elizabethan originals.

The first of the Shakespeare plays to be put on at the Odéon was *Hamlet*, on September 11th. Although ignorant of English, Dumas knew the general drift of the play well enough through Ducis's version and in any case, the free gesturing and lively facial expressions of the English players, so different from the wooden posturing traditional on the boards of the Théâtre-Français, conveyed almost as much as did the obscure lines they were speaking. 'The battlement scene, the scene of the two portraits, Ophelia's madness, the grave-diggers' scene, these shook me to the core. From this time on, but only then, did I have an idea of what the theatre could be, and out of all the broken fragments of the past I glimpsed the possibility of creating a world.'[7] He saw *Romeo and Juliet* on September 15th and *Othello* on the 18th. The tour had been planned to end on December 10th but the response of the public was so overwhelming that the visiting company went on playing all through the winter and into the summer of 1828. It seems probable that Dumas saw their productions of *The Merchant of Venice* in January, of *Richard III* in February, and of *Macbeth* in April.[8]

Under the stimulus of this revelation of the 'real Shakespeare', Dumas went to work on a verse tragedy based on the story of the assassination of Monaldischi, her chamberlain, by Christina of Sweden. The choice of subject was suggested to him, curiously, by a piece of sculpture representing the incident that he saw on the opening day of the official art exhibition which, that year, fell unusually late, on November 4th.[9] Why this bas-relief should have caught his eye rather than any of the colourful historical pictures which were also on show at this exhibition (Delacroix's *Decapitation of Marino Falieri*, Devéria's *Mary Stuart*, Delaroche's *Death of Queen Elizabeth*) is hard to explain, unless one supposes that he had already heard something about the extraordinary figure of Queen Christina from Adolphe de Leuven's father who, it will be remembered, was a Swedish nobleman.

Christine was written expressly for the Comédie-Française, even though Dumas had no contacts with any member of the company and no prospect of securing an introduction to its powerful director,

Baron Taylor. Lassagne, to whom he spoke about his predicament, suggested having recourse to Nodier, who was known to be a close friend of Taylor's. Many years before, Dumas had chanced to sit next to Nodier at the theatre, and had got into conversation with him without knowing who he was. Would Nodier remember the occasion? it seemed to Dumas most unlikely, but he could lose nothing by trying. The first call he paid was not too encouraging. He was received, graciously enough, by the daughter of the house, Marie Nodier, who explained that her father was extremely busy with a novel he was trying to finish and had given strict instructions to admit no one. Dumas pleaded so eloquently to be made an exception that the girl said she would try and see what could be done. She returned after a brief colloquy and, slightly embarrassed, told the young man that her father decidedly could not see him. Dumas bowed, smiled engagingly, and said he would return to try his luck again in a day or two; which he did. Marie found her father as ill disposed as ever to grant the importunate caller audience. He knew all about this Alexandre Dumas: a rascally theatre usher whose only reason for wanting to see him was to touch him for a small loan. This description did not seem to his daughter to tally at all with her impression of their visitor and finally, grumbling, the old writer said she could show him in. As soon as he set eyes on Dumas's tall, elegant figure Nodier choked with astonishment. It appeared there really was a theatre usher bearing the same name as his, and apt to pass himself off dishonestly as a 'man of letters'. Distressed at having mistaken the playwright for his disreputable homonym, and charmed, almost as much as his daughter had been, by Dumas's winning smile and pleasant talk, Nodier readily promised to speak to Taylor about his play.[10]

A few days later Dumas duly received an invitation to call on the director of the Comédie-Française—at seven in the morning. A little startled at being summoned so early in the day, Dumas nevertheless presented himself punctually at Taylor's door, rang the bell, and found himself practically pulled inside by an agitated maid who begged him to go straight up; he would find the baron in his bath. From the bathroom issued not the usual sound of splashing water, but a droning voice intoning endless Alexandrines; it appeared that another, uninvited playwright had forced his way in and was remorselessly reading to the defenceless theatre director an interminable tragedy he had composed on the subject of Queen Hecuba. Finally the intruder left; shivering, Taylor stepped out of his now less than tepid bath, wrapped himself in a dressing-gown, and motioned Dumas to follow him into the adjoining room. Deferential as always, Dumas offered to return at some more propitious moment, but it seemed that Taylor was genuinely anxious to hear his play. Possibly the fact that the subject was drawn from modern and not ancient history counted in its favour, for Taylor was sympathetic to the budding romantic movement and keen to promote any new work which seemed to offer an escape route from the cul-de-sac of neoclassical tragedy.

His views, however, were not shared by all members of the august company of the Comédie-Française, the majority of whom were conservative in outlook and in consequence found much to object to in *Christine*. But Dumas, well aware that, as a mere beginner, he had a great deal to learn, and that as a newcomer it was incumbent on him to adopt a propitiatory stance, readily agreed to make the changes they wanted and, on a second reading (April 30th, 1828) the play was accepted. This in itself was a great triumph, but, once again, viewed with sour disfavour by Dumas's employers. Deviolaine sent for him to give him another dressing-down. He told him it was obvious the actors were leading him up the garden path; they might put his wretched play into rehearsal but they would never actually put it on, and even if they did, the audience wouldn't give it a hearing. 'Dammit, you're not going to tell me that you, with your education at three francs a month, you'll succeed when people like M. Viennet, M. Lemercier, M. Lebrun come a cropper. Get along with you!'[11]

Deviolaine's prediction proved correct in one respect: *Christine* was never produced at the Théâtre-Français. As ill luck would have it, another play on the same subject was submitted shortly after Dumas's, with an urgent recommendation it should be shown with the minimum of delay, since its author was in the last stages of a terminal illness. It was put to Dumas that the poor man ought to have the satisfaction of seeing his work performed before he died. This appeal to his good nature was irresistible and Dumas withdrew his play, which was in consequence not shown until 1830, and then at the Odéon, not at the Théâtre-Français.

His compliance with the company's request gave him, however, a certain claim on their goodwill, and it was important to cash in on this at the earliest moment. So, in July, he started work on a new play, *Henri III et sa cour*. As with *Christine*, the starting-point came to him by sheer chance; Dumas was still far too poorly versed in the history of his own country to be able to select from its annals the incidents that would best lend themselves to dramatic treatment. At the Palais-Royal one day, having run out of paper, he went into a friend's office to borrow some. His colleague was out of the room; while waiting for him to return, Dumas started leafing through a history book lying on his desk. His attention was caught by a story about the Duc de Guise who, suspecting an intrigue between his wife and a young courtier called Saint-Mégrin, charged her with it and bade her opt between death by poison or by cold steel. She chose poison but the

Duke, who merely wanted to give her a fright and teach her a lesson, brought her a potion to drink which turned out to be nothing more deadly than cold broth. Pursuing his researches, Dumas discovered in L'Estoile's memoirs the account of Saint-Mégrin's assassination in 1578 by a gang of armed ruffians in the pay of the Duc de Guise. The idea of having him lured to his doom by a decoy letter sent by the Duchess herself, in bodily fear of her husband, was taken from another story in L'Estoile's chronicle, told about quite a different trio; but Dumas decided it was too good not to incorporate in his play, however it might conflict with historical truth.

Having drawn up his plan, he dashed off the play inside eight weeks, documenting himself as he went along. He gave a few private readings, the last one before Firmin and Samson, both of the Comédie-Française,[12] and *Henri III et sa cour* was officially accepted by the company on September 17th, 1828. Only then did complications set in. Dumas had promised the part of the Duchess's pert page to a pupil of Firmin's, a certain Louise Despréaux; Firmin had given him stalwart backing all the way through, and he owed the actor this small service. In any case, Louise was an attractive little thing. But Mlle Mars, who was playing the Duchess, disapproved strongly of this choice, arguing that Mlle Despréaux could never appear in doublet and hose, being grotesquely bow-legged. Dumas had to admit that he had never seen the young lady except in long skirts but whatever the case, a promise was a promise. In the end, Mlle Mars had to give way. 'Only, my dear fellow,' she said, 'ask to see your page's legs.'[13] Dumas almost certainly had ample opportunity to do this, and not just when Louise appeared in her page's costume. But it was the start of a long quarrel with the great actress, who disliked Dumas intensely, firstly because he was a romantic, secondly because of his racial origins. She used to pretend that she knew when he had called in her absence by the smell in the room. 'He's been here!' she would cry on her return, 'he's been here! Open the windows, open them all!'[14]

News of the forthcoming production was, of course, printed in the papers and reached the ears of Dumas's superiors. This time it was neither Oudard nor Deviolaine but the director of the secretariat, M. de Broval, who sent for him. 'In fairly silky tones, he explained to me that literature and bureaucracy were two enemies who had always lived at daggers drawn, and that having been told I was proposing, in spite of their natural mutual antipathy, to cement an alliance between them, he felt he should press me to declare my allegiance to one or the other.'[15] Stripped of the verbiage, it amounted to an ultimatum: if Dumas persisted in writing plays for public performance, he would have to leave the administration. Naturally, he refused to back down; but equally, he refused to accept his dismissal unless the Duc d'Orléans himself were to signify it; so he was provisionally given leave of absence without pay.

He had his revenge when the Duke consented to attend the opening performance of *Henri III et sa cour*, which turned out to be a triumph far beyond Dumas's wildest dreams; overnight, he found himself a celebrity. It must be said that Baron Taylor had spared no expense to ensure success; the costumes were eye-catching—Mlle Mars's were particularly gorgeous—and the sets were of a lavishness never before seen at the Théâtre-Français; the astrologer's laboratory in the first act was considered a marvel. But these were, after all, only accessories; it was the play itself that swept the audience off its feet (almost literally: the opera-singer Mme Malibran was seen to be hanging half out of her box, clinging to one of the pillars to save herself from tumbling out in her excitement).[16] Read today in cold blood, the work can be seen to have glaring faults. The plagiarisms are crude; to cite but one, the business of the dropped handkerchief picked up by a jealous husband is lifted straight from Schiller's *Fiesko*. The historical details, such as the rarity of clocks in early sixteenth-century France or the craze for cup-and-ball at Henry III's court, are far too artificially introduced. Worse, the characters lack all psychological depth; they are drawn straight from the stock-in-trade of the writer of melodrama, the Duc de Guise an ambitious, unscrupulous ruffian, the Duchess a passive victim, Saint-Mégrin the conventional hot-blooded, tender-hearted lover. At the same time, it is completely understandable that the audience should have reacted as it did on that memorable evening of February 10th, 1829, for *Henri III et sa cour* demonstrated beyond any doubt that here at last was a dramatist with an instinctive feeling for the theatre, able to establish a hold on his audience from the start, to carry each act through to its close without a moment's dullness, and to arrange infallibly for the curtain to fall on some pregnant piece of business—the dispatch of the fatal letter at the end of the third act, Saint-Mégrin's departure, at the end of the fourth, for what he imagines is a love-tryst but what the audience knows will be a rendezvous with death. Within each act, everything was calculated to whip up excitement and terror; the physical torture inflicted on his wife by the Duc de Guise to compel her to do his will was an extraordinary piece of audacity at the time, and was greeted with cries of delighted horror from the auditorium. This was the romantic drama which the younger generation had been sighing for, full of brio and sparkle and movement; it lacked only the poetry that Hugo was to provide, a year later, with *Hernani*.

Not only did the play end the period of Dumas's obscurity, it delivered him too from the grinding poverty he had had to contend with since he arrived in Paris. The day after the first performance, he sold the publication rights in the text for 6,000 francs—a sum it would have taken him four years to earn as a clerk in the service of the Duc d'Orléans. The royalties from the first run would bring him in, as he told Deviolaine with pardonable pride, another 15,000 at a conservative estimate. All for two months' work.

'So, in two months, you have earned the combined annual salaries of three departmental heads, including bonuses?'

'Get your three departmental heads together and tell them to do what I've done.'

'Be off with you! Listening to you talking like that, I wonder the ceiling doesn't fall on your head.'[17]

v Don Juan on the Barricades

Eighteen months before the sensational première of *Henri III et sa cour*, that is, in the summer of 1827, Dumas, finding himself at a loose end one evening, consented to accompany a friend of his, a young man of intellectual bent called Delanoue, to a public lecture billed at the Athénée, which was a government sponsored adult education centre functioning in a hall in the Palais-Royal. Delanoue was going for the sake of the lecturer, Professor Villenave; a highly erudite man, he assured Dumas, and a really fine speaker; I'll see you meet him afterwards, he added. Delanoue was as good as his word and once the evening's business was over introduced Dumas to the lecturer, a tall, slightly stooping man in his late sixties with a splendid head of wavy white hair; accompanying him was his wife, their son Théodore and their married daughter, Mme Mélanie Waldor.

Dumas learned that it was a custom of the Villenaves, after each of these lectures, to invite home a few of the younger members of the audience for tea and cakes. He readily agreed to join them, and the party set off on foot through the warm June evening, Dumas arm-in-arm with Mme Waldor. He was rather at a loss to know what to say to this slim, reserved, delicate-looking young lady, so different from any woman he had consorted with before; fortunately Delanoue, walking on the other side, kept up a flow of conversation. The young clerk judged her to be turned thirty. He learned that her husband, a captain in the regular army, was stationed away from Paris, at Thionville, and that they had a daughter, Elisa, a cherubic little girl with curly golden hair, whose birth had all but cost her frail mother her life.

He had never known a family quite like them, all of them so alive, so cultivated, so eager to discuss those questions of literary doctrine which he had thought were of interest only to professionals like old Arnault and aspiring writers like himself and Lassagne; and even the Arnault circle, when it came to the point, seemed more interested in cards than in cultural matters. Villenave, who had edited one of the leading Paris newspapers before his retirement, devoted most of his time to classifying and cataloguing his extensive collection of autograph letters; five rooms on the second storey of the house were entirely given over to housing his treasures. This was long before such

material came under the auctioneer's hammer; Villenave made his
acquisitions at no great expense, by arranging with the local grocers to
let him rummage through the old papers that people sold them to be
used as wrapping for candles, sugar-loaves, and other such commodities. Few visitors were ever allowed into his sanctuary; but Dumas
obtained access on one occasion, when he made the old man a present
of a bundle of letters addressed to his father by Napoleon and some of
the Marshals of the Empire. After this, he could count on a smiling
welcome in the little drawing-room, which M. Villenave rarely graced
with his presence, however, preferring to spend his evenings collating
his precious manuscripts.

But it was not for the sake of this pompous and self-opinionated old
scholar that Alexandre multiplied his visits to the house in the Rue de
Vaugirard. The attraction was Mélanie Waldor, with her gently
caressing eyes and low-pitched, honey-and-gravel voice. Suppressing
any pangs of conscience he may have felt when the thought of Catherine
Labay, so faithful but so very humdrum, crossed his mind, he launched
himself into a passionate courtship of the young woman, stimulated
rather than deterred by the difficulties of the enterprise; for they were
rarely alone, and in any case he noticed soon enough that, flattered
though she may have been by his attentions, she gave little sign of
being touched by them. Not that she found him unattractive, with his
tall, athletic figure, his burning blue eyes, thin face and sparse, downy
black beard. But the truth was that, though far from passionately
attached to her husband, she was terrified at the thought of giving
him cause for jealousy. They had parted, temporarily, on good terms,
and she felt perfectly content with the situation she now found herself
in, that of a married woman who was as much her own mistress as
married women of her class were allowed to be at the time. So when
Dumas, seizing his opportunity when her mother had briefly left the
room, started speaking to her in low-toned, urgent accents of his
desire to transform their friendship into something stronger, more
exclusive, the shocked horror with which she silenced him was not
altogether feigned. The little she had learned of love-making from the
perfunctory embraces of her soldier husband had left her with no
curiosity for further experiment, and the difficult, painful pregnancy
it had led to had left her desiring only that her untroubled grass-
widowhood should continue uninterrupted.

Dumas pretended to respect her wishes; so be it, a platonic friendship only; would she not, all the same, consent to meet him outside
the parental house? He had rented, he told her, a discreet bachelor's
establishment where they might converse in greater freedom than was
possible under the watchful eyes of Mme Villenave. He sent her the
address in a letter in which he affected to give guarantees of good

behaviour: 'Yes, yes, I won't lay a finger on your pretty dress, never fear. I won't ask you to remove anything apart from your hat and veil.' But he could not help adding: 'Confess, all the same, that there is a refined cruelty in telling me: "I will make myself beautiful to come and see you", and then imposing conditions . . .'[1] The conditions, however, were not long observed; on September 12th, ashamed and too confused to know quite what she was doing, she allowed him to take off the 'pretty dress' and much else besides.

Dumas soon discovered that breaking down her resistance was only the first step; to awaken in her an ardour equal to that which he felt required endlessly renewed solicitation and a whole course of persuasive indoctrination. He had never taken a married woman to bed before and supposed, optimistically, that she would have more to teach him than he had ever discovered in the arms of such untutored demi-virgins as Adèle and Catherine. Whether disappointed or not, he was undoubtedly taken aback by the prudishness that prevented Mélanie abandoning herself to the pleasure she should be experiencing. After an entire day spent together, he wrote hopefully: 'It seems to me that, although far away from me, you must still feel the impression of my kisses—kisses of a kind you have never been given by any other. Ah yes, in love you have the candour—I would say almost the ignorance—of a girl of fifteen.' But as the weeks passed, Mélanie's inability to respond to his embraces in the way he expected cast a shadow over their relationship. Lingering fearfully on the threshold of this paradise of sensual delight into which he sought to entice her, she appeared still to prefer the exchange of confidences to the exchange of caresses. 'It is happiness to write to you, but a much greater happiness to see you; and there is the same difference between seeing you and kissing you as between kissing you and . . . don't be afraid, I shan't press the comparison farther.' His never sated appetites offended her, and he found himself in the strange position of having to excuse and justify himself. 'Please believe that I only take such delight [in love-making] because it seems to link us more closely together. The moments of tranquillity that follow are delicious, even sweeter perhaps. Please believe that I can appreciate all that is most delicate in love, just as much as I enjoy all the delirious excitement it gives.' Since she still appeared unconvinced, he tried laughing her out of her frigidity. 'When you are sitting on my lap, when I press you to my heart, what does it matter what you say? For in the last resort, even though your lips tell me you hate me, your touch tells me the contrary.' And he ended his letter as though he were Catullus addressing Lesbia, sending her 'a thousand kisses on the mouth, kisses that burn, that send corresponding shudders through the whole body, and contain such felicity that they almost give pain'.

He had to cope too with her religious scruples, real or feigned.

Were they risking damnation? 'Regarding the other world—this world as it is being such a mixture of joy and sorrow—believe only that whatever portion of me may survive, even though it be but a spark, will love you as the body loves you from which that spark will have sprung. So, my angel, give me what happiness you can in this world, and let us hope for happiness in the next without counting on it, for we might be sorely disappointed.' Present mirth hath present laughter; what's to come is still unsure . . .

But there were other, more tangible threats to their idyll. As a married woman, Mme Waldor was freer to come and go than she would have been had she been younger and unmarried; but she was still the daughter of the house, and in her husband's absence her parents regarded it as their duty to keep watch over her. Her impatient lover had occasionally cause to resent the claims they made on her time, and their embarrassing questions about her mysterious, sometimes day-long absences. It is all very well living in a free country, grumbled Dumas; but what has happened to personal liberty in a modern civilization? 'We make all sorts of small concessions to those we live with, which time and habit eventually impose on us in the name of duty, so that we incur censure if we neglect them.' However, neither could forget the one overriding duty Mélanie had undertaken when she pronounced her marriage vows; the possible return on leave of Captain Waldor was a nightmarish prospect, not because of the inevitable interruption in their meetings, but because of the intolerable thought that she would be obliged to submit to her husband's intimate embraces. Mélanie was staggered by the violence of her lover's reactions, to judge from certain lines in a letter he wrote her after they had discussed this contingency. 'At last you understand me; you know what love is, since you realize what jealousy is. Have you ever experienced anything approaching it? And to think that those idiotic inventors of religions paint us hell as a place of physical torment! It's pathetic. Hell for me would be to see you continually in the arms of another. Damnation! The very thought would drive a man to crime! . . .' Mélanie tried to mollify him with the flattery all women use in such situations: true, he is my husband, but does it matter what he does with my body when you know my heart is yours and only yours? This balm was thin medicine for his wound; his inflamed imagination continued to show him in disgusting detail the authorized love-making in the conjugal chamber. 'You just can't understand all the torment I should undergo, far from you and knowing that *together in the same bed*, close to one another . . . oh, I am on the rack!'

Was he sincere in these protestations or was he simply echoing the conventional rantings of the romantic lover, imagining himself the Moor of Venice or some saturnine Byronic hero? Mélanie was not, after all, the only woman in his life. He still saw Catherine Labay from time to time, though he was no longer living with her; with his share in the profits of *Henri III et sa cour* he had established her and their baby son in a small house at Passy, on the outskirts of Paris. As for his mother, he had set her up in an apartment in the same street (Rue Madame) to which the Villenaves had recently moved, so that she and his mistress were now close neighbours. He had his own bachelor chambers at yet another address, on the fourth floor of a house at the junction of the Rue de l'Université and the Rue du Bac. Here he lived in some style, entertaining from time to time actors and actresses, theatre managers, and writers of the Romantic school who now regarded him as one of theirs.

Dumas had found his ties with Arnault's circle of neoclassical dramatists painlessly dissolved very shortly after the memorable first night of *Henri III*. He had been a regular dinner-guest at Arnault's house for several years, but on presenting himself as usual on the Sunday evening following this performance he found no one at home but Mme Arnault, who said to him: 'Dumas, when you are kind enough to come and dine with us, let us know in advance, because otherwise you would sometimes risk having to dine with no one but myself for company, and that would be poor entertainment for you.'[2] The old lady's husband, furious that the hallowed boards of the Théâtre-Français should have been desecrated by one of these barbaric, new-fangled romantic plays, had obviously decided he could no longer remain on speaking terms with the author. Dumas took the hint and never knocked on that door again. He could make do without the Arnaults now; throughout the winter of 1829, the stream of invitations was uninterrupted, for Dumas was now a coming man. The celebrated romantic artist Devéria executed his portrait, using the relatively new technique of lithography which permitted production of multiple copies, so that before long Dumas's youthful, smiling likeness was propped up in the windows of every print-shop in Paris and the provinces.

The house where he was surest of a warm welcome was that of Charles Nodier, director of the Arsenal Library, who held regular literary *soirées* every Sunday. The tone here was informal, not to say unceremonious. Nodier, with his jacket unbuttoned, remained seated to greet his guests, who for the most part belonged to the younger set of romantic poets, novelists, and artists: Vigny and Hugo, Musset and Nerval, Balzac and Mérimée; the aristocratic Delacroix and his melancholy fellow painter Tony Johannet; Barye, the sculptor, remote and reserved; another sculptor, as talkative as Barye was silent, David d'Angers; and Achille Devéria, Dumas's portraitist, an amazing dandy with his Spanish cape, stove-pipe hat, velvet faced dinner-jacket and satin waistcoat designed to look like a doublet. Most of these were, properly speaking, after-dinner guests, and arrived in the course of the evening to join in a game of cards (Nodier was a keen but unskilful whist-player) or, if they felt so inclined, to dance to the polkas played by Nodier's gifted daughter Marie on that recently perfected musical instrument, the pianoforte. The dinner-guests, who presented themselves at a somewhat earlier hour, constituted a privileged inner circle, to which, however, Dumas was rapidly promoted. He had his regular seat between Marie and Mme Nodier, where he rattled away gaily, to the gratification of his host, who declared himself delighted to have the meal-time enlivened by an even more entertaining conversationalist than he was himself.

Coffee was taken at table, and at eight the diners moved into the *salon* to await the rest of the company. There were more men than women among them, though of course Adèle Hugo accompanied her husband, and both Sophie Gay, the song-writer, and her ravishing fair-haired daughter Delphine, later to marry the newspaper tycoon Girardin, mingled with the cheerfully chattering throng. In due course, Dumas obtained Mme Nodier's consent to introduce Mélanie Waldor with her brother Théodore, presenting them both as poets; Théodore was listened to respectfully as he read his tedious elegies, tinged with the fashionable Byronic philhellenism of the time, while afterwards his sister took a turn on the floor at the invitation of Paul Foucher, Hugo's brother-in-law. Dumas, whose dancing days had ended before he left Villers-Cotterêts—we have seen in what mortifying circumstances—never invited Mélanie to waltz. His real relations with her remained unsuspected, which was just as well, for there was nothing bohemian in the librarian's social gatherings; Mme Nodier was said to have refused to receive the poetess Louise Colet, whose reputation in polite circles was slightly fly-blown. So for more easy-going feminine society Dumas relied on the parties he gave at his own establishment in the Rue de l'Université, to which members of the theatrical profession were invited, but never Mélanie.

Here, the presiding nymph was a sprightly young actress, by name Virginie Delville, whose acquaintance Dumas had made in 1828, at a time when he was still waiting for the Comédie-Française to overcome its reluctance to start rehearsing *Christine*. Mlle Delville or, to give her the curiously graceless name she had chosen for the stage, Mlle Bourbier—as one should say, Miss Puddle—was a *pensionnaire*, that is a probationary member of the Comédie-Française. A pert little piece with the French equivalent of a Cockney accent, she made an ideal girl-friend for the dissipated dramatist: always available when he wanted her and never concerned to know what he was up to when he didn't; in between love-making, she kept him amused with the stories she had to tell of the in-fighting among her colleagues at the Comédie. She may well have been counting on Dumas to reserve her a small part in the play that finally replaced *Christine* in the repertoire: *Henri III et sa cour*. That of the cheeky little page Arthur would have suited her well, but it had already been bespoken, as we have seen, and Virginie Bourbier was fobbed off with a walking-on part, that of one of the duchess's ladies-in-waiting.

Louise Despréaux, to whom the page's part was given in despite of Mlle Mars's acid observations about the shape of her legs, had started as a pupil of Talma when she was only ten. She was now nineteen, a lively and attractive girl; no doubt Dumas would have been delighted to pleasure her in place of Virginie Bourbier, who after her disappointment sulkily refused to continue her association with him. But Mlle Despréaux decided that one affectionate kiss was payment enough for the trouble he had taken on her behalf, and all his powers of seduction could never persuade her to go further. The truth was that she was more than just a pretty actress; she was intelligent, ambitious, and knew her own mind. Eventually she found a protector more to her liking in the neglected dramatist Alfred de Musset, whose comedies she succeeded in presenting to appreciative audiences in St. Petersburg long before they found a producer in Paris.

Yet another friend was Marie Dorval, an infinitely more talented actress than either of these two. She had introduced herself to him, in a highly original way, on the evening of the second performance of *Henri III*, as he was crossing the Place de l'Odéon. Sliding down the window of the cab that was taking her home, she called out to him. 'You are M. Dumas?' 'Why yes, madame,' he answered, walking over to her. Opening the carriage-door, she offered him a lift back and her lips to kiss. 'You've a fine talent, especially with women,' she declared with calculated ambiguity. The acquaintance, so auspiciously begun, ripened into a firm friendship which lasted all the rest of the actress's life.

Marie Dorval was no beauty, with her big, bulging forehead, sallow complexion, tiny nose and wide mouth. 'She was a truly heroic woman, for nature had given her no advantages,' wrote one of her admirers. 'Her face was sad and commonplace, her eyes a watery blue, her lips thin, her voice an oyster-woman's, her body a kitchen-maid's. She had to fight all the way. She battled with herself so fiercely that bit by bit she acquired a woman's grace and a lover's charm. Everything about her was warmed by the fire consuming her soul.'[3] Who, having seen her in one of the pathetic roles for which she was famous, could ever forget, wrote another contemporary after her death, 'the divine, super-human expression of that grief-stricken face, those lips writhing with passion, those eyes burning with tears, that quivering, trembling body, those thin, pale arms . . . and the graceful head hanging like a flower?'[4]

Thus, in a very short space of time Dumas acquired a not undeserved reputation as a Don Juan. 'I was credited with a whole string of adventures just as, subsequently, I have been credited with any number of clever sayings.' But he certainly originated some of these sayings, just as he certainly engaged on some of these adventures. He benefited from the myth, already current, of the superior sexual prowess of men of African extraction: 'people pointed to my crinkly hair and my swarthy skin, proof of my tropical ancestry.'[5] Most women were fascinated by him and very young men, like the Duc de Chartres, a junior member of the House of Orléans, saw him as a guide, philosopher and friend. Dumas talked endlessly to the seventeen-year-old prince about the dramatic art but more particularly about the younger and lovelier interpreters of this art.

All this while his discreet meetings with Mélanie Waldor continued; she may have suspected his infidelities, but if so she was content to overlook them, relieved, perhaps, that this too vigorous lover was able to expend some of his energies on transients. In the spring of 1830, being in poor health, she left the city to spend the hot season in the country; the Villenaves had a small estate called La Jarrie, at a short distance from Nantes. By this time Dumas had got over the first fever of passion and though he continued to write to her, his letters tended to be filled with specious excuses for not carrying out his promise to join her in Brittany: there was so much work he had to finish before he could free himself from his commitments and treat himself to a holiday. It is true that he was busy at the time, as we shall see presently, getting his new play *Antony* accepted for production at the Théâtre-Français; but that was not the only piece of business detaining him in Paris.

In the early part of the nineteenth century it was the accepted practice for a star professional from Paris to 'introduce' the latest stage hits to provincial towns, acting alongside regular members of the local repertory company. Accordingly Firmin, the Comédie-Française actor who had had the part of Saint-Mégrin in *Henri III et sa cour*, went on tour with the play at the end of its Paris run and produced it for audiences at various regional capitals, with the rest of the cast drawn from whatever talent the provincial theatre happened to boast. At one of his stops he was much struck by a performance given by the actress supplied for the part of the Duchesse de Guise and persuaded her to return with him to Paris and meet the author of the play. Dumas responded as Firmin guessed he would to the magnetic charm of this vivacious débutante, with her jet-black hair, deep blue eyes, Grecian nose and pearly white teeth. Unfortunately it was already June, too late in the season to secure her an engagement at any of the theatres at which Dumas had influence. However, he urged her strongly, now that she was here, to stay for a while; it was essential to be on the spot to seize whatever openings might present themselves, and there would surely be opportunities. In any case, he went on, speaking rapidly, 'if an opportunity doesn't arise of its own accord, I am the kind of man who can create one, and my reputation stands high enough for any play I sign, delivered to a theatre manager, to cause him to offer an immediate engagement to the man or woman who brings him the manuscript.' A little staggered, and perhaps somewhat amused, by such blatant self-assurance, Belle Krelsamer—for this was the young woman's name—agreed to prolong her visit, relying on Dumas's good offices, and Firmin's good will, to start her off on her theatrical career in the capital.

Dumas's first objective, however, was to win her for himself. After an intensive courtship lasting three weeks, she surrendered and, as he remarked with characteristic coolness when relating the story in his memoirs, 'to withstand me for three weeks is to put up a highly honourable resistance and there are very few strongholds, however well fortified, that can hold out against a siege longer than that.'[6]

Belle may well have regretted giving way so easily; for less than a month later, this inconstant lover was planning to interrupt their honeymoon so that he could take a trip to North Africa. The city of Algiers had fallen to a French expeditionary force on July 5th, 1830; and nothing would satisfy the irrepressible Dumas but that he should cross the Mediterranean and see for himself the newly conquered Barbary kingdom just as his father, when he was his age, had sailed the same sea to participate in the subjugation of Egypt. It was far too dangerous an expedition for a woman to undertake, but Belle was to accompany him as far as Marseilles. Resignedly, she set about packing a trunk.

On the day fixed for their departure (Monday, July 26th) she was astonished to receive new instructions from Dumas: they were not leaving after all, things were likely to be much more amusing here in Paris, so she had better unpack. The revolution, long anticipated by impatient republicans, seemed on the verge of breaking out. Charles X, exasperated at having his domestic policies thwarted by a rebellious Chamber, had pronounced its dissolution. He had also decreed an even tighter limitation of the franchise, so as to ensure that, in new elections to take place in September, a more biddable parliament should be returned; finally, he had suspended the clause in the constitution guaranteeing the freedom of the press, and issued orders that in future no newspaper was to appear until its contents had been seen and authorized by the Prefect of Police. 'People aren't going to like this,' said Dumas gleefully; 'and they aren't going to take it lying down.'

3*

Belle looked at him despairingly. 'What's the matter, my sweet?' 'Well, as you know, I couldn't understand your reasons for wanting to go on this African jaunt, and I understand even less your reasons for wanting to stay in Paris now.' 'Curiosity, my dear girl, in both cases.' Belle tossed her head; he might, she said, have found a more flattering reason for changing his mind.

The following day (Tuesday, July 27th) Dumas set off to tour the offices of the three opposition papers which, it was safe to predict, would be printing in defiance of the ordinances. On the way he fell in with Armand Carrel, former army officer, author of a *History of the Counter-Revolution in England*, and co-founder, with Thiers and Mignet, of *Le National*, a paper which had distinguished itself by its campaign against the ministerial decision to invade Algeria. Dumas and Carrel were in time to see the police arrive at the offices of *Le Temps* to dismantle the presses. Anticipating this move, the editorial staff had locked the doors, obliging the police officer to send for a locksmith. In the end the representatives of public order had their way and the doors were forced, but not before one of the journalists on the staff of *Le Temps*, a man with a stentorian voice and a splendid red beard, had challenged the legality of this action, reading out in ringing tones the article in the Code laying down the penalties for illegal entry.

Later the same day they heard firing coming from the direction of the Palais-Royal. Dumas, impelled by his 'curiosity', wanted to go and investigate, but Carrel was in favour of going home. He was convinced the revolution would fizzle out. Paris was full of soldiers, and what could civilians do against seasoned troops? Their commander, Marshal Marmont, had ordered the occupation of all strategic buildings, and it was only at the Palais-Royal that barricades had been erected; hence the firing. Dumas arrived to see soldiers clearing the Rue Vivienne at bayonet-point, and he watched Etienne Arago, with a small group of friends, going from theatre to theatre, summoning the management at each establishment to ring down the curtain and evacuate the auditorium.[7] But although he did see one woman killed by a stray shot, there was no concerted resistance on the part of the civilian population. After nightfall, however, while at supper in a nearby café, Dumas heard a few shots and the sound of a violent struggle. A guard post set up in front of the Bourse had been stormed by a daring band of revolutionaries, who succeeded in overpowering the detachment posted there and relieving them of their arms. Then they set fire to the blockhouse which went on burning through the night until it was reduced to a heap of ashes.

He got home about midnight and early the following morning (Wednesday, July 28th) went round to see Belle Krelsamer. Though unable to persuade him to remain safely indoors, she asked him at least to promise to keep out of trouble—a promise he readily gave and immediately broke. Back in his own apartment he changed into his hunting outfit and, with a gun in his hand, sallied forth into the streets. He spent a little time directing the construction of a barricade in the Rue du Bac and then set off to see what was happening at the offices of Carrel's paper, *Le National*. Finding his way barred by troops occupying the Rue de Richelieu, he turned off into the Palais-Royal and slipped upstairs to find out if any of his former colleagues had come in to work. Oudard was there, and asked him in astonishment the reason for his visit. 'I've come to see whether by any chance the Duc d'Orléans was here,' Dumas answered maliciously. 'What do you want with him?' asked the secretary. Dumas laughed. 'I want to address him as Your Majesty.' With the uncanny prescience in political matters he was to show on several other occasions during his life, Dumas had already, on the second day of the revolution, guessed that although the Bourbons were doomed, there would be no republic as most people expected, but instead a new monarchy, with the Duc d'Orléans, as head of the cadet branch of the royal family, on the throne. But officially, the duke was still a loyal subject of Charles X, and Oudard was unutterably shocked at Dumas's subversive sally.

From the windows of the Palais-Royal he could see the troops march up the street; just as soon as they moved on, people came out of their homes and reoccupied the pavements. The mood was clearly more defiant than it had been the previous day. Some were still shouting 'Long live the Constitution!' but now there were others crying: 'Down with the Bourbons!' and using paint and distemper to obliterate the fleurs-de-lys, the royal insignia, on all the walls and monuments. After leaving the offices of *Le National*, where he had some further talk with Carrel, Dumas continued wandering around and, emerging near the river, felt a prickling in his eyes when he saw the tricolour, banned in France since 1815, flying from the top of Notre-Dame.

The tall man striding along, with a gun in one hand and his bandolier slung from his shoulder, acted as a magnet for any would-be combatant; before long Dumas found himself leading a scratch company of some fifty men, of whom perhaps thirty carried weapons, though hardly any had powder and shot. He headed them in the direction of the Hôtel de Ville; but they halted when, at a distance, they could see other insurgents attempting to cross the bridge in the face of grapeshot; the military dispersed them after three or four discharges and Dumas's improvised company, sobered at the sight of this resolute defence, melted away into the side-streets. He himself spent the rest of the day with a family of his acquaintance, the Lethières. It was still touch-and-go, but there were rumours of widespread defections by troops under arms and the revolution might yet succeed.

No one realized more clearly than Marmont how dangerous the situation was. Orders had been given, as he knew, to regiments stationed at Orléans, Beauvais, Rouen and Caen to march on Paris, but these reinforcements would take a day or two to arrive. Faced with the risk of broken communications were his troops to remain dispersed through the city, the field marshal decided to regroup them in the quadrilateral formed by the Rue de Rivoli and the Seine to the north and south, and the two royal palaces, the Louvre and the Tuileries, to the east and west. The operation had been completed by the beginning of the third day, Thursday, July 29th, and as the revolutionaries were concentrating their fire on the Swiss guards in the Louvre, Dumas decided to position himself just opposite the Pont des Arts, taking cover behind one of the four bronze lions that stood, until 1950, in front of the Institut de France. The day was hot and airless. Only occasionally did the smoke from the enemy's guns lift sufficiently for him to distinguish the red-and-white uniforms of the Swiss mercenaries lining the parapets of the Louvre. He was surrounded by workmen, students, shop-assistants, all intent on the same deadly business. The most daring were the street-urchins, later to be immortalized by Delacroix in his semi-allegorical canvas *Liberty on the Barricades*. Lacking the physical strength to carry the heavy muskets, they brandished useless pistols and cutlasses; but they were always in the forefront of the fighting, and when the attackers, growing impatient, decided to try and storm the palace by rushing the bridge, it was the boys who led the men across. Dumas stayed where he was, having noticed a field gun at the far end of the bridge. The grapeshot, followed by a volley of musketry, killed the first half-dozen and sent the others scurrying for cover. Momentarily, Dumas found himself alone on the deserted quay-side. Taking advantage of the smoke-screen produced by a second battery discharge, he raced back to the Institut, dashed inside and then, finding a back exit into the Rue Mazarine, made his way home. His throat was parched, he had used up all his ammunition, and his shirt was stiff with sweat.

By the time he had refreshed himself and was ready to sally forth again, the fighting was over. At precisely five minutes past midday Talleyrand, who had been following the action from the window of his house, pulled out his watch and observed to the deputies standing beside him that the elder branch of the Bourbons had at that moment ceased to reign. The question still to be settled was whether the junior branch would pick up the crown of France. Dumas, after mingling with the crowd that had burst into the Tuileries, and watching four workmen dressed up in court robes performing a can-can to the sound of a fife and violin—it may well have been the first time this outrageous dance had ever been seen in public—went in search of Oudard, whom he managed to intercept just as he was leaving the Palais-Royal. He wanted to know whether his former chief would still think it treasonous to suggest that the Duc d'Orléans would be the next King of France. Oudard gave an evasive answer; in fact, as Dumas later discovered, he was even then on his way to Neuilly, where the Duke had remained discreetly inactive since the start of the revolution, to deliver him a curt ultimatum from the banker and king-maker Laffitte: 'You have the choice between a crown and a passport; which is it to be?'

Dumas spent the night of July 29th–30th at the Hôtel de Ville where La Fayette, the 73-year-old hero of the War of American Independence, had set up his headquarters as commander-in-chief of the National Guard. In the course of the afternoon he overheard Etienne Arago reporting to the general that there was a grave shortage of gunpowder in Paris; if Charles X decided to move against the city, its defenders could hardly count on being able to fire more than a few thousand rounds. Dumas saw this as a golden opportunity to cover himself with glory; breaking into the conversation, he offered to travel down to Soissons, where there was a military depot, and bring back whatever store of powder he could find there. Although judging the enterprise dubious, if not foolhardy, La Fayette raised no objection to his being given written authority to requisition the munitions.

Soissons was notoriously a hotbed of royalism; since nobody could be sure, at this point, who exercised lawful power in the country, it was far from certain that the local commander, a certain Vicomte de Liniers, would comply with the order. Nor would he at first. There was a heated argument after which Dumas, desperate at his obstinate refusal to countersign the requisition-note, pulled his pistols from his pockets and declared he would give the viscount five seconds before blowing his brains out and dealing similarly with the three other officers accompanying him. What would have happened if he had not been interrupted in his counting is hard to say; but before he had got beyond three, a side-door flew open and a hysterical woman—the commandant's wife—burst in, pleading with her husband to give way, and babbling about 'another black rising'. As a girl, she had seen both her parents massacred in the revolt of the slaves on San-Domingo in 1791. Dumas, with his tightly curling hair, his slight Creole accent, his face burnt in the July sun and with the blood of battle still staining his boots and gaiters, could easily have been mistaken by a traumatized woman for a black Haitian brigand. At all events, her intervention gave M. de Liniers a chance to yield gracefully and Dumas was allowed to load the gunpowder on to a requisitioned waggon and drive it back to Paris. For all the difference it made to the political outcome, however, it might just as well have stayed in Soissons; for, as he discovered on his return, during his two days' absence Laffitte, Talleyrand,

and Thiers had so manoeuvred that the republic Dumas wanted to see set up had been stifled at birth, and Charles X had simply been replaced by the Duc d'Orléans, who on ascending the throne took the name Louis-Philippe.

This week of effervescence, excitement, danger and final disappointment left Dumas in a state as near apathy as his normally mercurial disposition permitted. He persuaded La Fayette to send him on a semi-official fact-finding mission to Brittany, which enabled him to pay a visit, at the government's expense, to Mélanie Waldor who was still recuperating at La Jarrie. When he returned to Paris, he found the new royal administration firmly in the saddle; the part he had played in the revolution had earned him no credit, but rather the dangerous reputation of a hot-head. 'What are you doing now?' Deviolaine asked him. 'Nothing,' replied Dumas briefly. 'Lazybones!' exclaimed his relative. Stung, the young man retorted: 'But I'll be doing something before long, you'll see.' 'What are you going to do?' 'Fight, of course.' 'Fight? What's there to fight?' 'Why, the status quo,' answered Dumas defiantly. Deviolaine flew into one of his usual rages, but all ended, as it always did, with the two men embracing affectionately, while the elder prophesied that he would end up 'dying without a penny, just like your father'.[8]

Certainly, something had to be done to restore his finances, and Dumas started wondering about the theatre again. In the relaxed climate that succeeded the July Revolution, there was a strong demand for the kind of politico-historical drama that had been banned under the previous régime, and in particular for plays dealing with the career of Napoleon. Félix Harel, the bumptious manager of the Odéon, was pressing Dumas hard to write such a play, in which he hoped to cast his new star, Frédérick Lemaître, in the title role. At first Dumas turned a deaf ear, but Harel enlisted the help of Mlle George, the actress who had played the leading part in his verse drama *Christine* earlier that year, and together they hatched a plot to bring the recalcitrant author to heel. They invited him to an after-theatre supper party in the house that Harel and his leading lady shared and then, at three in the morning, told him they had something interesting to show him. Dumas was taken, all unsuspecting, upstairs and ushered into a room furnished with a writing-desk, bookcases, a couple of easy chairs and a comfortable bed with a purple eiderdown. 'A snug little room you've got here,' commented Dumas. 'I'm glad you like it,' replied Harel, 'because it's to be yours for the next few weeks. We'll let you out as soon as you've written your play on Napoleon.' Dumas, for form's sake, protested. 'You can't keep me prisoner like this. What about my mistress?' (thinking not of Mélanie Waldor, but of Belle Krelsamer). Mlle George pointed out that he had abandoned her for six weeks while he made his trip to Brittany, so it wouldn't cost him much to do without her for a few weeks more. In any case, if that was what was worrying him, her own bedroom adjoined the room assigned to him; in fact, there was no way out of his room except through hers.

Mlle George (Marguerite-Joséphine Weimer) was at this time forty-three years old. She and Harel, though living under the same roof, had a good mutual understanding which left both partners free to indulge any passing fancies. He appreciated her for her long acting experience and her ability to entertain his friends, while she never tired of his saucy wit and exuberant high spirits. Their political sympathies created a further bond, for both were ardent Bonapartists. Harel had been one of Napoleon's *préfets* during the Hundred Days, and had in consequence been driven into exile after 1815 until the amnesty, seven years later, made it possible for him to return to Paris. As for George, she had had in her youth a well-publicized liaison with the Emperor, and after his fall had refused to transfer her allegiance to the restored monarchy, even though the penalty was expulsion from the Comédie-Française and consequent loss of income and pension rights. The regal carriage, noble profile and ample bosom that had so impressed Napoleon were advantages that she retained unimpaired into middle age. But it was above all as hostess presiding at a supper-party that Mlle George was at her best; queenly, caustic of speech, a mixture, said Dumas, of a Greek hetaira, a Roman matron, and the cultivated niece of some Renaissance pope.

Harel had every reason to be delighted with his stratagem, for the play Dumas wrote under these rather unusual circumstances proved a great box-office success. Napoleon had been dead for no more than ten years and there were plenty in the audience who remembered him. Frédérick Lemaître was bombarded beforehand with advice and suggestions from marshals and princes of the Empire, though, being far too tall and quite unlike Napoleon in appearance, he made no attempt to play the part realistically. On the first night (January 10th, 1831) the Bonapartists turned up at the theatre wearing uniform, while during the intervals the orchestra played stirring military airs. Harel had not stinted money on the sets; that representing the passage of the Beresina was especially applauded. *Napoléon Bonaparte* continued to attract large audiences for the rest of that winter, though Dumas himself was anything but proud of his work, recognizing that it lacked all literary value and that its popularity was due to purely extraneous circumstances.

The drama he really wanted to have staged was one written immediately after the July Revolution, with a view to being put on, like *Henri III et sa cour*, at the Théâtre-Français, with Mlle Mars taking the part of the heroine as she had in the earlier play. The new work was, however, of a totally different kind, best described as a modern tragedy, that is to say, a play set in contemporary society but ending with a catastrophe. Previously, all plays with contemporary settings, from Molière down to Eugène Scribe, had been as a matter of course comedies, with the exception of a few experimental imitations of the German *bürgerliches Trauerspiel*; and conversely, any play written in the tragic mode, whether classical or romantic, was almost invariably set in the distant past. But with *Antony*, Dumas did away with this convention, and inaugurated the tradition that was to culminate, in the latter part of the century, in the dramatic masterpieces of Ibsen, Strindberg, and Chekhov.

His theme—adultery—was a peculiarly modern one too, at least in the way he treated it. Phèdre is no more than a would-be adulteress; Desdemona, an unjustly suspected one. In Adèle d'Hervey, however, Dumas created a heroine who is an unfaithful wife and yet an object more of pity than of reprobation. Here he may be said to have founded a different kind of dynasty, since Adèle is in some important sense the prototype of both Anna Karenina and Fontane's Effi Briest.

It is safe to predicate that Dumas would never have written *Antony* without the experience of his love-affair with Mélanie Waldor. In a letter written on June 13th, 1830, to give her the glad news that he had read the play to Mlle Mars and Firmin, both of whom were 'enchanted with their parts', he tried to reassure her about the autobiographical basis of the new work. 'You will recognize many details of our life in *Antony*, my angel, but only such as we alone have knowledge of. So you mustn't worry, the public won't notice anything, even though it awakens in us imperishable memories. As for Antony, I believe privately he will be recognized, for he's a madcap who much resembles me.'[9] In fact there is not a great deal of Dumas in the moody, violent hero, for ever brooding over his bastardy; the probability is rather that the author modelled him on Emile de Girardin, whose autobiographical novel *Emile*, published anonymously in 1827, is all about the moral sufferings of a young man born out of wedlock, whose parents for reasons of propriety refuse to recognize him. One of the difficulties Girardin faced when courting Delphine Gay was that his birth-certificate attributed to him a parentage which he knew to be fictitious; in Dumas's play, we learn that Antony did not marry Adèle when he might have because he could not name his real father and mother.[10] Adèle, on the other hand, with her one small daughter and her husband a serving officer stationed away from Paris, was easily recognized as Mme Waldor by those who knew her circumstances and suspected her liaison with the author of the play. Even the title was a veiled confession, for there had been a few weeks when Mélanie believed herself pregnant; Antony was the name Dumas invented for this unborn child. Having given his first-born one of the names borne by his grandfather, the Marquis Alexandre-Antoine Davy de la Pailleterie, it was only natural he should have given his second son his grandfather's second name, anglicized in accordance with the fashions of the romantic period.

On June 6th, 1830, *Antony* was accepted by the reading committee of the Comédie-Française and duly cast; but the actors were obviously in no great rush to get it into rehearsal. Even as late as December 15th, Dumas was still waiting, and Harel started badgering him to withdraw the play and have it put on at the Odéon as a successor to *Napoléon Bonaparte*. Finally, in the New Year, the Comédie-Française actors grudgingly started work; but they were clearly unhappy about the play, demanding one change after another until, as Dumas said, his tragedy began to take on the appearance of a light-hearted vaudeville. Then, at the dress-rehearsal, Dumas was asked by Mlle Mars whether he would mind if they put off the opening until May, by which time gas-lighting would have been installed in the theatre, allowing her expensive dresses to show to advantage. His old friend Firmin, adding insult to injury, advised him to profit by the delay to have the text revised by—of all people—Eugène Scribe, the most fanatic of the romantics' opponents. Raging, he retrieved his copy from the prompter, and went straight off to see Marie Dorval.

Imagining that he could take up where he had left off—six months before—he clasped her round the waist as soon as he saw her and was more amused than disconcerted when she promptly disengaged herself. Since she last saw him she had, as she explained, placed herself under the protection of Alfred de Vigny. 'Why, my dear,' declared Dumas, beaming, 'you couldn't have done better. In the first place, Vigny is an immensely talented poet. Secondly, he's a real gentleman; much more suited to you than a mulatto like me.' 'Well, as for that,' replied the actress, 'there could be more than one opinion.'

Antony, however, delighted her, and she was overjoyed with the part of Adèle. Listening to her reading it aloud, Dumas realized what a mistake he had made to offer it to Mlle Mars in the first place. He consented, though with some misgivings, to her plea that the title role should be given to Bocage, an actor he had seen only in a couple of small parts previously. Bocage had bandy legs and spoke with a slight nasal intonation but Marie's instinct had not been at fault; he succeeded in incarnating Antony to perfection, achieving a movingly wistful melancholy that Dumas could never remember hearing before except in Talma's interpretation of Hamlet, many years earlier. Finally, he had the satisfaction of seeing Belle Krelsamer in the small but not insignificant part of Mme de Camps, the young widow who, in the fourth act, chatters indiscreetly at a social gathering about Adèle's relations with Antony and out of sheer wantonness tears her reputation to shreds. By a curious coincidence, Mlle Krelsamer's stage name was the same as the real name of the woman on whom Dumas had modelled Adèle d'Hervey; she called herself Mélanie Serre.

The liaison between the playwright and Mélanie Serre (Belle Krelsamer) was no secret; it was moreover public knowledge that Dumas was the father of the baby girl born to her in March 1831. It had been impossible to keep Mélanie Waldor in ignorance of the identity of her successor. She was cut to the quick, and for a while threw all caution and all sense of dignity to the winds; she forced her way into the actress's lodgings and made a violent scene, she threatened to commit suicide, she wrote to Dumas offering to leave him in future completely free, provided only he agreed to break with Belle. He had the cruelty to send her tickets for the first night of *Antony*, promising to visit her in her box, and then forgetting to keep his promise; and after that Mélanie gave up the struggle, agreed to forget his ill-treatment, and talked to him, when they met socially, as though there had never been anything between them but a warm friendship.

The first night of *Antony* (May 3rd, 1831) was one of the most memorable premières in the annals of romantic drama. As had happened with *Henri III et sa cour*, it was the curtain lines that whipped up the fever; there was a particularly effective one at the end of the first act when Antony, in order to make it impossible for Adèle d'Hervey to have him moved out of her house to more suitable quarters (he had been brought in badly injured after a street accident) tears away his bandages, crying before he faints from renewed loss of blood: 'And now, I may stay, may I not?' But Dumas knew it was the third act that would make or break the play; the last scene came nearer to an enactment of rape than anything previously attempted on the stage. Adèle, not trusting to her powers of resistance, has left Paris to seek refuge with Colonel d'Hervey, her husband, at Strasbourg. Antony, setting out in pursuit, has overtaken her on the road and is secretly waiting at the coaching inn where he knows she will have to spend the night. The act ended with a vivid piece of dumb show. Antony appears on the balcony behind the window, breaks a pane of glass, climbs in, walks over to the door and bolts it; as Adèle, startled at the sound, emerges from her bedroom, he thrusts a handkerchief over her mouth and draws her back through the bedroom door. As the curtain fell, there was a brief moment of absolute silence in the theatre, and then a great roar followed by the sound of frantic clapping which went on for a full five minutes. Dumas's audacity had paid off once more.

At the end of the performance the audience was in a state of near-delirium.[11] As Dumas left his box to join Marie Dorval and Bocage on stage, he found the corridor blocked by a crowd of young men who 'pale-faced, panting, with staring eyes, bore down on me. I was tugged to the right, tugged to the left, hugged and kissed. I had on a green coat buttoning from the collar to the waist; the skirts were completely torn to pieces.' This ruined coat was carefully preserved by Catherine Labay, and right at the end of her life she would display it to a few select visitors as if it were a holy relic or the single surviving trophy of a battle fought in far-off days.[12]

Even when due allowance is made for Dumas's consummate stage-craft and for the excitement generated, in this post-revolutionary period of ideological effervescence, by the audacity of certain tirades he put in the mouth of his hero, the spectacular success of *Antony* in 1831 is not easily explained if one confines oneself to an examination of the bare bones of the text. How was it that Dumas managed to arouse in his whole audience, irrespective of differences of age and sex —and not just on this first occasion but whenever and wherever the play was put on in France during the July Monarchy—such a univers-ally responsive reaction, so that young girls dissolved into tears, young men shouted themselves hoarse, and even the respectable middle-aged burgher took off his gloves to clap and went home feeling some-thing akin to the cathartic purification of the mind that great tragedy is supposed to produce?

The answer appears to be that Dumas had, by a sleight-of-hand that almost amounts to a stroke of genius, succeeded in providing his play with an ambiguous message which satisfied the rebels and yet did not offend the conservatives. Antony, with his brandished dagger, had the air of threatening all the sacrosanct institutions of the time, and like a new Samson to be blindly shaking to pieces the two central pillars of bourgeois society, the sanctity of marriage and the inviolability of the home. This adulterer, this blasphemer against the holy of holies, was the undoubted hero of the play; every word, every act of his, from beginning to end, was calculated to arouse a thrill of sympathetic emotion among the younger members of the audience. Conversely, the wronged husband is given no say; he is not even in court, he remains an absent figure throughout, never appearing until the very last scene. He returns in the guise of an avenging angel to purge his dishonour; but our sympathies, by this time, are entirely on the side of the guilty pair whom public opinion would expect him to punish. The question is, how shall Adèle be saved, not from his violence but, what is far worse, from the blighting contumely that was the lot of the woman taken in adultery? In the few moments that precede his expected irrup-tion, as the locked door rattles and the angry man's shouts can be clearly heard, Antony asks Adèle whether she would prefer death to loss of reputation. 'I would beg for it on bended knees,' she replies. 'With my dying breath I would bless my murderer.' So he stabs her as he holds her in his arms, a second before the outraged Colonel d'Hervey bursts into the room.

But this is not all. The romantic hero, having committed the ultimate crime of murder, proceeds in effect to pay supreme tribute to established social values. The adulteress dies, her death being midway between suicide and execution; but, more fortunate than her successor Anna Karenina, she is spared the worse torture of public humiliation, and is even granted a complete posthumous rehabilitation. Antony, turning to the horrified husband and pointing to the butchered body of his wife, utters the sublime lie that will still all slanderous tongues: 'Aye, she is dead. She was resisting me, so I killed her.' In these two brief sentences, Antony transforms Adèle, in the eyes of the world, from a weak-willed wanton into a chaste martyr, more unsullied even than Lucretia, since Lucretia was at least raped before she fell on the sword.

Antony, as socially disruptive a play as had been seen in the nine-teenth century, thus ends in a superb gesture of reconciliation, and the values that had been so eloquently assailed from the start are finally seen to be implicitly accepted even by the rebel who had denounced and discarded them. It was not, after all, a revolutionary play, but one that played at being revolutionary; the last line put everything right. According to Dumas, the tumult on the first night was such that this last line could not even be heard. Later, it came to be regarded, rightly, as the key to the whole message of the play, and for that reason audiences waited for it with bated breath and burst into frenzied applause as it was spoken immediately before the final curtain fell. There was a performance at Rouen when, by mischance, it was omitted; the spectators' howls of rage at being cheated of this ultimate titbit testified to the importance it held for them. What happened on that occasion was that the stage-manager, mistaking the penultimate scene for the last, signalled for the curtain to be rung down immediately after Antony had stabbed Adèle, thus leaving no time for the husband to break in and for Antony to give the defiant and mendacious explana-tion for his deed. The spectators, in a fury, rose to their feet and shouted for the play to end 'properly'. The curtain was raised again but Bocage, playing Antony, had already left the stage in a pet and refused to come on again. Seeing that nothing else would pacify them, Marie Dorval 'came to life', rose from the chair where she had been lying with her arms dangling, walked over to the footlights and, in the sudden hush that fell, said in a clear voice: 'Gentlemen, I was resisting him, so he killed me.'

VI Melodrama on and off the Stage

Antony went on playing to enthusiastic audiences throughout the summer of 1831; it was one of the few theatrical attractions that could contend with the heat and the underlying restlessness of the times which discouraged peaceable citizens from venturing on to the streets in the evenings. The political settlement resulting from the July Revolution was still regarded by many, twelve months later, as a botched job which needed redoing. The Carlists or legitimists hankered after the restoration of the old dynasty, if not in the person of Charles X, at least in that of his grandson the Duc de Bordeaux in whose favour he had formally abdicated on August 2nd, 1830; the republicans, the so-called *réclamants de juillet,* remained unreconciled to the sleight-of-hand by which the banking and business community had imposed a compromise solution. Though one could not speak of a militant revolutionary movement as yet, there was undoubtedly widespread discontent and a pervasive mood of cynicism. Almost every evening, on the pavements of the boulevards, small groups would come together to argue and vociferate. The police would eye these impromptu debating societies warily, their hands on the guard of their swords. It was not long before one of the omnipresent gangs of street-urchins started yelling insults at the minions of the law and then, tiring of this tame sport, took to shying harmless but offensive missiles at them, cabbage-stumps or carrot-ends. Too often the disturbance would blossom into a minor riot which could rage for some hours before being brought under control.

Knowing how apt her hot-blooded lover was to take sides in any brawl he happened on, Belle Krelsamer decided it would be in his best interests, as well as hers, if they could get away from Paris until the long hot summer was over. Having contracted with Harel to write a historical drama in verse, set in the reign of Charles VII, Dumas was prepared to fall in with her suggestion, and on July 6th they set off for the seaside.

In 1831 the railways had not started to spread their tentacles over France, and to reach Le Havre, the nearest seaport to Paris, took a good twenty-four hours. The first part of the journey, as far as Rouen, was accomplished in the proverbially slow stage-coach, after which a river-boat conveyed travellers down to the mouth of the Seine. The couple had fixed on Trouville as their ultimate destination, having heard its secluded charms spoken highly of by the artist Huet.[1] At that time it was no more than a huddle of fishermen's cottages; nearby Deauville was still pasture-land. But the beach was a lively scene, with children scrambling among the rocks in search of mussels, and men and women wading through the shallows with nets to catch shrimps. There was only one inn, at which the landlady, when Dumas mentioned he knew Huet, gave them a cordial welcome; she recalled complacently how she once saved the artist from choking to death on a fish-bone, by forcing his jaws apart and thrusting a leek down his gullet. But she was much taken aback when Dumas insisted on having two separate rooms. This was not at all the way of 'her' painters when they arrived with their womenfolk, and she could make nothing of the explanation he offered —quoting an aphorism of Alphonse Karr's—that 'after a certain length of time, when a couple share a room, they cease being lover and mistress and become just male and female.'[2] He did not go into the other reasons Belle may have had for wanting a room to herself, as for instance that Dumas's working habits were not such as could be easily accommodated to a girl's need of her beauty sleep. He was up with the sun, pencilling verses for three or four hours before breakfasting with his beloved at ten. Snipe-shooting on the marshes occupied the rest of the morning; on his return, he would settle down to work again, taking an hour's break before dinner to go swimming. After the evening meal, he and Belle would go for a romantic stroll along the beach and back, but at nine o'clock he would settle down to another two or three hours' work before falling asleep.

In this way he managed his hundred lines a day, and *Charles VII chez ses grands vassaux* was all completed by August 10th. It may well have been, as he claimed, stylistically superior to his earlier verse play, *Christine*; but even so, he judged it full of faults. It was more a laborious pastiche than an original work: the starting-point had been a verse sketch by Musset, *Les Marrons du feu*, which he had heard the poet read at one of Nodier's *soirées*, and there were distant echoes of Racine's *Andromaque* and Goethe's *Götz von Berlichingen*. Worse than all this was the fact that the verse lacked all lyric fire. He was the first to admit this, when on his return to Paris he went and saw Hugo's latest play, *Marion Delorme*, in which the key roles were taken by the same pair of actors as had starred in *Antony*, Marie Dorval and Bocage. Although *Marion Delorme* was greeted with no more than polite applause from the body of the theatre—Mérimée, reporting on it to Stendhal, spoke of a 'semi-fiasco'[3]—Dumas, for his part, was carried away by enthusiasm, but at the same time felt so discouraged when he mentally compared

his achievement with Hugo's that he returned Harel the cash advance
he had received for *Charles VII*. In great alarm, Harel rushed round to
press on him five times the original sum, imagining that his star author
must have had a better offer elsewhere.

In fact, *Charles VII* did no worse than *Marion Delorme*, though it had
nothing like the success of *Antony*. Antoine Fontaney, an habitué of
Nodier's *salon* who was present at the opening performance, called the
play '*Othello* turned inside out', which was a fair description: the hero
Yakoub is a Moor whom his mistress incites to assassinate her husband.
Frédérick Lemaître had wanted this part but Dumas, who was not over-
fond of the great actor, demurred precisely because he feared Frédérick
would turn Yakoub into an imitation Othello. Full of apprehension as
the first night approached, Dumas decided to take his eight-year-old
son along with him, less as a treat for the boy than because he believed
he might bring him luck. The younger Alexandre never forgot their
silent walk home afterwards, through the moonlit streets of Paris, he
trotting along to keep up with his taciturn father, whose depression he
could sense clearly enough without fully understanding its causes.[4]

His next play, however, was a signal triumph which completely
restored his faith in himself. Discussing *Richard Darlington* after its first
few performances, the *Courrier des Théâtres* observed, with perhaps a
tinge of irony, that to say the play was a hit would be an understate-
ment; it was 'a furore, a mania, a need, a necessity.'[5] The audiences, to
Harel's delight, were even larger than those that had rolled up to see
Napoléon Bonaparte, and Frédérick Lemaître scored one of the greatest
successes of his career in the part of the eponymous hero.

The plot derived, distantly, from a late novel by Walter Scott, *The
Surgeon's Daughter*. Richard Middlemas, a child of unknown though
probably distinguished parentage, is brought up by a country doctor,
Gideon Gray, whose daughter Menie forms an unwise attachment for
him. Spurning the hard life of an ill-paid general practitioner, for which
his foster-father had him trained, he leaves for India, hoping to make
his fortune in that land of fabulous wealth. After various mishaps, he
enters into a compact with a sinister adventuress of Belgian extraction,
and at her instigation sends for Menie, now an orphan, pretending his
affairs have reached a prosperous enough state for them to marry. In
reality, her fiancé destines her for the harem of a native prince in return
for preferment in his service. At the last moment, however, the prince's
father, the formidable Hyder Ali, intervenes, frees the hapless Scottish
maiden, and has Richard thrown to an elephant of monstrous size who,
'stamping his huge shapeless foot upon his breast, put an end at once
to his life and to his crimes'.

It is unlikely that Dumas himself had read *The Surgeon's Daughter*
(published in 1827); the notion of extracting from it the scenario of a

melodrama had occurred to a couple of obscure playwrights one of whom, a banker called Félix Beudin, had visited him at Trouville to enlist his help.[6] The partners had hit on the idea that the central character, Richard, should be the disgraceful fruit of a liaison between a woman of the aristocracy and the public hangman; this would be revealed to the audience in a prologue, and would serve to explain why the mystery of his birth is so carefully kept from him. It was agreed to locate the whole action in England (even Harel might have baulked at having an elephant tread the boards of the Porte-Saint-Martin) and to inject into it a strong political interest. Although the historical setting of *Richard Darlington* is left indeterminate, the authors almost certainly counted on their audience reading into it an allusion to the contemporary agitation the other side of the Channel which preceded, over the space of a year or more, the passing of the Reform Bill in May 1832. Beudin had actually been in London at election time, and the animated polling scene, half way through the play, was almost certainly his work.

Richard Darlington is perhaps the closest Dumas ever came to writing a Shakespearian chronicle drama, in which the gradual moral disintegration of the hero, gripped by an inordinate ambition, is movingly unfolded before our eyes. The process starts when Richard resolves, on the spur of the moment, to propose marriage to the surgeon's daughter (renamed Jenny in the play), not from inclination on his part —though he knows he has inspired a deep passion in her—but simply because, as a parliamentary candidate, it behoves him to ally himself to a family in good standing. In the Commons, he becomes a spokesman for popular rights and a thorn in the flesh of the King's party, until he is seduced by offers of a title and an alliance with one of the wealthiest families in the kingdom. But to profit from this exorbitant bribe he needs to terminate his marriage to Jenny and, since she refuses to countenance divorce, he firstly orders one of his henchmen to abduct her and smuggle her abroad, and when this plan goes awry, he finally murders her himself.

Dumas was concerned that this murder, coming immediately before the dénouement when all Richard's crimes are brought to light, should be carried through in a novel and startling fashion. The goblet of poison, the dagger-thrust—these were so hackneyed; and to have Jenny smothered in her bed would have been too obvious a plagiarism. The play was already in rehearsal and the problem had still not been solved, when Goubaux, Beudin's partner, called on the master early one morning to ask if he had any new suggestions. Dumas was still in bed, though awake; he greeted his collaborator with a shout and, throwing aside the bedclothes, he leapt to the floor, his long, dark-skinned legs protruding from his nightshirt. 'I have it, my dear fellow,' he roared. 'I'll chuck her out of the window.'[7] The window in question opened on to a balcony overlooking a deep ravine. The audience would see Jenny dragged offstage, struggling, and hear her last cry as she plunged to her death.

The enormous popular success of this play owed much, undoubtedly, to the brutal talent of Frédérick Lemaître, whom the part of Richard fitted like a glove. In the first act, when he brusquely decides he must win Jenny in order to present himself to the electors as a solidly respectable married man, Dumas had written a whirlwind courtship scene; but he had not anticipated that Frédérick, enacting Richard's feigned ardour, would go so far as to brush the actress's lips with his; something that French theatrical conventions had never before permitted though, as one of those who witnessed it later observed, such a kiss would have provoked no comment in the supposedly prudish atmosphere of the British theatre.[8] As for the murder scene, Frédérick's performance could not have been more electrifying. Dumas had devised an agonizing build-up to this climax. The unscrupulous politician, confident that his wife is even now unwillingly embarked for the Continent, has arranged that the marriage contract should be signed by himself, the bride, and the bride's father, in his country house; he arrives a little before his visitors, only to discover that Jenny, having escaped from her abductor, is there in the house, innocently awaiting his arrival. Frédérick gave orders that at this point a green spot should be directed on to his face from the wings; he looked so ghastly on the night that Louise Noblet, who was playing Jenny, let forth a scream of pure terror and fled from him in such haste and confusion that she let her veil slip from her head. Returning on stage, the deed done, Frédérick calmly picked the incriminating piece of muslin off the floor, stuffed it carelessly in his pocket, and walked across to open the door and admit his guests.

Meeting Alfred de Musset in the corridors of the Porte-Saint-Martin after the first performance, Dumas noticed he was looking pale and distraught. 'My dear poet,' he inquired solicitously, 'what is the matter with you?' 'The matter?' answered Musset. 'I'm suffocating, that's what's the matter.' But Musset, who had failed lamentably to get his own, delicately diaphanous comedy accepted by the sensation-seeking theatre public of the day, had other reasons to feel 'suffocated' than those Dumas supposed, in his naïve vanity.[9]

Richard Darlington had its première on December 10th, 1831. By the spring of the following year, the vicarious thrills it offered were no longer wanted; the Parisians were in the grip of a real melodrama more macabre than any Dumas or his fellow romantics could have devised. On March 29th the cholera struck.

It had been known for some time that the disease was raging in

London, ship-borne [...] tic. Sooner or later it was bound to reach a skinny hand [...] hannel, but the carnival crowds that year were as carefree [...] the forlorn hope, perhaps, that their hectic gaiety might l [...] lence at bay. Suddenly, at one of the public balls, a dance [...] nd fell to the ground, tearing off his mask as he did so; [...] rs saw with horror that his face was already violet. Then [...] ller, then more and more keeled over, to be transported to [...] ospital, where invalids suffering from less deadly sicknes [...] ement protests for fear the infection should spread to tl [...] r apprehensions were groundless; the cholera worked wi [...] that it was not even necessary to bring its victims into the [...] were dead on arrival, and in the frantic haste to dispose c [...] they were shovelled into the earth still wearing their har [...] es.

The effects of t [...] e as bizarre as they were terrifying. The municipal autho [...] ig not incorrectly that the unhygienic condition of the [...] nething to do with the relentless spread of the disease, ar [...] d up the removal of refuse by having it shovelled on to [...] n to tips outside the city. This overdue reform, howeve [...] ist the opposition of the dustmen who, working with [...] il two-pronged rakes and carrying V-shaped wicker [...] ieir backs, had from time immemorial picked over th [...] ed up at street corners for the sake of the discarded clot [...] er junk they found there. Seeing their livelihood thr [...] new sanitary regulations, the ragpickers rioted; they s [...] refuse carts or tipped them into the Seine; and this reve [...] ouchables was only finally quelled after a pitched battl [...] m and the National Guard.

More alar [...] is the sudden crop of rumours to the effect that the mo [...] -toll was not due to the cholera at all but to a deliberate a [...] he part of the government to solve the problem of urban o [...] ig by introducing poison into the food supplies and drinki [...] instead of ignoring or denying the story, the police issued a s [...] o the effect that no effort would be spared to track down the [...] s, who were probably *carbonari* (left-wing revolutionaries). Tl [...] able result was that the population became ten times more net... an before; any lantern-jawed passer who happened to wear a hangdog look now risked being lynched by maddened mobs. Heine, who unlike most foreigners had the courage to remain in Paris over this dreadful period, relates how

> in the Rue de Vaugirard, where two men found to be carrying a
> white powder were murdered, I saw one of the wretches breathing
> his last, and the old women taking off their clogs to hit him repeatedly

over the head until they had battered his skull in. His body had been stripped stark naked, bloodily beaten and smashed; it was not just his clothes that had been torn off him, but his hair, his genitals, his lips and his nose; afterwards, a brute of a fellow tied his feet together with a rope and dragged him along the street, shouting again and again: *Voilà le Choléra-morbus!* An extraordinarily beautiful girl, white with fury, her breasts bare and her hands covered with blood, was standing close by and as the corpse passed her, she stamped on it once more, then burst out laughing and asked me to spare her a few francs in consideration of this worthy act, so that she could buy herself mourning, her mother having died a few hours before—of poison.[10]

This outburst of public frenzy died down as quickly as it had arisen. The newspapers ridiculed the theory of mass-poisoning, explaining that the powders found in people's pockets were probably nothing more sinister than camphor or some other compound thought to ward off the sickness. After that a great stillness fell on the city; almost all the theatres had closed, and after dark it was rare to see anyone at all out of doors. Those who could afford to do so left for the country; on April 7th, paying a social call at the Arsenal, Antoine Fontaney found the Nodiers packing their belongings in readiness for a move to Metz. At the Place de la Bastille, on his way home, he saw three hearses cross the square at the gallop; the only pedestrians he encountered were groups of working-class mourners returning from the cemetery.[11] Soon the death-toll rose to the point where removal vans had to be pressed into service to supplement the hearses, and one even saw coffins loaded on to cabs, placed athwart so that each one protruded eerily from either window.

On April 15th Dumas, who had spent the evening with Liszt and Boulanger, all three drinking black tea which was supposed to kill the germs, was suddenly taken with a trembling in his legs; a deadly shudder ran down his spine; looking in the mirror, he saw he was as pale as a ghost. He called his maid and told her to bring him a lump of sugar soaked in ether. She brought him the ether in a sherry-glass with the sugar-lump separately; in his confusion he drank off the opiate and, as a result, fell back on his pillow in a coma which lasted two hours. The doctor brought him round by steaming him under his bedclothes. Whether the drastic treatment had stopped the cholera in its tracks, or whether he had been suffering from nothing worse than a severe chill in the first place, Dumas never knew; but the experiment of imbibing so massive a dose of narcotic was in itself very nearly fatal, and he had to keep to his bed for several weeks.

While he was still convalescing he received a visit from his garrulous impresario Harel, who had been one of the few theatre managers to refuse to close down during the epidemic, even though on one evening the audience had dwindled to a single spectator; the man, Harel went on, refused the offer of a refund, insisted on having the performance put on for him alone, and then had the gall to hiss it. But things were picking up now, the epidemic was almost over, 'the cholera isn't covering its costs', so would Dumas be kind enough to cast his eye over this manuscript, a piece sent in by a totally unknown and obviously quite untalented young man, which had possibilities all the same. The invalid protested; he wasn't even up yet; but Harel would not take no for an answer, pointing out that Dumas always wrote his plays in bed anyway. This was perfectly true, as it happened. When a very young man, still obliged to put in a full day's office work at the Palais-Royal and often returning to do a couple of hours' overtime in the evening, he had got into the habit of going to bed at ten, with pen and paper on the bedside table, leaving word with his mother to wake him at midnight, when he would write another scene or two of the play he had on hand. The habit had remained even after the necessity had disappeared.[12]

The draft Harel had brought turned out to be a revision by Janin of a play by a certain Frédéric Gaillardet, set in the reign of Louis X (1314–16). The plot was based on various legends, alluded to by Villon and narrated at greater length by Brantôme, concerning the secret orgies supposedly indulged in by the Queen of France, Margaret of Burgundy, and her sister-in-law Blanche de la Marche. The scene of these licentious revels was the upper chamber of a tower, long since demolished, which overlooked the Seine and was known as the Tour de Nesle.

In Dumas's hands, Gaillardet's amateurish sketch was turned into a five-act prose tragedy, which eventually proved to be his most lasting contribution to the repertoire of nineteenth-century French drama, judging by the number of performances given and the frequency of revivals. It was originally written with Frédérick Lemaître in mind for the part of Buridan, Mlle George playing the Queen. Frédérick, however, had fled from Paris to escape the cholera, so Bocage had to step in until Frédérick returned to take over the part in September. In October the royal family attended a gala production. Later, Daumier drew a cartoon of Parisians queuing in the snow to see the play. *La Tour de Nesle* probably deserves equal credit with Hugo's *Notre-Dame de Paris* for inaugurating the extraordinary vogue the Middle Ages enjoyed in France in the early 1830s; hatters marketed *chapeaux à la Buridan*, and it became the fashion to medievalize one's name; Jean Duseigneur, the sculptor, took to signing himself Jehan du Seigneur.

There were periodic revivals of *La Tour de Nesle* throughout the

reign of Louis-Philippe. Under the Second Republic Mlle George, now
the senior actress in France, was warmly acclaimed in a special production put on at the Odéon. In the early years of the Second Empire *La
Tour de Nesle* fell victim to Napoleon III's oppressive theatre censorship,
but it re-emerged in 1861, with a revival that ran to over a hundred
performances, and the Porte-Saint-Martin staged it again in 1867 for
the benefit of the thousands of visitors who flocked to Paris for the
World Exhibition. It was seen again in 1877, when the leading theatre
critic of the period, Francisque Sarcey, wrote that the work remained
'as amazing and terrifying as it was the first day it was produced'; in
1882, what the avant-garde producer André Antoine called ruefully
'the eternal *Tour de Nesle*' had yet another five-week run at the Théâtre
de la Gaîté.[13]

Too little systematic investigation has been undertaken of the
factors that give certain works of dubious literary merit lasting popularity on the stage for one to do more than speculate on the cause of the
perennial fascination that *La Tour de Nesle* exerted over its audiences
in the nineteenth century. In a Europe where monarchy as yet retained,
whatever constitutional checks may have been introduced to mitigate
its abuses, much of its ancient aura and prestige, the average man could
still experience a delicious thrill at the spectacle of a solitary individual,
without rights or privileges, defying, and successfully defying for a
while, the limitless power of the wearer of the crown. This theme,
which Schiller was probably the first to exploit in *Wilhelm Tell*, gave
Dumas the inspiration for the climactic prison scene in his third act,
where Buridan, bound hand and foot, lying in a dungeon, facing the
prospect of execution without trial on the morrow, is visited by the
Queen, come to gloat sadistically over her captive. By revealing to her
his knowledge of the guilty secrets of her past and by threatening to
have the documentary proof placed in the King's hands unless she not
only releases him but has him appointed first minister, he turns the
tables on her; it is the Queen now who meekly obeys the dictates of
her transfigured subject. Such a sudden reversal of fortunes derives, no
doubt, from the stock-in-trade of the traditional melodrama, but the
fact that the tiger, in this instance, is a woman and the tamer a man
introduces an element of paradox into the situation, for in terms of the
conventional scenario, it is always a male potentate, in one guise or
another, who is shown lording it over the quailing girl martyr.

As one examines more closely the problematic mechanics of the
spell cast by *La Tour de Nesle* over several generations of playgoers, the
core image demanding evaluation reveals itself as this sinister 'dark
tower', as mysterious as Browning's, which on certain nights blazes
with lights, while in the grey dawns that follow, the sluggish currents
of the Seine regularly cast up on to its banks the blood-boltered corpses

of handsome young men, always strangers to the city and, to judge by their apparel, of no mean birth. The nymphomaniac queen and her accomplices have no trouble in attracting, on tempting assignations, young blades always ready for an intrigue spiced with mystery. Having spent the night in their arms, these Messalinas leave them to hired ruffians to despatch; the lifeless bodies are then thrown into the river and the great ladies' bouts of debauchery remain a well-guarded secret. The myth this story incarnates reaches beyond the fairly hackneyed correlation between love and death or, more properly, between carnality and mortality; it connects with the creepy horror aroused in most men by accounts of female spiders devouring their diminutive mates after copulation, or worker-bees stinging to death the males of their species once the queen of the hive has been fertilized. Queens, as Simone de Beauvoir has pointed out, are exceptional and in a way sacred in a male-dominated society, for they alone among women are invested with the power of life and death. Probably Dumas was playing unwittingly, in his drama of the duel between Buridan and Marguerite, on the deep-seated psychic fear from which few men have been exempt, at least down to the present century, of losing their over-lordship; the symbol of such deposition being woman's successful establishment of her claim to the same right to indiscriminate sexual adventure, unattended by remorse or dread of consequences, as man has traditionally enjoyed.

La Tour de Nesle had only just started its first, sensationally successful run when performances were abruptly interrupted by a fresh outburst of street violence. This was occasioned by the public funeral of a left-wing figurehead and popular Napoleonic general, Jean Lamarque; public funerals, by bringing large crowds of people on to the streets, always risked turning into riots since if disorder broke out the police were hesitant about suppressing it by force for fear of provoking unseemly scuffles round a coffin. Dumas could not have avoided attendance at these obsequies, supposing even he had wished to; he had known the dead general personally, his own father and Lamarque having been close friends, and the family had in consequence asked him to act as marshal of the detachment of artillerymen who were to march behind the gun-carriage that bore the coffin.

The procession started from the General's house in the Faubourg Saint-Honoré at eleven in the morning of June 5th, 1832. The day was hot and sultry, and heavy rain had started to fall even before the solemn march began, a long train of national guardsmen, students, workmen, Polish refugees, and Napoleonic veterans, winding its way silently round the Madeleine and up the Boulevard des Capucines. There was at least one unscheduled deviation from the prescribed route, so that it was three o'clock before the great crowd came to a halt at the entry of the Pont d'Austerlitz where the funeral orations were to be delivered. Dumas, still weak from his recent illness, felt too exhausted to stand and listen; so he took a couple of artillerymen off with him to help him eat a nourishing fish-stew. In this way he missed the lacedaemonian allocution pronounced by Etienne Arago: 'A few words must suffice, and here they are: General Lamarque began his career to the sound of the battle-cry "Long live the Republic!" and it is to the sound of "Long live the Republic!" that his ashes should be committed to the earth. Long live the Republic! and let those who count themselves my friends, follow me!' This was the signal for the insurrection, by which the republicans hoped to snatch back the victory of which they had been cheated two years previously. When Dumas emerged from his restaurant, the barricades were already up in the Rue de Ménilmontant, and on the boulevard he found his path barred by troops of the regular army. Dashing over to the nearby Théâtre de la Porte-Saint-Martin he kicked in the locked door and made his way backstage to the property store where he knew Harel kept a stock of guns originally acquired for the production of *Napoléon Bonaparte*. Seeing the street door standing ajar, a group of insurrectionists followed him inside and, disregarding Harel's vehement protests, Dumas distributed among them all the weapons he could lay his hands on.

After this he staggered home in a state of utter exhaustion and fell into bed; it was only later that he learned, in a letter from Arago, how the rising had been crushed. Fighting had gone on for the rest of the day and, sporadically, through the night, but when day broke on June 6th all resistance had ceased except in two working-class districts to the east of Paris. Battling in the maze of little streets around the church of Saint-Merri, the republicans held out for several hours more until by the afternoon every man among them lay dead or dying.

Arago's letter ended with a warning that Dumas might expect arrest at any moment for having distributed arms to the revolutionaries. If this threat never materialized, the reason may have been that in the initial confusion the authorities were misled into thinking he had perished in the last massacre of the insurgents; on June 9th Dumas had the curious experience of reading a circumstantial account of his own capture in the cloisters of Saint-Merri and subsequent execution after a summary trial. Tribute was paid to the courage with which he faced the firing-squad, and the journalist was kind enough to add a few words deploring the premature termination of a promising literary career. Dumas sent him his card, inscribed with a message of thanks for the generous terms in which he had couched his obituary. His friends had read the news-item too, as became evident when a messenger brought him a note from Nodier: 'My dear Alexandre, I have just read in the paper that you were shot dead on June 7th at 3 a.m. Pray be kind

enough to inform the undersigned whether that will prevent you joining us for dinner at the Arsenal tomorrow . . . Your devoted friend,
Charles Nodier (who is dying to hear all you can tell him about the
other world).'[14]

A friend at court did, however, pay him a visit a few days later to
let him know quietly that the question of arresting him was being
seriously debated by the Cabinet. It might be as well to take a short
trip abroad. Since this well-meant advice happened to coincide with
what his doctor had been urging on health grounds, Dumas hastily
finished a bad melodrama commissioned by Harel, said farewell to his
friends and boarded the coach to Lyons, whence the road led to the
Swiss frontier.

VII The Tourist

Tourism in the modern sense—that is, visits to foreign countries lasting a few weeks or at most a few months and devoted primarily to sight-seeing—dates from the close of the Napoleonic era; there is no record of the word *touriste* being used in French earlier than 1816. The eighteenth-century 'grand tour' differed in a number of respects from the mass tourism that succeeded it; it often extended over two or three years, and was undertaken only by young men of rank and wealth, for whom it was supposed to fulfil an important educational function. The continental wars that lasted, with few intermissions, from 1792 to 1815 made travel difficult and hazardous, and the 'grand tour' fell into desuetude. When finally a lasting peace was established in Europe, the pent-up *wanderlust* of the British in particular released a flood of eager travellers, heading chiefly for France, Italy, and Switzerland.

The special attraction of Switzerland was due in the first place to several notable literary works: Rousseau's *La Nouvelle Héloïse*, Schiller's *Wilhelm Tell*, and the third canto of Byron's *Childe Harold's Pilgrimage*, to mention only the most outstanding. In addition, certain note-worthy exploits in recent years had focused public attention on this region of Europe, among them Saussure's ascent of Mont Blanc and Napoleon's crossing of the Alps, brilliantly commemorated in a famous canvas by David. Although Italy had more to offer the cultivated mind, Switzerland was the country that chiefly stirred the romantic imagina-tion, and so it was to Switzerland that the more adventurous and poetic spirits turned. As the number of these passionate pilgrims grew, so did the demand for reliable and up-to-date guide-books to give pro-spective tourists information about the places they would be likely to want to visit and practical hints on transport facilities, food and lodging. The first of the long and highly successful series of Murray's *Hand-books for Travellers* was devoted to Switzerland. The compiler, writing in 1838, was able to note even then that tourism was making a major contribution to the economy of the Confederation, or, as he phrased it in his stiff, early Victorian English: 'the great annual influx of travellers into the country is of the same importance to Switzerland that some additional branch of industry or commerce would be.'[1]

Dumas's motives for setting out on an expedition to Switzerland were primarily, as we have seen, concern for his own personal safety

4

and the full recovery of his health; but also, he reckoned from the start that there might well be a market for an account of his journey when he returned. The newly founded *Revue des Deux Mondes* accepted six articles recounting some of his adventures and published them in its columns between February and November 1833, and the entire work appeared, originally in five volumes, between then and 1837, under the title *Impressions de voyage en Suisse*. It was an enormously successful work, and remained Dumas's best-selling book until he embarked on his career as a novelist in the 1840s. He came to be regarded as the great expert on travel in Switzerland, and contemporary cartoonists liked to draw him as a frizzy-haired Struwwelpeter waving an alpenstock as he strode from one snow-capped peak to another. With the sure instinct of the professional author, who never strikes a profitable vein without exploiting it to the end, Dumas went on to write a whole series of 'travel impressions', relating his later experiences in Italy, the Rhineland, Spain, North Africa, and finally Russia. If he had been able to realize the idea he was toying with in 1866 to visit the United States, there can be little doubt that he would have returned with material for a further set of volumes of travel impressions which might not have been the least interesting of them all.[2]

The romantic period in France witnessed the appearance of a number of travel-books of outstanding literary merit; Dumas was competing in this field with some of the best writers of the age, Chateaubriand, Stendhal, Gautier, among others. If his books proved more popular than any of theirs, this was due in the first instance to his skill in conveying the raw excitement of travel, the thrill of seeing with one's own eyes all the wonders of the wide world, glaciers and volcanoes, old battlefields and ruined monuments, fierce nomadic tribes and exotic birds and animals. As he expressed it himself, 'to travel is to live in the full meaning of the word; the past and the future are swallowed up in the present; one fills one's lungs, takes pleasure in everything, holds all creation in the hollow of one's hand.'[3] But in addition, he was able to bring a personal touch to everything he wrote, modelling himself here chiefly on Sterne, whose *Sentimental Journey* was a well-loved book. The *Impressions de voyage* are packed with accounts of the strange and sometimes uncomfortable adventures that befell him and of his encounters with odd, or occasionally famous people on his way. Lastly, Dumas used the framework of the travel-book to engage in a form of literary activity which was eventually to give him a far wider and more lasting reputation than the stage plays which had been his staple until then; that is, story-telling. The *Impressions de voyage en Suisse* include fewer descriptive passages than passages of narrative; whole chapters are given over to the retelling of local legends which Dumas set down —or so he assures us—as he heard them from the lips of the mountain-dwellers in the remote fastnesses of the Alps. Some of these are pure fairy-stories, involving magical animals or encounters with the Devil, others represent popular versions of historical events, which Dumas noted down even though he was well aware they were in part apocryphal. 'I deserve, I confess it, to figure in a category of travellers forgotten by Sterne, that of the credulous traveller; my imagination has always found it paid not to try and get to the bottom of this kind of thing . . '[4] Whether all the tales Dumas consigned to the pages of his book represent a living oral tradition is something that perhaps only a Swiss folklorist could tell us; occasionally, no doubt, he cheated, using an earlier printed source and pretending to have heard the story from some garrulous herdsman.[5] But whether the legends he narrates were really related to him or whether they were picked up in the course of his desultory reading, he retells them with an inimitable mixture of simplicity and gusto which stamps them as his own. His journey through Switzerland had the unforeseen result of revealing to his public, and to Dumas himself, a rare talent as a teller of tales, justifying Heine's tribute: 'Assuredly, after Don Miguel de Cervantes and Madame Scheriar, better known as Queen Scheherezade, you are the most amusing spinner of yarns I know.'[6]

The extent to which Dumas mixed up truth and fiction in relating the adventures he himself encountered on the way is, of course, another question. The *Impressions de voyage en Suisse* are not, strictly speaking, a diary of his journey; they were written for a public that looked as much for entertainment as for instruction and had no objection to being told tall stories, provided they were amusing; accordingly Dumas saw nothing wrong in embroidering the truth from time to time, in the interests, as he put it, of art.

Of all the traveller's tales he ever told, the most famous, undoubtedly, was the story of the bear steak of Martigny. The incident occurred in the first stage of his journey when, having explored the salt-mines at Bex, he continued on foot via Saint-Maurice (the town where, it will be recalled, his father rescued four men from the guillotine in 1794) and arrived in the evening at Martigny, where he put up at the Post Inn. Seating his guest at the supper-table, the landlord told him he was in luck. Had he ever eaten bear steak? No? Well, that was the *pièce de résistance* of the evening, a delicacy he must not miss. Dumas speared the first chunk in some trepidation, under the eye of his host who swelled with satisfaction when he took a second mouthful with much improved appetite. He had almost finished the steak when the innkeeper sauntered back to his table and remarked, hands on hips: 'Ah, what a bear that was! Do you know, he half ate the huntsman who killed him.' Dumas choked, returned the last mouthful to his plate, and demanded to know what he meant.

The story concerned a certain Guillaume Mona, of the nearby village of Fouly, who owned an orchard of pear-trees. Noticing that the fruit was regularly stolen as soon as it ripened, he stayed up one night to keep watch, and discovered that the thief was none of the village boys, as he had imagined, but a gigantic bear. The following night he loaded his gun with the sawn-off prongs of a hay-fork and took up his position in a corner of the orchard, having first climbed into a sack which he hoped would conceal his presence from the bear. In due course the creature lumbered across his field of vision; Guillaume let fly and hit it, wounding but not killing it outright. Unfortunately the animal picked up the man's scent and charged over to deal with its assailant who, his feet being entangled in the sack, was unable to free himself in time to take flight. Hearing his desperate screams, a neighbour ran up and despatched the bear with a shot through the chest; but of the unlucky Guillaume nothing was left but a bleeding corpse from which the head had been wrenched off and almost totally devoured. It was a fillet of this bear that had been served up to Dumas for his supper.

Travellers should be wary of telling tales that can be too easily verified. Switzerland was near enough for those who read his *Impressions de voyage* to visit the country themselves and check up on his assertions, which is what his friend Roger de Beauvoir did. Having toured the thirteen cantons, he returned to Paris and announced to all their mutual friends that Dumas had been having them on: 'there isn't a bear to be found any more anywhere in Switzerland.'[7] (He was forgetting, perhaps, the tame bears kept to this day in a pit in Berne.) Dumas himself later admitted that, although the story of the peasant who tried to shoot a marauding bear and was savaged to death was perfectly true—it had happened only three days before he arrived at Martigny— the sequel, in which he described how the bear's flesh had been cooked and served up to passing strangers, was a piece of poetic licence. Having acknowledged this much, he went on to draw an unexpected moral. Ever since the publication of his *Impressions de voyage en Suisse*, travellers had been dropping in at the Hôtel de la Poste at Martigny and calling—to the stupefaction of the proprietor—for bear steaks. His protests that there was no bear on the menu, never had been and never would be, always met with the same objection from the dissatisfied diners: 'But you served M. Dumas with bear.' The consequence was that the hotel manager regarded this M. Dumas as a practical joker whom he would cheerfully strangle if he could lay his hands on him. 'A French innkeeper,' continued Dumas, 'would have turned this to his advantage; he would have changed the inn-sign, and instead of Hôtel de la Poste it would have read Hôtel du Bifteck d'ours. He would have had the surrounding mountains combed for bears, and if there was no bear to be had, he would have served up beef, wild boar, horse, whatever was available, provided it was disguised with some out-landish sauce. He would have made a fortune within three years and retired, selling his stock for 100,000 francs and calling down blessings on my name.'[8] Swiss honesty contrasting with French enterprise . . . Today there are three hotels at Martigny, not one of which is called the Hôtel du Bifteck d'ours.

Meals—or the lack of them—play an important part in Dumas's recollections of his travels in Switzerland, as, indeed, they do in the later *Impressions de voyage*, whether the setting be Spain, Italy, or Russia, for although never a greedy eater, he took a great interest in food and delighted in practising his culinary expertise whenever occasion offered. At Obergestelen, where the other hotel guests were a chamberlain of the Danish court and an architect from Paris, the fare consisted, he tells us, of boiled marmot, which when it appeared on the table so resembled a human baby that only Brunton, the architect, had a strong enough stomach to face eating it. Dumas, however, saved the situation by descending into the kitchen and frying an excellent omelet for the Dane and himself. At Bex he ordered river trout, having heard they were superb in that part of the country, and was astonished to hear the landlady rouse one of the inn-servants and tell him to pick up his lantern and sickle and fetch a basketful of the fish from the river. Did they reap the trout in these parts? Impelled by his never failing curiosity, Dumas followed the lad through the night and watched the operation, seeing him wade into the ice-cold water, holding the lantern above his head to attract the trout to the surface; then, with a neat blow of the sickle, he would sever the head of the fattest fish, and start again. Bloody but effective—unless, of course, this counts as another bear steak story.

Later, when he was spending the night at Arth, on the Zugersee, Dumas remembered the display of skill he had witnessed at Bex and embarked on a similarly unorthodox fishing expedition. The brilliant moonlight had woken him up and he decided he would waste no more time but set out immediately for Lucerne. What followed was worthy of a Maupassant *conte*. Searching the hotel in the middle of the night to knock up his host and settle the bill, he blundered into another tourist's room and had to apologize for disturbing his slumbers. This other traveller, a young Belgian solicitor, explained that in any case the pangs of hunger had woken him long before Dumas's intrusion; he had arrived too late the previous evening to be served supper. 'Let's eat together,' cried Dumas gaily. 'It'll be supper for you, and breakfast for me!' So together they went foraging in the kitchen; but the larder contained nothing but eggs, which the Belgian said disagreed with him. Then Dumas remembered the lake was famous throughout

Switzerland for its freshwater fish; true, they had no tackle, but this did not worry the resourceful writer, who proposed they should borrow a boat and go out and *shoot* one. The method he used was to take on board a portable stove, which when held over the water drew the fish up from the depths, exactly as the inn-servant's lantern had hypnotized the trout in the River Rhône. Dumas took aim at a magnificent pollan, shot it through the head, and a few minutes later they were able to row ashore with it, gut it and cook it.

Nowhere in Switzerland did he find a hostelry totally devoid of provisions, a risk that travellers always incurred in other parts of Europe, though at Vaduz, when he made a detour through Liechtenstein, the only dish offered him was sauerkraut, for which he had the strongest aversion. Could he not have cutlets? eggs? potatoes? There was sauerkraut; what was wrong with that? Remembering the principality's reputation for succulent mushrooms, he thought of asking for a plate of these, but unfortunately had no idea what they were called in German; so he drew one on a piece of paper. The servant-girl, after examining the sketch, went away and returned with . . . an umbrella. On that occasion Dumas went supperless to bed. But no misadventures of this kind matched his experiences three years later when, crossing Sicily from south to north with a small party of companions, he found no provisions at the wretched inn where they were to spend the night beyond a few chestnuts and a cruse of oil. One lived off the land in these parts and, by dint of purchase and poaching, the travellers eventually assembled the wherewithal for a satisfying supper: a pigeon, a chicken, three hen's eggs, a rabbit, two pomegranates, and a dozen figs. In the end, however, Dumas had to do without his share of this improvised banquet. Drawn by the unusual odours of meat cooking, two tiny ragged starvelings, trembling with malaria, squatted beside the pot, and refused to be dislodged even by the hired cook's vicious kicks. 'What's wrong with them? what do they want?' Dumas asked his guide. 'They are hungry and they want to eat,' the man answered glumly and, after recording this reply, Dumas continued: 'That, alas, is the cry of the Sicilian people, and throughout the three months I spent on the island I heard nothing else but this. There are poor wretches whose hunger is never appeased from the day when, lying in their cradle, they start sucking their mother's withered breast, until the day when, stretched on their deathbed, they expire in a last attempt to swallow the consecrated wafer that the priest places in their mouth.'[9] Dumas abandoned his portion of the stew to these two skinny children, knowing that until their dying day they would treasure the memory of the one, blissful occasion in their lives when they had been able to eat their fill.

Switzerland, though of course far from being the prosperous

country it now is, was very different from Sicily, inhabited by a debilitated population permanently undernourished. The Swiss formed a pacific, civilized, well-policed nation; the wayfarer could move from town to town with no fear of brigands, along roads which, at least in certain cantons, evoked Dumas's admiration; who could fail to be impressed by the solicitude of an administration which had taken the trouble to place benches at intervals along the highroads with stone pillars nearby on which pedlars could hitch their packs as they rested? The inns were mostly clean, and if the beds were none too comfortable —the stuffing of the horsehair mattresses tended to protrude through the sheets and cause the sleeper to dream he was lying stretched out on a gigantic hairbrush—at least Dumas did not find himself obliged to share them with a colony of voracious insects, as so often in South Italy; while in Russia, as he discovered when he went there in 1858, there were no beds anywhere outside the mansions of westernized aristocrats; at the inns, the traveller made do with whatever vacant patch of floorboard he could find.

Another unexpected bonus for the traveller in Switzerland was the availability of baths even in remote wayside inns; something one never expected to find in French hotels at that period. After a long day's march—for, except when he had to cross a lake or, on one occasion, descend the Rhine, Dumas went everywhere on foot—there was nothing more soothing to the spirit and refreshing to his weary limbs than to loll in a tub. So delightful did he find this amenity, indeed, that he adopted the habit of writing up his notes at the end of the day with his body immersed in warm water and with paper and inkwell to hand on a board laid crosswise over the bath. The euphoria induced by such sybaritism contributed greatly, he claimed, 'to the mood of benevolence towards mankind and admiration for the world of nature which even today is apparent in my journal from the first page to the last.'[10] The most memorable experience of this kind befell him when he was on the road to Biel, travelling south along the banks of the Aare, and, having reached the village of Solothurn in the late afternoon, decided to stop there. The *gasthaus* offered him a choice between a hot water bath (5 francs) and a bath in warm milk (10 francs)—rather expensive, said the landlady apologetically, but at this season in the year the herds were being driven down from their mountain pasturage, and milk was not as plentiful as it would be in August and September. But Dumas decided the novelty would be well worth 10 francs, and so it was; luxuriating in his milk bath, set by the window so that he could watch the sun go down, with a plentiful and succulent supper laid within reach, he doubted whether any Roman emperor could ever have wallowed in greater luxury.

Although Switzerland was not yet the 'playground of Europe', its lakes and mountain scenery attracted even at this date a cosmopolitan crowd during the summer months. Visitors from the British Isles may not have been more numerous than those from other parts but they contrived to make themselves more conspicuous. The Englishman abroad conformed to no particular stereotype; he could be misanthropic, or he could be gregarious; cheerful or quarrelsome, or else taciturn, devoured by a mysterious melancholy. On the Faulhorn Dumas fell in with a party of Americans (father, mother, and seven children) to whom one of these eccentric Britishers had attached himself; this man, a poker-faced humorist, horrified the guides by his clowning on the edges of precipices, and laid a bet with the American that, at a distance of sixty feet, using his alpenstock as a javelin, the other could not touch him. In fact, the Yankee's bolt went clean through his cheek and knocked out a tooth. Then there was the splenetic sort. On his way up the Righi, Dumas met an agitated Englishman hurrying down, having heard that a large party of sightseers had preceded him to the top; this shy and introverted compatriot of Byron had come to Switzerland to escape society. A third variety was irascible, pugnacious, the type that would start a bout of fisticuffs with a London cabman whom he suspected of overcharging him. At Lucerne, Dumas found he had to act as second to a French commercial traveller in a duel with a certain Sir Robert Leslie, baronet,[11] who had thrown a bottle of wine at his head during supper. The duel ended with the Frenchman badly wounded and the baronet's brains bespattered over the grass.

Dumas had the good fortune to arrive at Lucerne while Chateaubriand was staying in the town, at the Adler, a hotel that still stands today in the Weggisgasse. The great writer had come to Switzerland as a voluntary political exile after the July Revolution, having judged it incompatible with the oath of loyalty he had sworn to the Bourbons —even though he had little reason to feel grateful to their house—to remain in France while a usurper was occupying their throne. Dumas had never met Chateaubriand, but had long wanted to; like all the young romantics, he looked up to him as the true founder of their movement, the first to have defied the outworn conventions of classicism, 'the rock,' as he wrote, 'against which the seas of envy, which still boiled round us, had beaten in vain for fifty years'.[12] That apart, it has to be admitted that there was in Dumas a touch of the celebrity hunter, attributable, however, less to ingrained snobbery than to his deep feeling for contemporary history which led him to miss no opportunity to meet and converse with the men who had played, or who might in the future play, a leading part in public affairs. Chateaubriand was not just a major author; he had held ministerial office during the Restoration and indeed had occupied a central position on the political stage ever since the publication of *Le Génie du Christianisme*, happily coinciding with the ratification of the Concordat by the French legislature in 1801, had brought him to the favourable attention of Napoleon Bonaparte.

When Dumas inquired at the Adler Hotel after their distinguished guest, he was told Chateaubriand was not in his room—he was 'feeding his hens'. Mystified—had the great man started keeping poultry?— Dumas left a message, and was overjoyed to receive two hours later a courteous invitation to breakfast the following morning. Over the meal they discussed the current political situation in France, the republican and the Carlist finding that there was, after all, more common ground between them than either might have supposed; for Chateaubriand, in spite of his sentimental attachment to the old monarchy, was clear-sighted enough to realize that a fresh restoration was out of the question. Fifty years hence, he predicted, all the European royal dynasties would have been swept away and replaced by elective presidencies, in France as elsewhere.[13]

Breakfast over, they went along, at Chateaubriand's suggestion, to look at the 'Lion of Lucerne', the monument designed by Thorvaldsen as a memorial to the Swiss guards who fell defending the Tuileries on August 10th, 1792. Dumas, remembering his own fairly recent skirmish with Swiss mercenaries firing on the people from the roof-tops of a royal palace, observed that they could hardly be called heroes; they were doing only what they had been hired to do. But at least they paid their debt, which is more than a lot of people do these days, answered Chateaubriand drily. Afterwards the two men went down to the river's edge and Dumas at last understood what the waiter at the hotel meant with the reference to 'M. de Chateaubriand's hens'; they were moor-hens, which the old exile fed every day with a few crusts of bread crumbled into the water.

The strongest testimony of the overwhelming impression made on Dumas by the great man's affability is not what he says in his travel notes, where he compares Chateaubriand, rather bombastically, to one of the Alpine peaks of which he had now explored all the slopes; rather, it lies in the fact that he says nothing in these pages of the numerous other curiosities of Lucerne which, had he been on his own, he would not have failed to visit and describe: the old wooden bridges with their curious panel paintings on walls and roof, and the *Wasserturm*, rising from the waters of the Reuss. The hero-worshipper in Dumas had temporarily eclipsed the conscientious sightseer.

He paid one other visit flattering to his self-esteem before leaving Switzerland; this was to Hortense, one-time Queen of Holland and, as the child of Joséphine Beauharnais by her first marriage, a stepdaughter of Napoleon. Like all members of the Bonaparte family, she was not

4*

allowed to live in France, and had settled in a fairly modest country house five miles west of Constance, on the shores of the lake. Once again, Dumas had no letter of introduction, and hoped merely that the name of the author of *Henri III* and *Antony* might have reached her ears. Evidently it had, for after leaving his card at her place of residence he received an invitation to dinner, where he met, besides the ex-Queen, her companion Mme Récamier, the same elegant beauty that David had painted in a world-famous portrait, wearing white muslin and reclining on a couch. When Dumas saw her she was wearing black; even her head and neck were draped in a black veil; but to judge by the brilliance of her eyes and the youthful timbre of her voice she might have been, he recorded gallantly, no more than twenty-five. In fact she was already well into her fifties.

Dumas, an excellent conversationalist, proved very good value to the middle-aged ladies starved of news from France in their out-of-the-way Swiss retreat, and he was pressed to join them for lunch the following day. Arriving a little early, he was taken out into the garden where his hostess turned the conversation on to the future of France. Dumas admitted frankly that his sympathies lay with the republicans. The 'aristocratic' monarchy of Charles X had been swept away, and replaced by a 'bourgeois' monarchy which, however, he was confident would be succeeded in its turn by a presidential republic on the American model. Hortense then asked him how he would assess the chances that a member of Napoleon's family might one day restore the glories of the First Empire. The question was possibly premature, but none the less apposite. Napoleon I's only son, the Duc de Reichstadt, had died only a month before this conversation took place; it was for him, no doubt, that Mme Récamier was wearing mourning. The male heir and Bonapartist pretender was at present Hortense's son by her marriage to Napoleon's brother Louis, and this young man, the future Emperor Napoleon III, was even now harbouring visions, which troubled his mother, of returning in triumph to pick up the sceptre that had dropped from his uncle's hands in 1815.

To the question thus put, Dumas answered firmly that no revival of Napoleonic pomp and power was possible in modern France. Her son, he said, would do better to 'seek the annulment of the sentence of exile, purchase an estate in France, stand for election as deputy, use his talents to try and win over a majority in the Chamber, and, with the help of his supporters, have Louis-Philippe deposed and himself elected king in his place.'[14] What is so remarkable about this advice is that it constitutes a fairly close prediction of what actually came to pass. After the abdication of Louis-Philippe in 1848, the National Assembly was persuaded to repeal the law forbidding members of the Bonaparte family to return to France. In the elections to the presidency that autumn, Louis-Napoleon easily beat his rivals and, having won the nation's consent in a plebiscite, assumed the imperial crown. When this happened Dumas, who retained his republican convictions throughout, was far from pleased, and it is not to be supposed that his prescience in outlining these events with such uncanny accuracy so long before they took place afforded him much retrospective gratification.

His tour of Switzerland was now almost at an end. The itinerary he had followed had taken him, by an erratic and circuitous route, through nearly every part of the country. There still remained one canton to visit, the Ticino, with its beautiful lakeside capital Locarno, but he needed to hurry if he was to cross the Simplon pass before the first snows closed the road. He got as far as Baveno, on Lake Maggiore, visited the Borromean islands, and at Arona, despite his fear of heights, climbed the colossal statue of San Carlo, 66 feet on top of a 40-foot pedestal, from which, seated in the saint's left ear-hole, he was able to contemplate the magnificent vista of the Lombardy plain. The following day, however, a letter was delivered to him of such disturbing import that he felt obliged to abandon all plans of further travel and return to Paris by the fastest mode of transport available.

VIII Father and Husband

Discretion prevents Dumas from revealing, at the end of the *Impressions de voyage en Suisse*, either the contents of the letter that summoned him back post-haste from the Italian-Swiss frontier, or the identity of the writer. A reasonable guess, however, is that the letter came from Belle Krelsamer; as for its contents, these can be surmised with greater confidence once we have seen how his relations with her had been developing since the honeymoon period of 1830. The couple still remained linked, but not as united as they had been, the bonds having started to loosen even before he left for Switzerland. A new stage divinity had thrust herself on his attention, and Belle found herself in danger of relegation to the role of the tiresome, querulous ex-mistress.

In the interval between completing *Richard Darlington* and starting work on *La Tour de Nesle*, Dumas had found time to write another play, *Teresa*, much inferior in quality to these other two, the scenario of which had been provided by a hack-writer called Anicet Bourgeois.[1] It had been his old friend Bocage who introduced the two and persuaded Dumas to listen as Anicet went over the plot. The central theme was the rivalry between an older man and a younger for the love of a beguiling Neapolitan beauty, Teresa. The complications were to arise from the fact that the younger man was betrothed to, and in the course of the play marries, the older man's daughter, and that Teresa was this older man's wife. It seemed to Dumas a pointless and unpromising imbroglio, but Bocage had his eye on the part of Teresa's elderly husband—possibly because he was afraid of being type-cast as a *jeune premier*—and so, to oblige him, Dumas wrote the play during the Christmas holidays he took that year in Villers-Cotterêts. Shortly after receiving the manuscript, Bocage called on him with the rather surprising news that *Teresa* had been accepted for production at the Opéra-Comique. A certain Ida Ferrier was to make her début as Amélie Delaunay, the pathetic little wife whose husband deceives her with her own step-mother, Teresa of the fatal charm. Bocage had high hopes of this new actress, whom he described to Dumas, intriguingly if enigmatically, as a *crystal statue*.

Dumas continued sceptical about the whole undertaking but, contrary to his expectations, when the play opened on February 6th, 1832, it proved a great popular success. However improbable the plot, it threw up a sufficient number of harrowing situations to satisfy the audience and at the end the cast was warmly applauded. Ida Ferrier was even recalled on stage after the final bow had been taken; after which, in a transport, she darted into the wings where Dumas was standing and threw herself into his arms, crying: 'Ah sir, you have just done me the greatest possible service; I'm a poor girl and you have made my reputation; I shall owe my future career to you . . . and I just don't know how to thank you!' The too susceptible playwright found it impossible not to warm to this charming spontaneity, these flushed cheeks, sparkling eyes and prettily heaving bosom. He took her off to supper and, subsequently, Ida 'thanked him' in the way actresses usually did in those days, at least when the dramatist was young and handsome.

This was the start of a long, tempestuous liaison which ended, eight years later almost to the day, in marriage. The marriage itself did not last, but there was no other woman with whom Dumas spent a larger part of his life. In the beginnings, at least, the physical attraction was powerful, for Ida had the kind of radiant blonde beauty that called forth admiring tributes even from such fastidious connoisseurs as Théophile Gautier, who penned a dithyrambic description of her perfection of colouring. 'Perhaps you have always imagined that lilies were white, that snow was white, that alabaster was white,' he asked rhetorically. 'Alas, you are mistaken; there is nothing so white in creation as Mademoiselle Ida's hands.' Then her hair: there was no harvest corn, no golden crocus to match it for colour. Her whole head, with that mass of yellow hair and that incomparable complexion, 'was the one thing in the world to put the beholder most in mind of springtime.'[2] Bocage's 'crystal statue' becomes rather more explicable, as a description, in the light of Gautier's poetic rhapsodies.

Ida Ferrier was born Marguerite-Joséphine Ferrand, the daughter of a postmaster in the neighbourhood of Nancy who died when she was seventeen, that is, four years before Dumas met her. He had made a good enough living out of his coaching-inn to be able to afford to send Marguerite to a first-class convent school at Strasbourg, where she was educated alongside the daughters of the local squires. Her taste for acting was developed at this school, for the nuns encouraged their charges to participate in amateur theatricals.

Her father, however, was found to have made no adequate provision for his family after his death, and Marguerite, rather than accept menial employment in Nancy, made up her mind to try for a career on the stage in Paris. Her mother, by all accounts as ugly and vulgar as her daughter was refined and beautiful, accompanied her to the capital and, having shared her initial privations, remained at her side when more prosperous days dawned. At the start, undoubtedly, Ida had a hard struggle to make her way. A certain impresario called Seveste consented to employ her, for a miserable fee, in the flea-pits of Belleville and Montmartre, but disaster struck when she forgot to turn up at the theatre one evening and no adequate stand-in could be found. Seveste sued her for all she was worth and more; fortunately she had an admirer rich enough to bail her out. But her relief and gratitude at being given the chance of starring in a play by Dumas were, in the circumstances, understandable. The tide of fortune was turning for her at last.

It so happened that when *Teresa* had its opening performance Belle Krelsamer, Dumas's *maîtresse en titre*, was away from Paris, carrying out a professional engagement in the provinces. When she returned she had no great difficulty in reasserting her prior claim, but this was only because Ida, too proud to share with a rival, temporarily severed her relations with Dumas, much to his discomfiture. It was when things were at this pass that he escaped from the complications of the situation by disappearing into Switzerland.

On his return, he thought of a characteristic subterfuge to satisfy both the young women. With some help, once more, from Anicet Bourgeois he wrote a new play, *Angèle*, with parts for Belle as well as for Ida. The new favourite, admittedly, came off better: the character she was to enact had some similarities with that of Amélie in *Teresa*, a very young, innocent and much wronged girl, of the type that endured in the French theatre for generations and still survives to our day, after a fashion, in the plays of Anouilh. Belle, on the other hand, must have been less than pleased with the part of Ernestine, the discarded mistress who, after a couple of scenes in the first act, disappears from sight until almost the end of the play when she returns to take her revenge.

Dumas had originally thought of entitling his new play *L'Echelle des Femmes*, since the central character is an ambitious young man without fortune or prospects who resolves to climb to the top using women as the rungs in his ladder, according to the terms of the author's metaphor. This would have been a much more explicit title, and the change to *Angèle* was probably made simply in order to give greater prominence to the role Ida was intended to fill; the dramatic interest remains centred, however, on the figure of the social climber Alfred d'Alvimar. Dumas had linked this play more closely to contemporary political events than any other he had put his name to, for Alvimar, when it opens, is just in the process of switching his allegiance to the Orleanist monarchy after the July Revolution has blown his hopes of preferment under the previous régime. In an opening scene of unexampled brutality, he breaks with Ernestine, who he reckons can no longer be of any use to him in the changed political circumstances. In her place he courts, assiduously and successfully, the sixteen-year-old daughter of a Napoleonic general who was killed in the year of her birth, calculating, as he explains to his confidant Jules Raymond, that 'the new government, still shakily based on its appeal to fickle popular sentiment and too weak to institute a change of system, has no alternative but to turn to the principal survivors of the imperial administration; within a month, all the top men of 1812 will be back in charge of the country's affairs.'[3] As the son-in-law of a senior officer who fell at Waterloo, Alvimar might land a plum job; but the marriage would, of course, require the agreement of Angèle's mother, whom he has not yet met. Once he does so, Alvimar decides he will achieve his ends more easily as her lover than as her son-in-law, and in consequence abruptly drops Angèle.

In the fluid society of the 1830s a character like Alvimar, using his sexual attractions to entrap women of influence who might help him up the ladder of preferment, was of peculiar topicality. Stendhal had provided an unforgettable prototype in the hero of *Le Rouge et le Noir*, a book that had provoked scandalized reactions when it was published only a year or so before *Angèle* was staged. A little later, Balzac was to introduce the same theme into *Le Père Goriot* where it is Eugène de Rastignac who profits by the hold he gains over Delphine de Nucingen to lift himself out of the sordid lodging-house environment to which his poverty had condemned him. At this stage in his literary career, Dumas had closer affinities, in some ways, with the new school of realist novelists than with the romantic dramatists, Hugo and Vigny, with whom he was popularly associated. One can go even further and say that his 'modern dramas' of the post-1830 period, *Antony*, *Richard Darlington*, and now *Angèle*, read today almost as though they were novels that had taken the wrong turning, written by a dramatist who had mistaken his medium. What is curious, and some would say regrettable, is that when in the following decade Dumas finally turned to the novel, the lengthy sagas he wrote had more affinities with the historical fiction popularized by Scott in the 1820s than with the contemporary social analysis that Balzac was providing in *La Comédie humaine*.

Alvimar's audacious schemes are, of course, necessarily frustrated in the end; so immoral a man could never have been allowed to triumph on the stage, no matter how his real-life analogues fared in the society of the July Monarchy. His seduction of Angèle in between the first and second acts results in her giving birth to a child between the third and fourth acts; here again, there is a close analogy with Mathilde de La Mole's pregnancy in *Le Rouge et le Noir*. But whereas the hero of Stendhal's novel is ready and anxious to set matters right and marry Mathilde, Alvimar sees more advantage in abandoning Angèle, once he has realized that her mother has nothing like the political influence he had credited her with earlier. He is on the point of slipping away to St. Petersburg when an old friend of the family, having divined Alvimar's secret intentions, challenges him, kills him, and marries the girl himself, knowing that in any case the pulmonary consumption he is a prey to will leave her a widow within a short space of time.

If Dumas were the kind of writer who makes a habit of relieving the itch of personal discomfort and guilt by projecting his problems into his work, one would be tempted to link the theme of the father's refusal to assume legal responsibility for his child with Dumas's own uneasiness at having, so far, brought two children into the world both of whom, by his fault, bore the stigma of illegitimacy. Angèle had her forerunners in her creator's own life; their names were Catherine Labay and Belle Krelsamer; and neither had had the good fortune to find a champion who could compel their seducer, at pistol's point, to make amends or risk the consequences. Such a theory, however, is scarcely tenable in face of the complete lack of evidence that Dumas ever felt the slightest twinge of conscience at having fathered two bastards (he was later to father at least two more). What made Angèle's position utterly different from that of Catherine or Belle was that she belonged to a distinguished and respectable family. The conventional morality of the time ruled that, although it was scandalously un-principled to get with child the unmarried daughter of a countess, an unmarried sempstress or actress came into quite a different category.

In 1833, when *Angèle* was created, Alexandre, his natural son, was a boy of nine, and Marie-Alexandrine, his daughter by Belle Krelsamer, an infant not yet two years old. Having little inclination for family life, he visited Catherine Labay and her child at Passy only from time to time as the fancy took him or the necessity arose. But, though a neglect-ful parent, he was not indifferent or cold-hearted, and once when the little boy had a bad fall and suffered concussion the father, summoned from town, actually fainted away with emotion at seeing his son white-faced and all bandaged up. The doctor had prescribed leeches, but the child refused obstinately to allow the nasty creatures near his skin, and stared misgivingly at his father when he gave his word they wouldn't hurt. 'But you wouldn't let them bite you,' said the little invalid; whereupon his father picked out two from the jar and applied them to the palm of his own left hand, swearing he felt nothing.[4]

On the other hand he showed no compunction at all in taking young Alexandre away from his mother, to whom the boy was passionately attached, when his new mistress, Belle Krelsamer, expressed a desire to bring him up herself, along with her own baby daughter who was his half-sister. Catherine tried to get custody of her son, but the law normally came down on the side of the father in such cases, and she was forced to give way. Belle, however, found she had taken on more than she bargained for. She complained to Dumas, in a long, angry letter, that she found the boy (eight years old at this time) quite uncontrollable. 'I can't even manage, however much I beg or threaten, to get him to allow me to comb his hair; he won't let me give him reading and writing lessons and behaves so wilfully and so violently that I am always having to scold him.' It was a great mistake, she went on, to have given him permission to visit his mother on Thursdays and Sundays. 'The more he sees of her, the worse his mood when he returns; he is sulky and bad-tempered with us all; I firmly believe his mother is turning him against us and even against you; he no longer asks for you as he did in the beginning; he has only one idea in his head, his mother, nothing else counts for him.' Dumas ought really to have been firmer. 'There are cases where it is less dangerous to make a clean break than to try and effect a gentle separation . . . It is essential that for a period of time this child should see only you and have only you to love, unless you want him to drift away from you and come to look on you, judging you through his mother's eyes, as a tyrant rather than a friend.'[5] It may well have been this letter that brought Dumas post-haste back from Switzerland before he had completed his projected tour.

There is a certain ironic justice in the fact that, barely two years later, when Dumas set up house with Ida Ferrier, the writer of this letter was punished for having tried to drive a wedge between Catherine and her son when her rival succeeded in taking Belle's child, Marie-Alexandrine, away from her. Belle was made even more unhappy than Catherine, for her daughter grew very fond of Ida and in a short while forgot about her mother, whereas Alexandre remained loyally attached to his throughout the whole of her life. Marie was a quiet, undemonstrative little girl, quite unlike her turbulent half-brother. Physically, she took after her father more than he did; she inherited in particular his sapphire blue eyes and dark complexion. But Ida did not extend the same affection to both Dumas's children; she was bitterly jealous of Alexandre, disliked having him around, and indeed made life so difficult for Dumas when the boy did come visiting that father and son found it more agreeable to meet outside.

By the end of 1833 Belle Krelsamer had finally been banished and Ida and Dumas were living together in an apartment in the Rue Bleue. For an unmarried couple openly to cohabit in this way was unusual at that date, more especially when they both enjoyed leading a social life. It meant that their dinner-parties were always rather short of women, since ladies who observed the proprieties refused to come, and Ida did not believe in allowing Dumas to enjoy the company of other sorts of women to any greater extent than she could help. The only actress suffered with a good grace at her table was Mlle Mars, possibly because she judged her too old to present a serious danger; in any case, Mars and Dumas always tended to rub each other up the wrong way. Ida was a skilful and accomplished hostess; with her mother's help, she ran the household without waste and yet on a fairly sumptuous scale, and in spite of the irregularity of her situation, invitations to her dinner-parties were much sought after. As the circle of their friends widened, it became apparent that the rather pokey set of rooms in the Rue Bleue would no longer suit, and Dumas took the lease on a fourth-floor apartment in the Rue de Rivoli, with a balcony overlooking the Tuileries Gardens. Ida made sure it was furnished appropriately.

Deep in its inner recesses, she had her sanctum, her 'laboratory', as it was called by one of the few woman friends permitted to enter.[6] Here she would spend up to four hours a day getting herself ready for the evening's appearance; hair-dyes in phials and creams in jars, powders and rouges and eye-shadow in their several boxes, were all to hand and all arranged in a set order, and once her toilette was completed 'even the news that her mother had just died would have left her unmoved . . . Not for the world would she have permitted a tear to form; her blond eyelashes, dyed brown, one of her greatest attractions, would have been discoloured.'[7] Not for another thirty years did it become generally accepted that society ladies might paint their faces; Ida Ferrier could claim to have invented the art of *maquillage* and to have practised it, in advance of her time, with a talent rarely exceeded.

She had a passion, too, for clothes, and spent Dumas's money freely on them. Having thick ankles and not very dainty feet, she started the fashion for floor-length dresses. Apart from her irregular teeth, about which nothing could be done at that period, she had a flawless face, and liked to wear her hair in a mass of fair curls. She had well-shaped arms and shoulders, and her bosom was dazzlingly white; unfortunately, however, she did not keep for long the slim silhouette that had so entranced Dumas when he first saw her; and once she started to put on weight, her former attractions were seen to be no more than what the French call *la beauté du diable*, meaning that what the devil has given the devil can as easily take away.

Temperamentally, she was an actress first and foremost, and not just in the professional sense; those who knew her well were sometimes astonished at the multiplicity of façades she could present to the world. She was a shrewd judge of character, and adapted herself unerringly to the company in which she found herself. In the society of respectable women, she posed as the fallen angel, one whose errors of conduct were due to her warm heart, never to lack of principles. At a pinch, she could even pretend to be a prude. But put her in a relaxed, bohemian circle, and no one was more capable of outrageous pleasantries and wild behaviour. In her dealings with servants, she showed yet another side of her nature; if they crossed or annoyed her, she would pour forth a stream of vulgar abuse couched in the sort of language normally heard only on the lips of fishwives or the lowest kind of street-walker. Totally lacking in natural modesty, she observed the conventions of polite behaviour only because it was politic to do so; ambitious and cold-hearted, she put forth all her charm to win over those who could render her the kind of services she needed to promote her own interests, and treated all others with haughty disdain.

The summit of her ambitions was to be offered employment in the Comédie-Française; and after some bargaining between Dumas and the administration, a contract was signed on February 24th, 1837, giving her a five-month engagement, at a fee of 4,000 francs, for the 1837–8 season. In return, Dumas had to promise to write a 'tragedy' for the Company; the word implied a verse play set in classical times and involving historical characters of some eminence.

A suitable subject had, in fact, occurred to Dumas the previous year, while he was staying at Naples and visiting the ruins of Pompeii. He subsequently went to Rome and was fortunate enough to be granted an audience with Pope Gregory XVI, to whom he explained his idea: he would write a play concerned with the early Christian martyrs, set in the reign of the Emperor Caligula. When His Holiness objected mildly that the first persecutions of the Christians in Rome were supposed to have occurred some time after Caligula's death, Dumas referred to a popular tradition which might allow him to falsify the historical record in the interests of true religion, whereupon the Pope replied—if one may accept Dumas's version of the conversation— 'Do it then, my son; what you purpose may not succeed in the eyes of men, but the intention will at least have merit in the eyes of the Lord.'[8]

The first part of the Pope's prediction came close to being verified in the event. *Caligula* had its defenders; Gautier called it 'the one conscientious poetic work to have been produced in 1837';[9] but on the whole it had a bad press, and was taken off after only twenty per-formances. Dumas was not well served by the august company for which he had written his tragedy. The Comédie-Française was chronic-ally hard up, and disinclined to spend money on the accessories that Dumas wanted. He reached the point of threatening a lawsuit when they refused to allow him horses to draw Caligula's triumphal chariot. 'Fancy asking us to provide horses,' exclaimed one of the *sociétaires* wrily, 'when we can barely afford, in our classical indigence, to act on foot!' In the end the author had to agree to have the chariot drawn by a team of female slaves. The banquet scene, which should have been a brilliant orgy, was lit by three smoky torches, and all that was

provided for the imperial feast was a plate of anachronistic oranges and
a few apples in a bowl; as Delphine de Girardin remarked witheringly,
the general effect, with the guests lolling languidly on divans, was of a
town-hall used as a temporary hospital ward during an outbreak of
cholera.

The casting proved difficult too. One of the members of the company
had refused to play Messalina on the grounds that she could not
reconcile it with the purity of her own private morals to impersonate
so notorious a nymphomaniac; she had to be replaced by another
actress, Louise Noblet, who had a clearer idea of the proper division
between life and art. As the Christian slave-girl Stella, the object of
Caligula's lust, Ida Ferrier had been given the leading feminine part
and by all accounts failed to make much of it. Her elocution, like that
of many other actresses in the Comédie-Française at the time, left much
to be desired. In *Angèle* she had lisped; this was tolerable, since her
part was that of a simple-hearted, tearful girl of sixteen; but as Stella,
defying the tyrant Caligula, her adenoidal sing-song bordered on the
grotesque. Then again, her physique was quite wrong for the part.
'Mlle Ida,' as the actor Samson recorded in his memoirs, 'had a very
pretty head on top of a thick, squat body. Her monstrous girth
hampered her freedom of movement; she tripped and fell two or three
times . . .'[10] Delphine Gay, writing under the pseudonym of the
Vicomte de Launay in her husband's newspaper *La Presse*, reckoned
she was totally miscast.

> How can anyone take the part of *ingénue* with as thick a waist as
> that? In the roles played by Mlle George, that actress's ample form
> is acceptable; it could even be said that too slender a frame would
> be quite wrong for such parts . . . But Mlle Ida's fatness, in the part
> of a wistful, sentimental girl always wearing white, a shy, light-
> footed virgin fleeing an infamous libertine, a sylph, an angel with
> invisible wings—Mlle Ida's fatness is both ludicrous and disgusting.
> One should at least be transportable if one's fate is to be kidnapped
> every evening.[11]

It is not difficult to imagine how Ida Ferrier reacted to this public
ridicule of her ungainliness, nor how hard a time Dumas had of it
trying to mollify her.

But although in many respects his private life was passing through
a difficult phase at this period, the tribulations he was enduring were
nothing compared to the sufferings he had, for some years, been
unconsciously inflicting on his son. About the same time that he and
Ida started living together, he had placed Alexandre in a private board-
ing school, the Pension Saint-Victor, run by Prosper Goubaux, one of
the two playwrights who had collaborated with him in the writing of

Richard Darlington. Goubaux had a genuine vocation for teaching, but unfortunately no great talent for organization and administration. Reminiscing about his schooldays later in his life, Alexandre referred to Goubaux as 'the worthiest of men, but also the most happy-go-lucky' and to the school he ran as a 'bizarre institution in which I learnt very little'.[12] Had the headmaster been a little more aware of what was going on out of class, Alexandre might have had a less unhappy time of it. He wrote of these early trials in an autobiographical passage included in the preface to one of his plays, *La Femme de Claude*; in the same preface he refers to the opening chapters of a novel, *L'Affaire Clémenceau*, in which he told the story of his own wretched schooldays under the cover of fiction. These two texts, taken together, present a lamentable image of a boy persecuted by his schoolfellows, who came mainly from rich and aristocratic families, both because of his father's notoriety and because his mother had borne him out of wedlock. They started by ignoring him, went on to make him the butt of cruel jests, and proceeded by stages to ragging and outright bullying. At night he would be woken up with a start when one of them flung a book at his head; or else he would find that a saucepan of water had been emptied over his bed and he had to sleep as best he could between wet sheets. In the refectory, the boys made sure he was the last to have the dish as it passed round the table and that by the time it reached him it contained only uneatable scraps, or nothing at all; so that his meal often consisted of a crust of bread and a glass of water. One evening he was urgently summoned downstairs, found the lamp in the stairwell had been extinguished, and caught his foot in a cord that had been rigged up to trip him.

He was badly hurt as a result of this prank, and Goubaux read the whole school a lecture on bullying, after which his persecutors became more circumspect. He was still addressed as 'bastard', and still apt to find his exercise-books covered with obscene drawings above which his mother's name had been written. Finally the psychological stress began to tell on his health and his father, noticing this at last, took him away from the Pension Saint-Victor and boarded him in a small, family establishment, the pupils of which attended classes at the Collège Bourbon.

In this new environment he rapidly recovered his health and spirits. Ladies with whom his father was on visiting terms started to invite the boy to their houses. Nodier's daughter Marie, now Mme Mennessier, with a son of her own rather younger than Alexandre, was one of these, and another was the Marquise de Saint-Mars, the widow of a high-ranking cavalry officer who, having fallen on hard times, started writing highly successful society novels using the pseudonym Countess Dash.[13] Strangely, he even struck up a friendship with Mélanie Waldor, who encouraged him in his hopes of putting an end to his father's long-standing liaison with Ida Ferrier. The letter the boy wrote to his father, to plead with him to get rid of the woman who came between them, has not survived, but the text of the older man's reply has come down to us, and few stranger letters can ever have been addressed by a father to his adolescent son. The principal argument he used to convince Alexandre that the continuation of the liaison was in his best interests was founded on—of all things—the presumption of Ida's sterility. 'Not having had a child for six years, I am *certain* not to have any and thus you will remain my only son . . . If I were to marry another woman than Mlle Ida, I might have three or four other children, whereas with her I shall *never* have any.'[14]

As one reads these lines, and remembers how quickly after the birth of each of his illegitimate children Dumas deserted their mothers, one is driven to the conclusion that the last thing he wanted was to follow the example of his friend Victor Hugo and found a family. It would be through his own literary achievement, not through the begetting of progeny, that his name would pass to posterity. This streak of egoistic vanity may well have dictated the postscript to this letter, in which Dumas seems to be denying his son even the right to use the family surname. 'Instead of signing Alex. Dumas as I do, which might one day cause grave difficulties for both of us, since our signatures are so similar, you ought to sign yourself Dumas Davy; my name is too well-known, you understand, for there to be any doubt—and I can't add the word *père*; I am still too young for that.' The suggestion that, in order to save his father the embarrassment of acknowledging their relationship, he should take his great-grandfather's surname, must have cut the younger Alexandre to the heart.

Yet in spite of appearances, there can be no question that Dumas felt a strong affection for the boy, and was as deeply troubled as his normally cheerful nature allowed by the apparent impossibility of establishing friendly relations between Ida and Alexandre, the two persons to whom, since his mother's death,[15] he felt most deeply attached. His torn affections found expression in the oddest ways, as when he wrote to his fifteen-year-old son: 'If you were a hermaphrodite and if in addition to bisexuality God had also granted you a talent for cooking, I would have no other mistress but you. But unfortunately God had other views when he created you. So, once and for all, be magnanimous enough to allow our hearts always to touch and meet in spite of the material obstacles that may stand between us. You occupy, as you always will, a special place in my heart, as my eldest, and you will always have a special claim on my purse, though my heart is rather more to be depended on than my purse.'[16]

However much he may have wanted to respect his father, the

younger Dumas, confronted with this incurable frivolity, had eventually to renounce the attempt, at least on the personal level, and reserve his esteem for the playwright and the novelist that his father later became. When introducing him to ladies of his acquaintance he would say, with wry humour: 'Permit me to present to you my revered parent, a big child I had when I was very young.'[17] He knew the child to be petulant and self-willed, and he had no power to stop him making a fool of himself. His attempts to reason his father out of his infatuation with Ida failed completely, and before long Dumas announced his intention to legalize his relations with her. The marriage was solemnized at a civil ceremony on February 1st, 1840, followed four days later by a church wedding at the Eglise Saint-Roch. The witnesses were Chateaubriand and François Villemain, the Minister for Education. Chateaubriand, always mindful of his attachment to lost causes, and in particular to that of the fallen Bourbon monarchy, stared morosely at the bride's pendulous breasts stuffed into a white corsage and, turning to Roger de Beauvoir, remarked to him *sotto voce*: 'You see, my destiny never changes, even now. Whatever I raise my hands to bless, collapses.'[18]

The news of this marriage caused a ripple of amusement among those who knew the couple, while the various women who had been, at one time or another, on terms of intimacy with Dumas reacted with righteous indignation. 'I expect you will have heard that M. Dumas has married his fat lady,' wrote Marceline Desbordes-Valmore, the poetess, in a letter to her husband. 'Mme Serre [Belle Krelsamer] came round here and fainted away. She is to start proceedings to gain custody of her daughter. Mme Waldor called too. She had supposed he was marrying some respectable woman, and had written him a note saying she was "relieved to hear he had at last extricated himself from his shameful liaison". Imagine the effect this letter will have had!'[19]

There was much indiscreet speculation about the reasons for this marriage, after so long a cohabitation which, as everyone knew, had not been without its occasional squalls. Inventive boulevard wits retailed all manner of fanciful stories, tricked out with corroborative circumstantial detail, to explain why this notorious rake had been forced to make an honest woman of the actress. Ida's interests, it was said, were looked after by a certain M. Domange who ran a sewage disposal business in Paris. Using her savings to buy up all Dumas's I.O.U.s, he was able to confront the improvident author with the choice between marriage and a debtor's prison.[20] Alternatively, it was said that Dumas had been so ill-advised as to take Ida to a ball given by the Duc d'Orléans who then said to him: 'It is understood, my dear Dumas, that you could not have introduced me to anyone but your wife.'[21] Dumas himself was alleged to have declared that he married her 'so as to have the chance of a legal separation'.[22] Although this jest is quite characteristic of Dumas's style of humour, its authenticity is all the same a little suspect, since he himself recorded hearing an identical explanation offered by Marie Dorval when she announced to him, back in 1831, her recent marriage to the impresario Jean-Toussaint Merle.[23]

The truth of the matter is probably that, in spite of her difficult, domineering nature, in spite of the jealous scenes she made whenever she suspected him of showing interest in some other woman, in spite of the lengths she went to—opening his letters, having him followed in the street—to make sure he was not playing her false, Dumas found he could not, when it came to the point, part from her. Readers of *Adolphe* will remember Constant's disabused reflections on how inde-structible a prolonged liaison between a man and a woman can become, even though the two people involved find little positive pleasure in the association. 'We reach the decision, calmly, in due course to make the break; we have the impression of awaiting impatiently the moment when we may carry out our intention; but when that moment arrives, it fills us with terror.' Some such process must have been in operation here. Their incessant bickering must have depressed Ida as much as it did Dumas—yet he would not let her go, even when she appeared to want this. At one point she entered into negotiations for a theatrical engagement in St. Petersburg, without telling Dumas what she was doing, until the contract actually arrived for her signature. Before appending her name, she showed it to him; he glanced through it and tore it up. Yet only a little later he made secret preparations for a trip to Corsica, planning to write from there and let Ida know it was all over between them; but he lacked the strength of purpose even to set off.

The marriage did not last above four years; Ida found a man she preferred, an Italian nobleman of the bluest blood with a wife and son living in Palermo. Divorce was out of the question for either of them, but by 1844 Dumas was happy enough to let her go and live with her prince on a permanent footing, no doubt gratified that she was leaving him for a man who was listed in Gotha. At least matters had turned out better for him than for his bosom friend Roger de Beauvoir, who had similarly contracted an inexplicable marriage with an actress, Mlle Doze, a pupil of Mlle Mars, but not particularly gifted, though she was very pretty. Although they had lived together, as lover and mistress, in perfect harmony for several years, once married they fell to quarrel-ling bitterly and incessantly. Worse, they made no secret of their dissensions, which were widely reported and eagerly discussed in the papers, and they embarked on painful, expensive, and pointless litigation. Eventually death came to release them both from their bonds; the wife was carried off by pulmonary tuberculosis and the husband, a little later, by dropsy.

Dumas paid a posthumous tribute to Roger de Beauvoir in the preface he wrote for a collection of his friend's miscellaneous pieces. The greater part of this preface is concerned with Beauvoir's literary achievement and his reputation as a supper-table wit. Of his disastrous private life Dumas says only this: 'The man least fit to be a husband married the woman least fit to be a wife.'[24] Did he stop a moment, after penning this phrase, to reflect how apt an epitaph he had written on his own preposterous excursion into matrimony?

ix The Novelist

Dumas's mutation from playwright to novelist took place as he was nearing his forties. The metamorphosis was not complete, since he retained a lively interest in the stage, and went on writing for it, almost till the end of his life; but his most important plays were all written before 1840. Even in the mid-1830s it seems that the two veins that had been so richly productive in the past—the historical melodrama and the domestic tragedy—were beginning to be worked out and that Dumas was feeling the need to discover some new form of dramatic expression. *Kean, ou Désordre et Génie*, produced in 1836, was different from anything he had attempted before: a play based on the life of the great British actor who had died only three years previously, written at the suggestion of Frédérick Lemaître and composed deliberately to allow the French actor to show off all his special talents. Frédérick and Edmund Kean were in many respects similar types, even off-stage; both given to drink and gambling, both notorious lechers. On stage both had the same dominating presence, with their magnetically staring eyes, their ability, on the right occasions, to make the rafters ring to their stentorian outbursts. Thus, the more Frédérick was himself in *Kean*, the better he incarnated Kean. The result, mortifying to Dumas, was that the actor got more credit for the play's success than did the author.

Three years later, Dumas experimented again, this time with a historical comedy. In point of fact, *Mademoiselle de Belle-Isle* was not a comedy in any but the purely negative sense that it did not have a tragic ending; the two young lovers are finally reconciled, but the agonies of misunderstanding, estrangement and despair they have first to endure border on the tragical, and *Mademoiselle de Belle-Isle* thus belongs roughly to the same class of play as Shakespeare's *Cymbeline* with which, incidentally, it has a number of analogies, possibly fortuitous. Staged at the Théâtre-Français, with Mlle Mars, now sixty if a day, enacting the virginal eighteen-year-old Gabrielle de Belle-Isle, it was a great success, though Gautier was uncharacteristically caustic about the veteran actress's insistence on grabbing the parts of unmarried girls. 'An astonishing *ingénue*,' he commented; 'still able to get about without a stick!' One has to admit even so that Dumas's first regency comedy[1] must have owed much of the impact it made at the time to the skilled interpretation of the Comédie-Française actors, Firmin and Lockroy as well as Mlle Mars, for its intrinsic merits are far from obvious. The plot is almost impossible to accept, turning as it does on the incredible circumstance that the Duc de Richelieu, one of the most notorious roués of the age, fails to realize that the woman he spends the night with, between the second and the third acts, is not the innocent Gabrielle whom he had wagered he would seduce, but an old discarded mistress, the Marquise de Prie. Even then it would need only a word from her to dispel the illusion, and in order to ensure she cannot utter it Dumas has to introduce a further *coup de théâtre*: a palace revolution, resulting in Mme de Prie's fall from favour and sudden banishment.

At the time *Mademoiselle de Belle-Isle* had its première, on April 2nd, 1839, Dumas had already started switching his allegiance from the stage-play to the novel. The point of junction was a work loosely based on the life of John Paul Jones, one of the heroes of the American War of Independence, which had first been conceived and written as a drama and was later turned into a piece of narrative fiction. While touring Brittany immediately after the July Revolution he had made a point of stopping at Lorient so as to find out more, if he could, about Captain Paul Jones, his interest having been stimulated by Fenimore Cooper's fictionalized account of his adventures in *The Pilot*. The local archives yielded little information, but Dumas elicited a few colourful details from an old clerk who remembered the stories his father used to tell of the American naval commander's exploits.

It was not, however, until five years later, when Dumas was cruising off the coast of Sicily in a chartered brig, that the data he had assembled crystallized in his mind in the shape, almost inevitably, of a play, since at that time it never occurred to him to compose except in the dramatic mode. *Paul Jones* was written in the space of a week when equinoctial storms compelled the captain to beach his ship near San Giovanni. On his return to Paris Dumas read the script to Harel and Mlle George, but the actress found much to object to in the part he had written for her, and so, for once, Harel felt himself obliged to decline an offering from his favourite author.

Dumas shrugged his shoulders and sent the manuscript to his agent, Porcher, to place if he could; but nothing happened for a further three years. Then, early in 1838, he was approached by a senior member of the editorial staff of *Le Siècle*, with a request for a two-volume novel to appear in instalments in the newspaper. As they wanted delivery within a month, Dumas had little time for reflection; he badly needed the fee, however, and so decided to use the material he had collected on Paul Jones. Porcher, apprehensive at seeing the plot of this still unplayed drama disclosed to the public in the form of a serial story, expressed his concern to the playwright who silenced him—or so he later related—with an uncannily accurate prediction: 'Porcher, harken well to the words of Nostradamus. There will come a time when no publisher will agree to bring out a book which has not appeared first in a newspaper, and when the only plays a manager will accept are those drawn from novels.'[2]

In France, the idea of publishing popular fiction by instalments in the daily press was pioneered by Emile de Girardin, who launched the first relatively cheap daily paper, *La Presse*, on July 1st, 1836. The recent increase in the proportion of the population that could read, coupled with a gradual rise in the standard of living as the industrial revolution gained impetus, convinced Girardin that there was a market for a low-priced popular daily. His profit margin would be small, but he reckoned he would cover his costs comfortably if increased circulation allowed him to raise his charges for advertisement space. Girardin had to face an initial setback when his idea was poached by another press magnate, Dutacq, who brought out the first issue of *Le Siècle* on the very day that Girardin had fixed for the inception of *La Presse*, charging exactly the same quarterly subscription rate of 10 francs. Nevertheless, in its beginnings *La Presse* did conspicuously better than *Le Siècle*, and since in all other respects the two newspapers were similar in style and content as well as being identical in price, Girardin's success must be attributed largely to his initiative in offering subscribers hitherto unpublished novels appearing in parts. The first work published in *La Presse* in this way was Balzac's *La Vieille Fille* (October 23rd–November 4th, 1836). With its slightly scabrous plot, it was not altogether suitable as family reading, and before long Girardin started commissioning lighter fiction from more innocuous authors. The other newspapers, *Le Siècle, Le Journal des Débats, Le Constitutionnel*, were forced to follow suit if they wanted to keep their readers, who bought a newspaper not, as formerly, because its political line coincided with theirs, but in consideration of the appeal of the particular author who had been signed up for the current *roman-feuilleton* (serial story).

One result was that the writing of fiction, which had previously been a far from lucrative occupation, suddenly became profitable, and indeed enormously profitable for the few who had the knack of writing stories that kept their readers on tenterhooks, all agog for the next instalment. Such authors found themselves the subject of hotly contested auctions between rival press barons. When Eugène Sue, who had received 26,500 francs from *Le Journal des Débats* for his *Mystères de Paris*, announced his next novel, *Le Juif errant* (*The Wandering Jew*), Girardin tried to secure it for *La Presse* by outbidding Bertin of *Le Journal des Débats*; both were disappointed when the enterprising Dr Véron, editor of *Le Constitutionnel*, chipped in with an offer of an astronomic

100,000 francs and carried the day. Véron had no reason to repent his rashness, for *Le Constitutionnel*, which had a circulation of less than 4,000 in 1843, started selling 24,000 copies a day as soon as *Le Juif errant* began to appear in its columns.

Though the vogue of the serial novel lasted until at least the end of the century, its honeymoon period, what one historian has called the stage of 'true *roman-feuilleton* mania',[3] endured for a mere six years, from 1842 to 1848, and Dumas took maximum advantage of it. In *Le Siècle* he published *Les Trois Mousquetaires* and its two long sequels, *Vingt ans après* and *Le Vicomte de Bragelonne*. Girardin gratefully accepted *La Reine Margot* on Christmas Day 1844 to replace Balzac's *Les Paysans* which had been driving the unappreciative readers of *La Presse* crazy with boredom; and when *La Reine Margot* came to an end he approached Dumas with a request to write a further romance concerned with the life of Cagliostro. Dumas accepted the commission and the result was the novel usually called *Joseph Balsamo* but occasionally known, in English translation, as *Memoirs of a Physician*. Bertin's *Journal des Débats* was fortunate enough to secure the rights on *Le Comte de Monte-Cristo*. *Le Chevalier de Maison-Rouge*, a romance centring round the imprisonment and execution of Marie-Antoinette, appeared in *La Démocratie pacifique*, while *Le Constitutionnel* was able to serialize *La Dame de Monsoreau* (better known in the English-speaking world as *Chicot the Jester*) and its sequel *Les Quarante-Cinq* (*The Forty-Five Guardsmen*), two novels set in the reign of Henri III. Dumas composed all these works, many of them of enormous length, not in sequence necessarily but often simultaneously, so that he was sometimes writing novels for several different newspapers at once. Arsène Houssaye once overheard a fair visitor at one of Mme de Girardin's *soirées* ask Dumas what he did for a living; he responded by lifting up a pile of newspapers lying on an occasional table and answering, with an ironical smile: 'I am a gentleman of leisure.'[4]

The problem that puzzled everyone was how he found time to do it all. The caricaturist Marcelin provided his own fanciful answer when he drew Dumas seated at his table with four separate pens between the fingers of each hand, while a waiter standing by his side ladled soup into his open mouth. There was a particle of truth in this last detail, for more than one memoir-writer mentions the trolley on which lunch was brought in to him as he worked and from which he would help himself without needing to stop writing. He covered the paper at great speed, rarely crossing anything out and never revising. As time went on, under the pressure of the commitments he had entered into, he found himself writing more and more, if not faster and faster. The eight large sheets that had represented his daily output initially increased progressively to ten, fifteen, twenty and more. He took no little pride in his ability to turn out work faster than anyone else, and was not above boasting publicly of his speed of execution. In 1845, when about to start his three-volume romance *Le Chevalier de Maison-Rouge*, he wagered a hundred *louis-d'or* that he would complete the first volume within 72 hours, including the time needed for eating and sleeping. He emerged from his study six hours before the deadline, holding the completed pile of foolscap paper.

Even in normal circumstances, he worked non-stop from the moment he woke up in the morning. 'He gets out of bed and, while half-dressed, writes a couple of pages; he calls for some hot water and while his man is bringing it he writes another twenty lines. He is told that breakfast is ready. "Good," he says, "let my wife know", and he goes on writing. When the others are taking coffee and cigars he escapes from the room to go back to his writing. He leaves the house to shop, to pay a few social calls; he gets home and continues where he has left off. He writes before meals and after meals; he goes to the theatre, has a late night supper and returns to go on writing.'[5] Like Napoleon, he was able to make do with a minimum of sleep at night, thanks to a habit of taking cat-naps during the day. Victor Hugo's son Charles recalls how, in the house he rented at Brussels, he had three couches at his disposal so that wherever he was working, if he felt too tired to continue he could throw himself down on a divan, close his eyes and fall sound asleep for perhaps five minutes, after which he would wake up and resume writing. But it was not even necessary for him to lie down. 'Often, after my long nights spent working, when I have only had an hour or two's sleep, my eyes close and if I happen to be sitting near a wall, I rest my head on the wall; or if I am sitting at a table, my head falls on the table. Then, however awkward the position, whatever angle my head makes with my body, I sleep for five minutes, and at the end of these five minutes I wake up sufficiently refreshed to start work again immediately.'[6]

Even with his phenomenally robust constitution, Dumas paid for these excesses; every so often—usually once a year—he would be laid low with a bout of fever. When this happened he would lie in bed and drowse away the hours, taking no food but only an occasional sip of lemonade. After three days his temperature would drop to normal and he was able to start the taxing round of work again.

He had his peculiar fads, one of which was to use different coloured paper according to what he was writing: yellow for a play, pink for a magazine article, azure for a novel, but never in any circumstances white. He had a theory that writing on white paper eventually ruined one's eyesight. Once, when he was at Tbilis, almost at the end of his journey through Russia, the stock of blue paper he had brought with him ran out and he visited every stationer in the city in a vain search for something similar; he was convinced that the stories he wrote during that halt suffered from being penned originally on the sickly buff paper which was all he could procure.

Writing as rapidly as he did, he never troubled to put in accents, commas, or indeed any form of punctuation. This may have been due, however, to the simple fact that the art of punctuation had never been properly taught him at school, for Dumas records how, when he was still earning his living as a clerk, his employer the Duc d'Orléans happened one day to look over his copy and, after expressing gratification at the legibility of his handwriting, suddenly exclaimed: 'Aha! You have your own ideas about punctuation, I see,' and, picking up a pen, proceeded to put in the commas in accordance with the rules of grammar.[7] When he became famous, Dumas left this finicky business to his secretaries, who were also expected to do his proof-reading for him and were encouraged to eliminate repetitions and elucidate obscurities in the finished text. One of them relates how he would good-humouredly shrug his shoulders when his attention was drawn to some sentence in which the syntax was so muddled that it was difficult to see what the meaning was. 'Dash it!' he said, grinning at his secretary. 'I mean, try putting in a few dashes here and there.'[8]

Even more necessary to Dumas than the succession of secretaries and copyists that worked for him were his research assistants or collaborators, of whom again there were many, though only one who counted, Auguste Maquet.

When still a schoolboy of sixteen, Maquet had distinguished himself as a doughty fighter in the 'battle of *Hernani*', that historic occasion on February 25th, 1830, when the young romantics organized a noisy demonstration at the Théâtre-Français to overawe the classicists in the audience and ensure the triumph of Hugo's epoch-making verse drama. A few months later, still before his seventeenth birthday, he fought at rather greater risk to life and limb alongside the republicans during the July Revolution, and participated actively in the storming of a police barracks. About this time or a little later, he got to know Gérard de Nerval, who introduced him to the joyous circle of the so-called 'Jeunes-France', of whom Gautier, who was also briefly an adherent, has left an entertaining account in his *Histoire du romantisme*. The group originally met in the studio of the sculptor Jean Duseigneur, situated above a greengrocer's shop in the Rue de Vaugirard; in the summer of 1831 most of them moved away from the Latin Quarter and emigrated to a quiet district in the north of the city. They dubbed their new quarters the 'Tartars' Camp' and proceeded to make a nuisance of themselves to the neighbours by sunbathing in the nude, giving loud and discordant brass-band recitals, and indulging in such pranks as enveloping a dressmaker's dummy in a shroud and leaving it on the pavement outside to terrify belated pedestrians.

Discontented with their humdrum French names, several of these dishevelled romantics adopted more exotic ones; something vaguely Celtic was aimed at; one member of the group, Théophile Dondey, took to signing himself Philothée O'Neddy, while plain Auguste Maquet became the wild clansman Augustus MacKeat. He did, however, have a sound practical reason for disguising his real name. Maquet had performed remarkably well as a classical scholar and now aspired to a doctorate at the University of Paris; but he knew that the examiners were hopelessly prejudiced against candidates known to have affiliations with the romantic movement, and it made sense, therefore, to adopt a pseudonym when it came to signing the occasional article or poem he was now beginning to publish in the literary periodicals.

His great ambition was the same as Dumas's had been at his age: to make a name for himself as a dramatist. While earning his living as a teacher of history at the Lycée Charlemagne, he collaborated with Nerval in the writing of a one-act play, *Lara ou l'Expiation*, the idea of which was taken from one of Zacharias Werner's fate-tragedies, and with Gautier on another dramatic piece, *Parisina*, deriving from Byron's poem of that title. Neither of them found a producer. Undismayed, Maquet wrote a third play unaided and submitted it, under the title *Un Soir de Carnaval*, to Anténor Joly, director of the Théâtre de la Renaissance, a theatre Hugo had founded for the express purpose of staging romantic plays. Joly rejected *Un Soir de Carnaval*, calling it 'well written but unsuitable for the theatre', whereupon Nerval, with whom Maquet had remained in close touch, suggested he should show the text to Dumas. Ever obliging, the author of *Antony* took the trouble to rewrite Maquet's play, and under the new title *Bathilde* got it accepted at the Renaissance, with the leading part taken by Ida Ferrier. Maquet, whose name, notwithstanding Dumas's material assistance, appeared as sole author of the piece, was overcome with gratitude, and expressed his feelings in a delicate sonnet addressed to Dumas's actress-mistress.

Bathilde was given a first performance on January 14th, 1839. The following year Maquet wrote a short historical novel, entitled *Le Bonhomme Buvat*, drawn from a contemporary chronicle of the abortive conspiracy of 1718 hatched under the aegis of the Spanish ambassador to France, Antoine de Cellamare. Having hawked the manuscript unsuccessfully round the Paris publishers, Maquet left it with Dumas, who was then on the point of leaving for Florence with his bride. He took the manuscript with him, liked it, and made Maquet a handsome offer for the right to rework it. The result was the first of Dumas's

(a) General Thomas-Alexandre Dumas (1762-1806) Dumas's father, one of Napoleon's generals

(b) Marie-Louise-Elisabeth Labouret Dumas's mother

(a) Dumas's birthplace at Villers-Cotterêts

(b) Le Château de Monte-Cristo
Dumas's house at Marly-le-Roi

(a) Alexandre Dumas as a young man. *From the lithograph by Achille Devéria, 1829*

(b) Ida (Marguerite-Joséphine Ferrand) Ferrier, actress. Dumas married her in 1840. *From the lithograph by A. Constant*

(a) The revolution of 1830: attack and capture of the Louvre, 29th July

(b) The cholera epidemic: Paris 1832.
From the wood engraving by Daumier

(a) Bestriding the Swiss Alps: a contemporary cartoon of Dumas, 1833

(b) Dumas and his pets: from the cover of *Histoire de mes Bêtes*

(a) Mlle Mars (Anne Boutet) (1779-1847)

(b) Mlle George (Marguerite-Joséphine Weime (1787-1867)

(c) Opening of the Théâtre Historique, Paris, 1847

Alexandre Dumas in late middle-age

(a) Edmond Dantès and the Abbé Faria imprisoned in the Château d'If: from an early edition of *The Count of Monte-Cristo*

(b) Garibaldi

(c) Alexandre Dumas *fils*, 1864

Dumas père with Adah Isaacs Menken c. 1

important historical novels, *Le Chevalier d'Harmental*, and the first of a long series of romances in which he and Maquet collaborated, though they were all published under Dumas's name.

Le Chevalier d'Harmental, still a highly readable book, is properly a love-story in a historical setting. Raoul d'Harmental, a young noble-man who won his spurs on the field of battle at Denain but subsequently shared in the disgrace that befell all Mme de Maintenon's protégés on the death of Louis XIV, allows himself to be enrolled in a conspiracy against the Regent, Prince Philippe d'Orléans. The plot involves nothing less than kidnapping the Prince and spiriting him off to Spain, and in order to escape the attentions of the Regent's spies, D'Harmental agrees to disguise himself as a student of theology of retiring habits, and takes lodgings in a narrow Paris street called, at that time, the Rue du Temps perdu, but later renamed the Rue St. Joseph. (The street exists to this day; in one of its houses, just a year before *Le Chevalier d'Harmental* was published, a child named Emile Zola was born to an Italian father and a French mother.) While awaiting the signal for the attempt to be made, Raoul finds time hanging heavily on his hands and becomes interested in a girl living in the house opposite his. Bathilde is, however, no ordinary *grisette* but the orphan daughter of an officer who had been killed, many years before, while serving under the command of Philippe d'Orléans. This circumstance will in the end prove the salvation of her lover; for the plot to kidnap the Duc d'Orléans miscarries on the first attempt, while at the second the police are forewarned and arrest the conspirators, including Raoul d'Harmental. The Regent, learning whose daughter Bathilde really is, allows Raoul to marry her in the chapel of the Bastille and then, instead of having him led to execution, grants him his pardon.

The sentimental streak in *Le Chevalier d'Harmental* is due not simply to the prominence given to the love-affair between Raoul and Bathilde which appears, almost till the end, to be doomed in view of the dangerous game the young man is playing, but also to the tender relationship between Bathilde and her guardian Buvat, a bumbling old bachelor working as a cataloguer in the Royal Library. (It was originally on the published memoirs of the real Jean Buvat that Maquet based his story.) Buvat is as honest as the day is long, totally disinterested, but somewhat timorous and not particularly perspicacious; it is he who, ignorant of Raoul's complicity, betrays in all innocence the secret of the conspiracy to the authorities.

The way *Le Chevalier d'Harmental* got written set the pattern for the future collaboration between Dumas and Maquet. It was not always Maquet who started the ball rolling, as happened in this first instance. There is strong presumptive evidence that Dumas was the first to have the idea of drawing a historical novel from the apocryphal memoirs of

5

D'Artagnan, published by Gatien Courtilz de Sandras in 1700, and it is certain that he progressed a good way with *Le Comte de Monte-Cristo* before involving Maquet in the work. But whether the initial impetus came from Maquet or not, it is quite clear that the form taken by their collaboration was fundamentally different from the pattern followed in other literary partnerships formed at a later date: that of the Goncourt brothers first and foremost, but also those of Erckmann–Chatrian (Emile Erckmann and Alexandre Chatrian), the Rosny and Tharaud brothers, and of Colette with her first husband Henri Gauthier-Villars. In all these instances, in so far as they have been documented, collabora-tion appears to have extended to the actual composition of the finished text. Neither with Maquet nor with any other of his associates did Dumas adopt this procedure. What he did was first to talk over the plan of the unwritten work in some detail with his collaborator, who would then be left to prepare a preliminary draft of a section of the book. Dumas would peruse this draft and entirely rewrite it, without, however, departing from its general lines. It was improvisa-tion on a theme already roughly worked out, so that he was spared the labour of invention to a large extent and could, at the same time, justly claim that the finished product was his own, every page bearing the stamp of his inimitable style, his verve, wit, and dynamic narrative thrust.

Dumas's long experience of writing plays with a variety of collabo-rators—with Leuven and Pierre-Joseph Rousseau at the start, and later with Goubaux, Beudin, Frédéric Gaillardet, Anicet Bourgeois, and even Gérard de Nerval[9]—must undoubtedly have given him a taste for this kind of creative cross-fertilization; he was, wrote Villemessant, 'the kind of man whose imaginative faculties flourished in informal talk and who in the last resort cannot manage without a collaborator, even if he only plays the part of a patient listener'.[10] But in addition, there was the point that Maquet was a professional historian of sorts, familiar with the likely sources and well equipped to do a piece of research on a specific topic. All the long novels they wrote in common were, in a broad sense, historical; even *Le Comte de Monte-Cristo*, the greater part of which is set in contemporary time, has a long and important section towards the beginning on the inner history of the Hundred Days in which the oddly imposing figure of the old king, Louis XVIII, is sketched in some detail. It is curious that Dumas should have been so successful in reviving the vogue for the historical novel in France, long after the original interest aroused by the transla-tions of Scott's novels had faded. But his treatment of the form was in one essential respect different from Scott's and from the way Scott's principal French imitators, Vigny, Hugo, and Mérimée, handled it. For them, what counted was 'local colour': the reconstitution of what they took to be the flavour of the period their novels were set in. For Dumas, however, this kind of conscientious authenticity was of minor importance. In a moment of candour, he once admitted that his way of dealing with history was 'strange'.

> I start by devising a story. I try to make it romantic, moving, dramatic, and when scope has been found for the emotions and the imagination, I search through the annals of the past to find a frame in which to set it; and it has never happened that history has failed to provide this frame, so exactly adjusted to the subject that it seemed it was not a case of the frame being made for the picture, but that the picture had been made to fit into the frame.[11]

History, in short, was used by Dumas in much the same way as science was used by Zola: to confer a semblance of veracity on his fiction. Apart from his very youngest readers, everyone knew that Cardinal Richelieu, Anne of Austria, the Duke of Buckingham, who figure so prominently in *Les Trois Mousquetaires*, were real people. There could be no argument either that Charles de Baatz d'Artagnan (1611–1673) had had a real existence, whatever doubts there might be about the exact truth of some of the stories Courtilz de Sandras told of his adventures in his *Mémoires de M. d'Artagnan*. But for Dumas, as presumably for Maquet, any detail found in print in a roughly contemporaneous record could be assumed to be 'true history'; they did not trouble themselves with the finer distinctions between memoirs and 'pseudo-memoirs'.

In *Les Trois Mousquetaires* we are given a peculiarly rose-tinted, partial, not so much distorted as disinfected view of the past, as anyone can see who compares the book with, say, Manzoni's *The Betrothed*, another historical novel of which the definitive edition came out just a couple of years before *Les Trois Mousquetaires*. Dumas's picture of the seventeenth century omits everything that would have made it a most uncomfortable age for any of his nineteenth-century readers were they to have been magically transported back into it. The epidemics, the famines, the injustices, the barbarous superstitions of the period have no place in his account. Even war is reduced to a gay picnic beneath the fortifications of La Rochelle.

This is no criticism. Only a pedant would cavil at the anachronisms,[12] the historical implausibilities, the glaring omissions, for in the final analysis history is for Dumas, paradoxically, a means of projecting his novel out of real time completely, and this is precisely what gives his fiction its perennial and endearing freshness. Athos, Porthos, and Aramis, like D'Artagnan himself, exist on a plane where none of the usual dull concerns of adult humanity have any hold. Money and possessions are not merely of no account, they are things one does not need to trouble one's head about, for in the last resort God will provide—God taking the form sometimes of their captain M. de Tréville, sometimes of the women they serve or love, for the musketeers, as Dumas frequently reminds us, are not plagued by the sad scruples of a later age, and gladly receive, from time to time, much needed subsidies at the hands of their mistresses.

Although the book is one that, ideally, should be read for the first time in one's boyhood, it is not, like other boys' classics—*Martin Rattler*, *Tom Sawyer*, *Treasure Island*—a story of pre-adult adventure. The heroes are brave, loyal, energetic and enterprising, but also strongly susceptible to sexual temptation. Each of the three musketeers is characterized by the special quality of his relations with women— tragic in the case of Athos, light-hearted in the case of Porthos, mysterious in the case of Aramis. D'Artagnan's attitude to the opposite sex is a somewhat ambiguous one, idealistic and materialistic in turn. Perhaps, like his creator, he is simply greedy. There is in the first place the romantic affair, never consummated, with Constance Bonacieux; but in addition he engages in a very unplatonic relationship with the charming Ketty, Milady's waiting-woman. The episode of his impersonating, with Ketty's help, Milady's lover the Comte de Wardes, to the point of finally substituting himself for the Count in Milady's bed—a variant on the improbable situation in *Mademoiselle de Belle-Isle* which so offended Sainte-Beuve—all this is not boy's stuff at all. However carefully the book is written so as not to offend the susceptibilities of the delicately minded, it is impossible to overlook a certain obsession with the various forms taken by the war between the sexes, which comes to the surface particularly in those parts of the book where the blonde siren Milady is in the foreground. There is one scene, in chapter LVI, which can only be described as sadistic; what makes it acceptable none the less is that it is related as a story within a story, and a palpably false one at that which the reader is not asked to imagine as having actually happened. Milady has been taken prisoner and is being kept under close guard in a castle near Portsmouth. She can escape, and carry out the mission entrusted to her by Richelieu, only if she can seduce the puritan officer Felton who has been detailed to guard her. She begins by pretending to be one of the elect herself; then, having won his interest by posing as a co-religionary, tells him the story of the violence done her by Buckingham when, as an innocent girl, she was abducted by that licentious nobleman and raped by him repeatedly after he had added a powerful narcotic to her drinking water. The whole salacious episode is related in a suitably chaste manner though in most convincing detail; and although a fabrication, it has the intended effect not only of winning Felton over, but of making him the blind instrument of Milady's political purpose under the illusion that he is avenging her lost honour. He arranges her escape back to France, and himself becomes the Duke of Buckingham's assassin.

However episodically composed, *Les Trois Mousquetaires* is solidly structured on the successive bouts of a protracted duel between D'Artagnan and Milady; the fact that he is fascinated by her beauty, from the moment he first sets eyes on her in the inn at Meung (chapter I), does not so much complicate the situation as enrich the novel with a powerful extra dynamic constituted by this love-hate relation. The duel, however, remains the basic motif of the book, and indeed, duels seem to have been one of the fundamental accessories needed to stimulate Dumas's imagination. *Le Chevalier d'Harmental* opens with a duel, arising as gratuitously as that between D'Artagnan, the three musketeers, and the Cardinal's guards in the fifth chapter of *Les Trois Mousquetaires*; while in *Mademoiselle de Belle-Isle* there is the fantastic duel proposed by D'Aubigny and accepted by the Duc de Richelieu when, since an actual encounter proves impossible, they agree to dice for the result; he who loses the throw undertakes to end his own life.

In his first conversation with the Count of Monte-Cristo, which takes place in a hotel suite in Rome, Albert de Morcerf asks his new friend whether he disapproves of duelling to the point of refusing to fight if challenged. Monte-Cristo replies that he would never decline an encounter if the cause of the quarrel was trivial—an insult, a blow, or being given the lie—all the more so since, being both a crack shot and expert with the rapier, he would have every chance of killing his opponent. 'Oh yes indeed, I would fight a duel for any of these things; but for a lingering, deep, unending hurt I would if possible give in return a hurt as lingering, deep, and unending as I had received.'[13] For the reader, who knows that Monte-Cristo is the *nom de guerre* of Edmond Dantès, an inoffensive sailor who was thrown into prison on the eve of his wedding; who knows further—or discovers shortly— that Albert de Morcerf, his interlocutor on this occasion, is the son of the woman he was betrothed to, whose present husband (Albert's father) was one of those responsible for his imprisonment;—for the reader these words have a sinister resonance they cannot possibly contain for the young man to whom they are addressed. It is an early instance of the use Dumas makes in this novel of a traditional device of melodrama, by which the actors in a scene, or some of them, are shown as being ignorant of matters about which the spectator is fully informed.

Le Comte de Monte-Cristo, a work that has a strong claim to be reckoned Dumas's masterpiece, is no doubt the greatest 'revenger's tragedy' in the whole history of the novel. Yet it was written not by some aggrieved victim of society for ever brooding over his wrongs, but on the contrary by the most blithely forgiving of men, who, though he could use a sharp tongue on occasion, never bore a grudge and never admitted to having enemies. Why he should have devoted the best of his talents to the elaboration of an epic fantasy of vengeance will always remain a mystery to those who insist on tracing a subjective origin in every great literary work. With Dumas, it often seems that what caused his imagination to catch fire most easily was whatever was most foreign to his own nature.

The book had its antecedents, one in particular, a shorter work entitled *Georges* which Dumas published the year before *Le Comte de Monte-Cristo* started to appear in the *Journal des Débats*. The setting for this earlier novel was Mauritius, an island Dumas had, of course, never visited; his information is supposed to have been supplied by a close friend, Félicien Malleville, who spent his boyhood there. The structure of *Georges* has a marked affinity with that of the later, longer novel, there being a time gap of fourteen years between the events related in the earlier chapters (the first three) and the sequel. The hero, Georges, is the son of a wealthy mulatto landowner; in 1810, during the seaborne invasion of Mauritius by the British, he endures a bloody affront at the hands of a boy of his own age who, as a white, enjoys absolute impunity in his dealings with the coloured population on the island. Georges is shortly after sent to France to be educated, but never forgets the burning injury he sustained; as a grown man, he returns to Mauritius determined to avenge himself. What he has in mind is a duel with his childhood aggressor; but the colour prejudice of the time forbids this—a white will never cross swords with a man of mixed blood.

The sensational outcome, in *Georges*, need hardly detain us, since it bears no relation to the dénouement of *Le Comte de Monte-Cristo*. But the essential elements are the same in each novel: an ancient wrong, to be avenged after a long lapse of time, during which the man who has suffered the wrong and thirsts for vengeance has been transfigured ('Transfiguration' is in fact the title of the sixth chapter of *Georges*); he returns to the scenes of his youth an educated, polished gentleman, widely travelled, a remarkable polyglot—he even speaks Chinese—and extremely wealthy. In all these respects the hero of *Georges* is identical with the hero of *Monte-Cristo*.

If one can trace the basic structure and subject of *Le Comte de Monte-Cristo* back to *Georges*, the broad outline of the plot of the later novel is known to have been derived by Dumas from a compilation made by a certain Jacques Peuchet, who had access to the record department of the Paris police and availed himself of his inside knowledge to write up the secret history of the more sensational *causes célèbres* of earlier times.[14] The particular story that caught Dumas's attention was concerned with the revenge taken by a poor shoemaker called François Picaud who, when on the point of marrying an orphan girl, heiress to a modest fortune, was denounced by a few of his boon-companions, actuated purely by malice and jealousy, as a secret agent of the royalist cause (the events took place in 1807). Picaud was arrested and stayed in prison until the fall of Napoleon in 1814, neither his fiancée nor his next-of-kin ever learning on what charge he was being held.

While in captivity, he became friendly with an Italian priest whom he nursed through his last illness and who, dying, bequeathed him the secret of a treasure hidden in the cellars of a deserted Milanese *palazzo*. After his release, Picaud located the cache and, returning to Paris, set about tracing the identity of the men who had been responsible for his arrest and imprisonment. He waylaid one of them on a bridge spanning the Seine, drove a knife into his body and threw the corpse into the river. He paid a good-looking gangster to seduce and then marry the daughter of one of his other enemies. He poisoned a third; and was finally able to come face to face with the ringleader, a café proprietor called Loupiau, whom he stabbed to death after bitterly reproaching him his treachery. Before this happens, Loupiau's wife—formerly Picaud's fiancée—had died of grief, Loupiau himself had been reduced to beggary when Picaud burned down his café, and his daughter Thérèse had been forced into prostitution.

Dumas, it is clear, reworked this sordid scenario in a number of ways. He altered the chronology—Dantès is arrested during the First Restoration, in consequence of being anonymously denounced as an agent of the Bonapartists. He kept the story of the Italian priest and the hidden treasure, but lifted the sequel on to a higher social plane, so that the main events of Le Comte de Monte-Cristo take place in the *salons* of the wealthy upper classes of the July Monarchy. But above all, he altered the moral standing of Picaud-Dantès; from being a vulgar assassin, in due course apprehended and executed for his crimes, Dumas's hero becomes an instrument of divine Providence with a self-imposed mission to chastise the wicked and reward the virtuous.

Monte-Cristo, unlike Picaud, acts always indirectly, which is why, although very much in the public eye, he is never suspected of engineering the disasters that befall those who persecuted him so cruelly and wantonly in his youth. They individually work out their own doom, and in most cases this doom is merited not because of the injury they did, in far-off days, to the hapless sailor Dantès, but because of the sins and crimes they have committed since then. Monte-Cristo needs to do little more than bring these to light; exposure is sufficient to confound and ruin them. It is not for having despatched the anonymous letter falsely denouncing Edmond Dantès to the authorities that retribution finally overwhelms the fisherman Fernand; it is because, subsequently, having joined the army and risen to high rank, he basely betrayed a heroic independence fighter to his enemies for monetary reward. This shameful deed is simply brought to public notice by Monte-Cristo years after the event; he can then safely leave it to the press to hound the unfortunate man—now a general and a peer of the realm—to suicide. Similarly Villeneuve, the magistrate who initialled the order consigning Dantès to perpetual imprisonment in the dungeons of the Château d'If, is not—and indeed could not be—punished for this callous abuse of his power. But in the intervening years he has committed other dark deeds, for an evil-doer will never stop at a first act of infamy. An intrigue with a titled lady had resulted in the birth of an infant boy whom Villeneuve, believing the child to have been still-born, buried in the garden of his own house. He has no idea that, in fact, his bastard son was rescued, restored to life, and brought up, far from Paris, by an honest Corsican couple. It is, once more, Monte-Cristo who makes this discovery and who, in addition, ascertains that the boy, as he grew older, went to the bad (for blood will tell) and was eventually sentenced for forgery. This young thug, having escaped from the hulks, becomes an unwitting instrument in Monte-Cristo's devastating plot to bring ruin and shame not only on Villeneuve, but also on the third villain, Danglars, the man who originally conceived the whole scheme of embroiling Dantès with the authorities. Since that time Danglars, like Fernand de Morcerf, has prospered astonishingly in a purely worldly sense, and is now a rich banker. Andrea Cavalcanti, the handsome ex-convict, is provided by Monte-Cristo with a putative father, an Italian nobleman with allegedly immense possessions, and Danglars, whose financial affairs have reached a dangerous pass thanks again to Monte-Cristo's secret machinations, is delighted to accept this apparently eligible suitor for his daughter's hand. In all this Monte-Cristo has merely, as it were, set up the game; he can leave it to the perverted passions of his victims to do the rest and bring down retribution on their own heads.

The grand design is, he thinks, God's; he himself, with his intelligence, single-mindedness, and fabulous wealth, acts merely as the catalyst. Long before his plots begin to bear fruit, he confides his secret purpose to, of all people, Villeneuve, in the form of a parable. Like Christ, he says, he was once carried aloft by Satan 'into an exceeding high mountain' and asked what desire he would want to have gratified in return for paying homage to the Spirit of Evil. Monte-Cristo, having reflected long, answered: 'I wish to be Providence, for there can be nothing in the world more splendid, greater and more sublime than to mete out reward and punishment.' Satan sighed and explained that this function had, from the beginning of time, been discharged by one of the daughters of God and could not be delegated to a mere mortal. 'You have seen nothing of her, for she works by hidden devices and walks along obscure ways; all I can do is to make you one of the agents of Providence.'[15]

So Monte-Cristo serves the inscrutable designs of Providence, and Providence in turn serves Monte-Cristo. A series of fantastic coincidences eases his task. The girl Haydée whom he had purchased from the Sultan of Turkey turns out to be the daughter of the brave Albanian warrior whom Fernand de Morcerf betrayed. The Corsican smuggler Bertuccio, who saved the life of Villeneuve's bastard child and secretly raised him, enters Monte-Cristo's service as his majordomo. Many years before meeting her socially in Paris, Monte-Cristo had happened to run across Villeneuve's second wife in Italy and observed then that toxicology appeared to be her favourite object of study; it needed only a little casual tutoring on his part, and she was ready to engage on the series of mysterious poisonings among Villeneuve's close relations which were traced to her only when it was too late.

There remains, however, a hint of ambiguity in this mission. Is it God-given or not? It was, after all, undertaken in consequence of a pact with the Devil. Monte-Cristo's error is to have forgotten the text that Tolstoy placed at the beginning of *Anna Karenina*: 'Vengeance is mine; I will repay, saith the Lord.' His enemies are all made to pay the penalty for the foul wrong they did him: Fernand de Morcerf, his rival in love, is publicly disgraced, abandoned by his wife and son, and commits suicide; Villeneuve is driven mad by the discovery that his second wife is a murderess and his natural son a murderer; Danglars's family is dispersed and he himself bankrupted and forced to flee abroad. But, in the process, the guiltless suffer alongside the guilty. When Villeneuve shows Monte-Cristo the corpse of his wife and young child, the count, we are told, 'turned pale at this frightful spectacle; he realized he had exceeded the rightful bounds of revenge; he realized he could no longer say "God is for me and with me" ';[16] and, with this revelation fresh in his mind, he chides Emmanuel, one of those whose virtue he has tried to reward, when he hears the young man speak of him as one hardly lower than the angels, 'a god about to ascend into heaven after having appeared on earth to sow good'. 'Never say that, my friends,' cries Monte-Cristo. 'The gods commit no evil, the gods can stay their hands when they wish. Chance is not their master, they, on the contrary, are the lords of chance. No, I am a man, Emmanuel, and your admiration is as misplaced as your words are sacrilegious.'[17]

Almost at the end of his long saga, Dumas shows his hero returning to Marseilles, where the whole disastrous train of events started. Here he hires a boat and has himself rowed out to the Château d'If, that Mediterranean Alcatraz where he spent the best years of his youth alone in a cell, not knowing what accusation had been brought against him nor by whom, and despairing of ever regaining his freedom. Ten years or more have passed since he made his fantastic escape and unearthed the vast hoard of jewels and bullion buried in the caves of the Isle of Monte-Cristo. The fortress of If still stands but is no longer used as a prison. Shuddering, he has himself taken by a guide down to the dungeon in which he was confined, and to the other cell occupied by the Italian priest Faria, who befriended him, undertook his education, revealed to him who his secret enemies were, and bequeathed him the means to exact his terrible vengeance. The reason why Dantès-Monte-Cristo undertakes this pilgrimage into the past is that he feels it essential to conjure the threat of madness that hangs over him whenever he is visited by the thought that he may have devoted his life to a sinful task, for 'Vengeance is mine, saith the Lord'.

From his guide, who has picked up certain stories from the jailers whom he replaced in 1830, he hears the popular tradition of his own imprisonment and attempted escape, resulting, as no one doubts, in his death by drowning. Listening to the story as it is related to him with all the distortions that time and ignorance have introduced, the Count of Monte-Cristo tastes once more the ancient wormwood of baffled rage and lust for vengeance, and emerges finally into the bright sunlight strangely comforted to think that vengeance has been taken and the rage slaked. For time blunts the edge of resentment, and once one has struck down one's enemies it is necessary to whet it anew for fear of forgetting why one took the action one did; and this can be done only by reviving, however artificially, the old poisonous hatreds, reliving in imagination half-forgotten sufferings, and keeping remorse at bay by breathing fresh life into bitter memories.

x The Triumphant Years

There can have been few better known nor more affectionately regarded public figures in Paris than Alexandre Dumas in his heyday,
that is, in the mid-1840s. He had no sooner to appear in the auditorium
of a theatre or a concert-hall, than

> in the twinkling of an eye, the entire audience was on its feet;
> everyone turned to look at the illustrious novelist, whose tall
> figure dominated the crowd and who, smiling right and left at his
> friends and even at strangers, progressed only slowly towards his
> seat in the stalls, detained as he was by all the hands held out for
> him to shake on the way. . . . The young author to whom he ad-
> dressed a word or two as he passed immediately became the focal
> point of every lorgnette. 'A friend of Dumas's,' people whispered.
> 'Obviously a man of consequence,' and the young ladies looking for
> a husband glanced covertly at the fortunate mortal who numbered
> such a man among his acquaintances.[1]

The fascination he exerted was due not simply to his notoriety as a
writer but also to his striking physical appearance. Dumas was no
longer the merry stripling that Devéria painted; he was now a robust
athlete in his prime. 'Everyone knows how tall he is,' wrote one of his
woman friends; 'his hands and his feet were nevertheless incredibly
small. Gentlemen still, at that date, wore knee-breeches to certain
balls. Dumas took pleasure in showing off a fine pair of legs which
would have helped him to innumerable conquests in the eighteenth
century when women were greatly susceptible to this attraction.'[2] Men
were intrigued by what they fancied they could detect of his Caribbean
ancestry, and by the spectacle—more imagined than observed—of the
primitive African held in check by the civilized Caucasian. They saw
in him

> as it were a composite specimen of the physical perfections of
> several different races: the negro in him came out in his crisply
> curling hair and thick lips, puckered in a humorously ironical
> smile which he owed to the European element; while his Nordic
> origins had given him his solid frame and broad shoulders, a tallness
> of build such as would make a Russian guardsman green with envy;
> and to cap all, a truly French elegance.[3]

He had always been a popular dinner-guest, who could be relied on to keep up a flow of entertaining talk throughout the meal. 'When he came to dine with us,' Arsène Houssaye recalled, 'it was a treat for everybody. He drank nothing but water, but water changed to wine for him.'[4] At one particular party, which must have taken place before the *coup d'état* of 1851 since Victor Hugo was one of the guests, the brilliance of his conversation so delighted the company that Houssaye's wife, assisted by Delphine de Girardin and Rachel the tragedienne, took all the flowers from the vases and scattered them over his head. As for his insistence on being served only with water, this was a matter of genuine preference. He had as discriminating a palate where water was concerned as a wine-connoisseur with regard to vintages and *cuvées*. In those pre-piped water days, servants habitually drew the household supply from the nearest well or fountain and Dumas was able to tell at the first sip which one it came from; but he professed himself incapable of distinguishing between a burgundy and a claret. At the same time he was no total abstainer; he could carry his wine, at a pinch, better than most men, and for a bet would down a dozen bottles of champagne without suffering any ill effects. Travelling in South Russia at a somewhat later date, he discovered that the Georgians, even at dinner, took their drinking a good deal more seriously than their eating, but knowing what a good head he had he was not too apprehensive when invited to a banquet arranged in his honour. In the event, he emptied more bottles than any of the other guests, and remained bright-eyed and sober when the rest were all snoring under the table; as proof of which his host, the editor of the local newspaper, delivered him a certificate duly signed and dated.

The art of conversation is, of course, the most ephemeral of all, and we only know that Dumas excelled at it because so many of his contemporaries have vouched for the fact and because he himself took such obvious pride in it; as witness the answer he gave to a friend who, knowing he had been invited to dine the previous evening with a minister of the crown, asked him how it had passed off. 'Well enough,' said Dumas wickedly, 'but I should have been bored to death if I hadn't been there myself.'[5] Even the greatest wits of the age paid tribute to his brilliance, among them Roger de Beauvoir. Calling on Dumas one morning and finding him not to be at home, he went into the kitchen to look for a piece of paper on which to leave a message, and chanced on the cook's account book lying open on a table; he could not resist improvising a quatrain for Dumas to read when he came in:

This is the book in which Dumas keeps tally
Of all that he spends on food and drink.

> But his lavish expense of quip and sally
> Is more than he'll ever keep count of, I think.[6]

He left the epigram unsigned, but Dumas, on his return, appended the author's name without a moment's hesitation.

People remembered, of course, and repeated some of his cleverer repartees, but too many of these depend on puns which were a form of wit more appreciated then than now, and in any case almost impossible to reproduce in another language.[7] But the dry humour he was famous for informed other types of remark, including many that he recorded in his own memoirs, for Dumas was never hampered by the false modesty that deters so many people from telling stories in which they figure to advantage. Thus he mentions how surprised he was, on a return visit to his home town, to find an innkeeper whom he had known well in his boyhood still hale and hearty, although the old fellow was well into his eighties. Dumas started complimenting him.

'You'll live till the day of judgement.'

'Oh no, my boy,' he answered. 'I've been very ill, didn't you know?'

'No, when was that?'

'Three and a half years back.'

'And what was the trouble?'

'Toothache.'

'It's your own fault, you've no business to have teeth at your age.'[8]

Elsewhere Dumas relates how Mlle George and he once clubbed together to buy Harel a pet pig for his birthday. Harel was delighted with the present and, not being a man of particularly fastidious habits, kept the animal in his chambers. 'One day, Harel came up to me during a rehearsal and said: "My dear fellow, I must tell you, I am so fond of my pig, I take him to bed with me!" "I know," I replied, "I met your pig just now, and he told me exactly the same thing in the very same words." '[9]

This little anecdote is typical of the kind of riposte Dumas indulged in at the expense of his interlocutor, though occasionally it must have been hard to know whether he was being intentionally facetious or not. A second-rate novelist called Amédée Achard sent Dumas a complimentary copy of his latest book and, meeting him after a few weeks, asked him if he had read it. 'Of course I have,' answered Dumas genially, 'and I was as much entertained by it as if it had been one of mine.'[10] Whether flattery was intended, or a veiled reproach of plagiarism, is something Achard never discovered. It was chiefly at the expense of his fellow writers that Dumas exercised his deflationary wit, sometimes gentle as here, sometimes devastating. At a social gathering one evening he chanced to see François Ponsard, an overrated dramatist who was notoriously adept at wangling state sinecures. After hearing about the latest pension he had been granted, Dumas remarked: 'My dear Ponsard, there will only ever be one thing lacking to set the seal on your fame.' 'What's that?' asked Ponsard a little suspiciously. 'Why,' rejoined the other, 'you can't hope to die destitute in a hospital ward.'[11]

It was never safe to try and put Dumas down. He happened to be with Soumet, a playwright of the old school, at the Théâtre-Français when one of Soumet's works was being performed, and could not help nudging him and pointing out one member of the audience who was fast asleep in his seat. 'You see the effect your plays have,' said Dumas maliciously. The following evening, when one of Dumas's comedies was billed, Soumet was enchanted to notice a spectator in the stalls snoring soundly, and tapped his rival on the shoulder. 'You see, my dear Dumas, it is possible to sleep through your prose too.' Dumas looked round. 'That?' he said. 'That's the same man as we saw yesterday, he hasn't woken up yet!'[12]

He nourished an inveterate grudge against another playwright whose unpardonable sin was to bear the same name as his; this was Adolphe Dumas. Mme de Bassanville relates how he once asked the manager of the Odéon about a certain writer of comedies called Moléri. 'An excellent fellow,' was the answer. 'He is really called Molière, but as he does not dare sign his works with so celebrated a name . . .' 'And quite right too,' interrupted Dumas. 'But why doesn't M. Adolphe Dumas show the same modesty where I'm concerned?' Unaware that the identity of surnames gave any offence to the author of *Antony*, Adolphe Dumas, in an exuberant moment, once slapped him on the back at a party, exclaiming: 'It'll be said one day that the nineteenth century boasted two Dumas, just as it's said there were two Corneilles in the seventeenth.' Now the great tragedian Pierre Corneille did in fact have a younger brother, Thomas Corneille, whose literary reputation stood high during his lifetime but whose stock had fallen considerably since. Dumas pretended to ignore his colleague's cheerful remark, but a few minutes later, when the company were invited to take tea in the adjoining room, he bowed to Adolphe, saying simply: 'After you, Thomas.'[13] The sally, heard by everyone, prompted universal laughter, and went the rounds of Paris. But Alexandre never relented in his hostility towards Adolphe. Victor Hugo records a short conversation between Edouard Thierry and Alexandre Dumas which he overheard in 1847.

'When are they performing your homonym's *Ecole des familles* at the Théâtre Historique?'

'Thursday,' answered Dumas briefly.

'And how long do you suppose it'll run?'

'Thursday.'

'I wasn't asking you when, I was asking you how long it would be played.'

'I know,' replied Dumas, 'and I'm telling you: Thursday.'[14]

His vanity, which was prodigious, was a by-word in Parisian society. Clever hostesses were said to make sure he was seated opposite a wall-mirror, so that he could occasionally glance up from his plate and catch sight of his own reassuringly intelligent features. 'He's so vain, Dumas,' drawled one smoking-room wit, 'he's capable of getting up behind his own carriage, to make you think he has a black footman'—negro servants being considered vastly chic at the time. At a supper party in Hugo's house, in the company of a number of truculent romantics engaged in their customary pastime of denigrating the achievements of the age of classicism, Dumas sat silently listening to Racine being denounced as a sorry scribbler, La Fontaine as a puerile composer of nursery rhymes, Corneille as a dramatist quite undeserving of his reputation—but at the mention of Corneille he raised his hand. 'I'm not entirely in agreement with you there,' he declared. 'Corneille has his good points. In any case, one must make allowances. I'm not so sure, if I'd been living in those times, I should have done much better myself.'[15]

Such artless self-satisfaction, diverting rather than offensive, reconciled all but the most jaundiced to the unique position Dumas had won himself in the world of letters. He had his enemies of course, of whom the most embittered was Balzac, perpetually irritated that this man, who had so recently taken up novel-writing, was able to command much higher prices than he could, even after the years of herculean toil that *La Comédie humaine* had cost him; whenever Dumas's name was mentioned in his hearing, Balzac would turn on his heel, muttering: 'That coon!'[16] The envy of less successful men was responsible for most of the hostility he incurred, but, as the French proverb has it, it is better to be envied than pitied, and Dumas had his own way of dealing with objectors. At an official function to which he had been invited he noticed that a barrister of his acquaintance, a certain Chaix d'Est-Ange, was staring rather rudely at the battery of medals Dumas was wearing strung across his broad chest; for it was another of his harmless foibles to solicit honours from reigning sovereigns, several of whom—King Leopold of Belgium, Queen Isabel of Spain, the King of Sweden and the Grand Duke of Lucca—had obliged by conferring on him orders of one sort or another. Observing the lawyer's critical eye fixed on these baubles, Dumas asked him whether anything was amiss. 'That cord you're wearing round your neck!' exclaimed D'Est-Ange. 'It's such an ugly green, it looks as though the top of your woollen undervest was sticking out.' Dumas laughed. 'I know why you don't like it, my dear Chaix; it's the colour of sour grapes, isn't it?'[17]

The unique combination of imperturbable affability and a barbed wit, which was Dumas's way of countering the malice of his rivals, could not altogether disarm them. To attack him for being the most widely read novelist in France would have been absurd, so they fell back on sneering at him for his supposed cupidity, and hinting darkly that he was engaged in unfair or at least unprofessional practices. As early as 1842, one malignant pamphleteer wrote that Dumas 'seems to have given himself up, body and soul, to the worship of the Golden Calf', and that it was 'materially impossible for him to write or dictate everything that appears under his name.'[18] The first of these accusations carried little weight, under a régime which openly subscribed to the theory that the accumulation of private fortunes was the best way of ensuring the prosperity of the country as a whole. The second charge was more serious, with its implication that Dumas was shamelessly exploiting his popularity by passing off as his own the products of hired scribblers.

This allegation gained wide currency; Charles Hugo summed it up in a wicked aside: 'Everyone has read Dumas, but nobody has read everything of Dumas's, not even Dumas himself.'[19] The most extraordinary rumours started circulating in the 1840s concerning his methods. 'Some people maintained that Dumas bought up complete manuscript novels from literary hacks toiling in garrets; others would tell you, with an air of total conviction, that he kept a dozen or so poor devils shut up in his basement, scribbling away from morning to night. There were also those who were sure all Dumas's novels were simply translations of old English or German works that had passed into semi-oblivion.'[20] Some of these stories came to Dumas's ears; he attempted a humorous rebuttal when describing an encounter he made in Bourg-en-Bresse when he was collecting material for his novel *Les Compagnons de Jéhu*. He had the misfortune to find, in the local archivist, a man who had heard of his reputation for getting others to write the books he signed, and who, when Dumas explained his business, asked him ironically: 'So this is a novel you are proposing to write yourself?' 'Why yes,' replied Dumas. 'I got my last one written by my valet; but as it proved a great success, the rascal wanted such a huge rise in wages that, to my great regret, I had to get rid of him.'[21] But such flippancy could not satisfy the more serious-minded of his critics.

In fact, it would have been difficult for Dumas to refute the charge entirely. The full list of his published works, running to over 300 titles, almost certainly includes a few that he had very little hand in. One of the clearest instances is the novel *Les Deux Diane*, published in 1846-7.

This is a work entirely lacking in Dumas's usual deftness of touch, but which an unwary reader could well imagine came from his pen, since several of the characters in the book appear in an earlier novel, *Ascanio*. There can be no argument about the authorship of *Ascanio*, though Dumas may have been assisted to a minor extent by Paul Meurice, one of Hugo's young disciples. A version of how *Les Deux Diane* came to be written and published under Dumas's name is given in the Goncourts' diary; the brothers are relating the story as they heard it from Jules Janin.

> One day, Meurice called on Dumas saying: 'I need 30,000 francs.' 'You know perfectly well I haven't the twentieth of that sum.' 'There's a very simple way to raise it, if you'll agree. I have a chance of bringing off a superb marriage, but it may all fall through for lack of those 30,000 francs. So here they are!' Saying which he laid out six manuscript folders he was carrying under his arm. 'You've only to put your name at the end and I'll have my 30,000 francs.' Dumas told him to come back the following day. Overnight he read the manuscript and appended his name. Meurice got married, and the world got *Les Deux Diane*.[22]

Corroboration of this story is found in Paul Foucher's memoirs, where it is stated that when Meurice later laid claim to the authorship of *Les Deux Diane*, 'not only did Dumas declare that he had no part in the work he had signed, but he asserted loudly that he had never even read it.'[23]

Such irresponsibility, which came close to defrauding the public, could not pass without protest. In addition, Dumas's shamelessness in signing contracts with several different newspapers for different serial stories to appear simultaneously aroused suspicions that the rumours were well founded and that he was employing ghost-writers to earn himself a fortune. A certain Jean-Baptiste Jacquot, writing under the pseudonym Eugène de Mirecourt, sent an indignant letter to the recently founded Société des Gens de Lettres complaining that certain authors—naming no names—had achieved such a stranglehold on the market that only novels to which they put their name, *whether they actually wrote them or not*, had any chance of being published. (It was said in fact that when Mirecourt offered one of his works to *La Presse*, Girardin returned it to him with the blunt message: 'Get that signed "Dumas" and I'll pay you one franc fifty the line.')

The Society duly set up a committee to look into the question, but of course it had no status in the matter and no authority to act even if action had been thought justified. A writer who assumed responsibility for works partly or even entirely written by others was breaking no law. Disappointed in this first attempt to character-assassinate Dumas, Mirecourt decided to torpedo him in a direct attack, and published a scurrilous pamphlet entitled *Fabrique de romans. Maison Alexandre Dumas et Compagnie*, in which the author of *The Three Musketeers* was accused of running a literary sweat-shop and of reducing his so-called collaborators to the condition of 'black slaves working under the whip of a half-caste overseer'. The lampoon was so violent and so ignominious (Mirecourt even descended to making tasteless remarks about Ida Ferrier) that it backfired. Dumas had no difficulty in winning a libel action and the pamphleteer was sent to prison for fifteen days to teach him manners. He emerged unrepentant and resumed his campaign against Dumas, this time publishing a series of articles in a scandal-sheet, *La Silhouette*. To put a stop to the nuisance, Alexandre Dumas junior, by now a young man of twenty-one, called round at the offices of *La Silhouette*, smashed up a few sticks of furniture and issued a challenge; but Mirecourt was canny enough to stall. His quarrel, he said, was with the father, not the son; and bringing forward his own son, who was all of seven years old, suggested that M. Alexandre Dumas *fils* might like to exchange shots with him.

The two Dumas, father and son, were never closer than in these years. Ida, who had been largely responsible for keeping them apart in times past, was to all intents and purposes settled in Florence. On October 18th, 1844, the young man announced triumphantly in a letter to Joseph Méry: 'Great news, my dear, good friend! The break-up of the Dumas household! Husband and wife are on the point of separating, like Abraham and Hagar, for other reasons than barrenness—and I imagine that before long you will see a fat lady on her way through Marseilles to live in Italy for good.'[24] The deed of separation was, in fact, dated October 15th, and no sooner was Ida off the premises than Alexandre joined his father in the commodious country residence, the Villa Médicis, which he had been renting since 1843. It was located in the small town of Saint-Germain-en-Laye which, it will be remembered, was where his grandfather the Marquis de la Pailleterie spent his declining years. Possibly family associations counted for something in the choice; but what was more important was that the town had recently been connected by rail to Paris, thus making it possible, if need arose, for Dumas to reach the city's centre within half an hour. Saint-Germain was an ideal retreat for a busy writer who needed the time for long, uninterrupted spells of work; but after a few weeks of peace and quiet Dumas began to find it all a bit dull, and was glad when his friends and his son's friends found their way out there on Sundays. The receptions were lavish; he laid on a firework display one evening; on another occasion he paid a small fortune to have the cream of the Comédie-Française actors come and give a performance in the local theatre.

Father and son lived together in the greatest amity like two raffish

bachelors, for at this time no one could have foretold that the younger
man would eventually evolve into the pompous moralist he became
under the Second Empire. His father had not waited for the boy to
leave school before initiating him into the boisterous pleasures he took
such delight in himself. One evening he carried him off to a masked
ball in the then disreputable district of Montparnasse. They danced all
night, with such abandon that the older man was still bathed in sweat
when they got home in the early hours, and the skin-tight trousers he
was wearing stuck so fast to his legs that Alexandre had to split them
down the seams with a pen-knife before they would come off. After
that, his father drank a great bowl of soup and, too excited to go to
bed, sat down at his desk, where he wrote steadily as the dawn came up
and on through the rest of the day till the following evening.

How far they went in sharing their pleasures can only be guessed;
but they did not scruple to give others the impression, at any rate, that
they passed their women from hand to hand, or rather from bed to bed.
'You know, father,' the younger man drawled one day, in the midst of
a group of mutual friends gathered in a knot on the boulevard, 'it's a
great bore, you always giving me your old mistresses to sleep with and
your new boots to break in!' 'What are you complaining about?'
retorted the other. 'You should look on it as an honour. It proves you
have a thick prick and a narrow foot.'[25] The bystanders were unsure
whether to snigger or look shocked. In mixed company the pair
expressed themselves a little more circumspectly, of course, but hardly
less cynically. Conversing with a middle-aged lady who commiserated
with the young man for having so dissolute a father, Alexandre
answered flippantly: 'At least, if he doesn't set me a good example, he
provides me with an excellent excuse.'[26] It is evident that he inherited
not merely some of his father's physical advantages, but a fair measure
of his gift of repartee as well.

One mistress the two men did not share, however, was the lovely,
fickle, pathetic Marie Duplessis, whom the younger Dumas was to
immortalize as the Lady of the Camellias, with reference to the bouquet
that she invariably carried, white camellias during twenty-five days, red
for the next three. He could not avoid introducing her to his father for,
as he remarked resignedly: 'As soon as a woman takes my arm, the
first thing she does is to lift her skirt to stop it getting dirty and the
second is to ask me when she can meet you.'[27] The meeting, in this
instance, was nothing if not sensational. Dumas had gone along to see
a performance of his *Demoiselles de Saint-Cyr* when his son emerged
from a box and caught him by the coat-tail. 'Close your eyes and put
your head through the door; don't be afraid, nothing's going to
happen to you.' Dumas obeyed, and felt his cheeks immediately
clasped by two soft hands, while two quivering, burning lips pressed

themselves on his. After that, he and Marie flirted gaily for as long as the interval lasted, and then he left her to Alexandre. He never saw her again. She had hoped to enlist his help to get a part in his next play, but it was only a passing fancy, as his son later explained. She would never have summoned up sufficient determination to learn her lines and attend rehearsals.

Neither of the men attached enough importance to their temporary liaisons to regard the other as a rival in love, and each was—at least during the period we are speaking of—more closely bound to the other by ties of affection than to any other soul, his mother excepted in the young man's case. 'I know of no two characters,' wrote the father, 'more diametrically opposed than Alexandre's and mine, which yet harmonize better. To be sure, each of us finds plenty of enjoyment away from the other; but I think the best times are those we spend together.'[28] He liked to imagine that the twilight hour which was when his son came into the world had been responsible for the 'amalgam of antitheses that constitutes his strange character'; active and indolent in turn, both credulous and mistrustful, blasé and ingenuous, neglectful and devoted, 'he uses all his wit to make fun of me and loves me with all his heart . . . From time to time we quarrel and like the prodigal son, he takes his portion and leaves his father's house. The same day, I buy myself a calf and start fattening it, certain that before the month is out he will be back to eat his share.'[29]

When Dumas laid his plans to tour Spain and North Africa in the autumn and winter of 1846–7, it went without saying that Alexandre would go along too, though he disappeared mysteriously on the way, no doubt in pursuit of some Andalusian beauty who had taken his fancy, leaving no word but rejoining the party imperturbably in Gibraltar. It was the first time Dumas had travelled abroad with a whole retinue of friends, servants, and hangers-on. In Switzerland he had been on his own, apart from the boy Francesco whom he picked up as a guide and interpreter on the way. The trip he took in 1835 in which, starting from Naples, he sailed round Sicily and then travelled through Calabria, had been made with as sole companions Godefroy Jadin, the animal painter, and a bulldog called Mylord; while on his 1838 excursion to Belgium and the Rhineland he had been accompanied by Ida and, from Frankfurt onwards, by Gérard de Nerval. But Dumas was now a person of much greater consequence, and would travel only with his court. Apart from his son, the principal members of his party were Maquet, the artist Boulanger whose responsibilities were approximately those of a professional photographer today, and an Ethiopian servant nicknamed Eau-de-Benjoin (Friar's Balsam), who had previously acted as factotum to a French colonel in Algeria and consequently knew something of the country.

The journey originated as a government-inspired project, part of a plan to advertise the recently acquired North African colony and encourage settlers from metropolitan France. Xavier Marmier, who accompanied the Minister of Education, Salvandy, on a tour of Algeria, had suggested that the best way to interest the average Frenchman in the newly opened territory might be to persuade Dumas to go there and write one of his popular travel-books on his return. Acting on this advice, Salvandy put the proposal to the writer over dinner and Dumas accepted, on condition however that he should have a warship put at his disposal to visit the various coastal towns. Salvandy reluctantly agreed, though he subsequently had reason to regret this when he had to face a barrage of criticism in the Chamber from opposition deputies, feigning patriotic indignation that a unit of the French navy should have been used for the transportation of this 'celebrated penny-a-liner.'

Originally, no doubt, the plan was for Dumas and his party to take ship at Toulon and sail directly to Algiers. But the day after this meeting with Salvandy, he chanced to be dining with the Duc de Montpensier, one of Louis-Philippe's sons, for whom a marriage had been arranged with the Queen of Spain's fourteen-year-old sister; the Queen herself, Isabella II, was to marry her cousin at the same time, so that there would be a double royal wedding at Madrid, and the Duc de Montpensier, who had a great liking for Dumas, suggested he should modify his itinerary so as to attend the ceremony first and travel on to Algeria afterwards.

Salvandy having consented to this change of plan, Dumas found himself with the prospect of visiting both Spain and North Africa on semi-official missions. The expenses, however, would have to be met largely out of his own pocket. Montpensier personally subscribed 12,000 francs, but the government could go only half way towards matching this princely generosity. 1847 was a year of acute economic crisis in France, and the régime was only able to keep going thanks to a massive gold loan from the Bank of England. Dumas, informed of the financial arrangements, acquiesced with a negligent shrug of the shoulders: 'Eighteen thousand? Well, that ought to be enough to pay my guides.'[30]

This sounds like a typical piece of Dumasian arrogance, but in fact a journey like this, stretching over three months, was almost as ambitious as a round-the-world trip today, and correspondingly costly. It was not possible to budget precisely; the first unscheduled disbursement was made even before they left France. They took the train from Paris to Bordeaux but, because of engine failure at Beaugency, they were late in arriving and so missed the mail-coach that was to take them on to the Spanish frontier. But time was of the essence; it was already October 5th and they were due in Madrid for the royal weddings on the 10th; so Dumas spent 1,300 francs on acquiring a private conveyance by means of which, travelling through the night, they caught up with the mail-coach and were able to transfer to it at Bayonne. At the border crossing he became seriously alarmed about customs checks, having heard that the Spaniards allowed no firearms of any description into their country; he was carrying no fewer than six cases packed with carbines, fowling-pieces and pistols, partly for self-defence in case of encounters with bandits, but chiefly in the hope of shooting game on the way. All turned out well, however. 'Reading my name, inscribed on brass plates on every box and trunk, the inspector of customs approached me, greeted me in excellent French, and addressing his underlings in Spanish which I found even more mellifluous, ordered them to let everything through without examination, down to my travelling bag.'[31] His pleasure was enhanced by the sight of the minute investigation made of the luggage of all the other travellers who were required to turn out their pockets and even submit to having the lining of their travelling cases ripped open.

At Cordoba, at a later stage in the journey, there was an internal customs examination which proved just as painless. Eau-de-Benjoin had been left in charge of the luggage, and reported subsequently to his master as follows: 'The chief customs officer saw your name on the trunks, sir. He asked if you were the author of *Monte-Cristo*, and when I said yes he answered: "Very well, pass along." '[32] Dumas realized that his name was his passport, and a far more effective passport than any delivered by the French Foreign Office. Reflecting on the many slanderous attacks made on him by envious fellow writers and carping critics in France, he decided that if he wanted to bask in the genial warmth of his own popularity, then he would need to travel more; as he expressed it epigrammatically: 'Posterity begins abroad.' What he meant by the oft-repeated phrase is implicit in the following passage of his travel journal:

> As you cross the frontier, it is as though you pass from this life to the next. It is not to you, but to your shade that all these testimonies of affection, at every turn of the road, are addressed; and I must say that my glorious shade is received in this country with such acclaim as to make my poor mortal frame quite envious . . . From the flattering picture the Spanish form of me, I can have some inkling of what people will think about me after my death.[33]

As an instance of the malice of his compatriots compared with the respectful admiration of the Castilians, one needs only to quote a couple of sentences from a letter written by Cuvillier-Fleury, the Madrid correspondent of *Le Journal des Débats*, to his wife on October 9th, 1846: 'Alexandre Dumas has this moment arrived, on that idiotic mission given him by Salvandy. He has got fatter and more ugly than ever and is terrifyingly vulgar.'[34] But ugly, fat, and vulgar though he may have been, he very soon became the centre of attraction even at the Court. Janin relates how one old diplomat, arriving late at the reception, asked his neighbour to explain what all the grandest grandees of the most ancient families of Spain were doing standing in a group around one tall, burly man, not in uniform but in ordinary evening dress, while the Queen, her consort, the Duc de Montpensier and the Infanta his bride were sitting, neglected by all the courtiers, in another part of the brightly lit hall. 'Bless you,' was the answer, 'it's Alexandre Dumas. Who else did you suppose it could be?'[35]

Madrid was packed out when he arrived. Having neglected to make hotel reservations, he was glad to accept the hospitality of a friendly French bookseller who stocked all his works and was honoured to have him under his roof. There remained the problem of the commissariat. As soon as his party entered Spain, they had realized with dismay that if they were to rely on the ordinary fare provided in the wayside inns, they were like to starve to death long before they reached the coast. So Eau-de-Benjoin was deputed to buy provisions in the market—the invaluable fellow could make himself understood in Spanish, English, and Italian as well as French—while Dumas, who prided himself on his cooking, was unanimously elected *maître d'hôtel*. At Toledo, their next stop after Madrid, an English gentleman, travelling for his pleasure, attached himself to their group solely in order to have something to eat and, on taking his leave, begged to be allowed to return the favour whenever Dumas should chance to be visiting London or Calcutta.[36]

From Toledo they descended the Tagus as far as Aranjuez and then took the road south to Granada through Don Quixote's country. After that they turned west, arriving at Seville on November 7th; in spite of the lateness of the season, the city authorities announced a special bull-fight in his honour, and a box at the theatre was put at his disposal for as long as his stay lasted. The great attraction here was the trio of dancers, Anita, Pietra, and Carmen. In common civility, Dumas lifted Anita's hand to his lips on being introduced, whereupon the artiste leapt back six feet uttering a scream of horror, and he realized that what is ordinary politeness in one country may be an infernal liberty in another. But when farewells were said, at the end of his stay in Seville, all three girls gladly allowed him to kiss them on both cheeks.

At Cadiz he boarded the French corvette, *Le Véloce*—ill-named, since it could never reach more than eight knots, having been equipped with too small a boiler. In this labouring vessel they voyaged first to Gibraltar which, amazingly, they found to be fog-bound. But the British, Dumas commented lightly, have a genius for upsetting the laws of nature. 'They have made dahlias to smell like carnations, they have made cherries without cherry-stones and gooseberries without pips; they are in the process of making cattle without legs. . . . There was no fog at Gibraltar before Gibraltar was annexed by the British; but the British were used to fog, and didn't feel at home unless they had fog, so they made fog.'[37]

In the mild, late November and December weather they cruised along the Algerian littoral, stopping occasionally to go ashore and carry out a great slaughter among the wild duck, snipe and partridge. They saw little of the interior, but Dumas had a curious encounter near Tunis, which was the furthest point east the *Véloce* took him. Together with the French consul Laporte, who acted as his host and interpreter, he made an excursion to a nearby shrine marking the burial place of a marabout. It was famous for a certain smooth rock, down which barren women were supposed to slide a certain number of times in a variety of positions in order to cure themselves of infertility. Laporte reassured the timid votaries by passing Dumas off as a Frankish doctor of high repute. After a while, he became interested in one girl in particular to whom Laporte, at his request, put a number of questions in Arabic, translating her answers as she gave them. She was an orphan, it appeared, and not yet married (she was, indeed, only twelve years old); yet she looked well dressed, well cared for, and her nails and eye-lids were painted in just the same way as were her companions'. Thinking, perhaps, of Monte-Cristo's Haydée, whom he had created an orphan too, Dumas asked her whether she would like to go with him over the sea. Once he had convinced her that there really were other lands beyond the horizon, and had promised her all she desired—silk blouses, a sequin turban, and scarlet trousers embroidered with gold—she readily agreed to the proposition.

'And would you come, just like that, without knowing me?'

'Did you not say you were a doctor?'

'I did.'

'Then, if Allah has given you knowledge, he must have given you goodness too.'[38]

Dumas was sorely tempted, especially when Laporte assured him that, in all probability, having no family, she really would leave home and country and follow him. But to return to Paris with a twelve-year-old Tunisian handmaiden would have been a little too outrageous even for him. So he took a handful of silver from his pocket, gave it her, and walked regretfully away with Laporte to where their horses were tethered.

On January 3rd, 1847, he boarded the steamer plying between Algiers and Toulon, his African adventure over. He stepped ashore with a heavy heart. The joy of the rover returning home was a feeling he never experienced; every time he set foot in France after a long voyage he was overcome with lassitude and depression. 'This is because what awaits me in France is a swarm of petty enemies whose hatred can never be disarmed. On the other hand, from the moment he crosses the frontiers of France and enters another country, the poet is really nothing but a living ghost, hearkening to the verdict of posterity. France represents his contemporaries, that is, the men consumed by envy. Why should that be so, when it would be so delightful if it were not so?'[39]

XI The Turbulent Years

Although in the end wiser counsels prevailed and Dumas decided against carrying off the little Arab girl he met at Sidi-Fathallah, he did return with two Tunisian craftsmen, Hadj'Younis and his twelve-year-old son Ahmed. They were skilled in the traditional Islamic arts of interior decoration, and he proposed to set them to work on one of the apartments in the country house he had started to build at Marly-le-Roi.

Marly-le-Roi was a quiet hamlet a mile or so south of Saint-Germain-en-Laye, where he had acquired half an acre of land on a charming site in wooded country overlooking the Seine. His original plan was for a modest, eight-roomed house, a kind of cottagey retreat which the architect with whom he first discussed the idea reckoned would cost him no more than twelve or fifteen thousand francs. Neighbouring landowners, however, hearing that they had a new Croesus in their midst, offered him several adjoining plots at inflated prices and Dumas, who saw his income rapidly increasing from year to year, allowed himself to be tempted. He would build the French equivalent of Scott's Abbotsford. It would be a renaissance style château, like the one at Villers-Cotterêts, with a neo-gothic pavilion to which he could retire to write his future masterpieces. His architect warned him that the soil was too clayey to support so large an edifice, but instead of agreeing to a modified plan Dumas told the builder to dig down to the bedrock and use the space, once excavated, to construct a capacious cellarage. The revised estimates kept mounting until finally he found himself committed to an expenditure ten times that originally envisaged. But what matter? it was only so many more columns for *La Presse* or *Le Constitutionnel* and since Girardin and Véron seemed happy to pay him large sums for writing books that it amused him to write anyway, why not spend the money—an incidental spin-off—on bricks and mortar and labourers' wages?

On July 24th, 1844, Dumas invited six hundred of his friends and hangers-on to an alfresco banquet on the site of his future house. 'In three years from now,' he cried, 'I invite you all back—to dine indoors.' The news spread quickly, as did any report of the activities of this phenomenal man, and sightseers came flocking down from Paris by every train. On Sunday the actor Mélingue, having got out at Le

Pecq, the nearest railway station, and not being too sure what directions to give the cab-driver, shouted up to him: 'Drive us to . . . Monte-Cristo!' After that Dumas's house, still half-built, had a name: Le Château de Monte-Cristo.

When he returned from Algeria it was nearing completion, and he was able to hold his house-warming party only a few days later than he had predicted. Everyone who saw the house and grounds came away deeply impressed, and Léon Gozlan wrote a dithyrambic article in which he declared: 'It would be possible to fall madly in love with this monument, much as one may fall in love with the moon when one is young.'[1] And Balzac, who had always cherished the ambition of building his own house and had never had the money to realize it, wrote to his future wife Mme Hanska: 'Monte-Cristo is one of the most delicious follies ever built. It's a lodge fit for a king.' He added that Dumas had already spent 400,000 francs on it and would need to spend another 100,000 before it was finished.[2]

The house, with its dependencies, was certainly a curiosity. As one approached it one noticed a profusion of coats-of-arms carved in stone, and a frieze of sculptured heads representing the poetic geniuses of all ages, from Homer to . . . Casimir Delavigne. The façade was surmounted by a Turkish minaret, while from the weathercock flew a banner bearing the device of the Davy de la Pailleterie family, for Dumas was toying about this time with the idea of establishing his claim to the title of marquis which had lapsed at the death of his grandfather, long before he was born. Inside, the visitor wandered up and down the three storeys through a succession of little rooms all furnished in different styles. The principal novelty was the 'Arab room', on which Hadj'Younis had lavished great care, covering walls and ceiling with arabesques interspersed with texts from the Koran picked out in vermilion and gold.

At some two hundred yards distance, surrounded by a token moat, stood the pavilion, an even stranger structure. It was built of stone blocks, each with the title of one of Dumas's works engraved on it. The customary warning: Beware of the dog! was written in Latin, but for the benefit of those who lacked the advantage of a classical education there was a statue of a snarling bull-terrier, modelled, it was said, on Mylord, the animal that he and Jadin took with them on their tour of Sicily. The ground floor consisted of one single room, Dumas's study. His desk was a refectory table at which an abbot had once presided over silently munching brethren, and above the chimney-piece, incongruously, was affixed a fan-shaped cluster of daggers and broadswords. A spiral staircase led up to a sparsely furnished bedroom with a balcony from which, when he felt like it, he could observe his guests strolling on the lawn below.

These guests, as often as not uninvited, arrived every weekend in droves to gawp at the château and examine Dumas's private zoo and aviary. The latter consisted of two parrots (one red-and-blue, the other yellow-and-green), a peacock and a peahen, a few golden pheasants, and a vulture named Jugurtha after the great Numidian challenger to Roman power in North Africa. This fierce bird had been a parting present from the Tunisians, but it was given him uncaged, and Eau-de-Benjoin had understandably shrunk from attempting to haul it along to the ship by the chain that was attached to its neck. So Dumas borrowed a riding-crop and drove the creature before him as if it were a turkey; the vulture was, he claimed, quite tame by the time they reached the harbour. Eventually, after Monte-Cristo had been sold and its contents dispersed, Jugurtha became the property of the landlord of a nearby inn, forced against his will to accept the bird in settlement of his account with the now bankrupt proprietor of the 'château'.

The four-footed beasts in Dumas's menagerie were less exotic, consisting of an indeterminate number of dogs, at least one cat, and three monkeys. Each animal had been given a fanciful name. One of the dogs was called Pritchard, after the fanatical English missionary who got himself expelled from Tahiti in 1844. The monkeys had been mischievously baptized Pichot, Kératry, and Mlle Maxine, which were the names, respectively, of the editor of a literary review, a reactionary politician, and a Comédie-Française actress, all of whom had, at one point or another, aroused Dumas's animosity. The cat bore the extraordinary name of Mysouff the Second. Dumas, like Dick Whittington, had a cat when he first came to Paris. This was the original Mysouff, a highly intelligent animal who used to walk by his side every morning as he went to the office and would return punctually at five to greet him as he came out and accompany him home.

All these birds and beasts were devotedly cared for by the gardener, Michel, an unlettered rustic who developed in addition a much-valued talent for dealing with impatient creditors and bailiff's men. Dumas came by his staff in all sorts of unorthodox ways. Marie Dorval, having fallen on hard times, once brought him a diminutive black boy called Alexis in a basket of flowers, begging him to take charge of the child since she could no longer afford his keep. Alexis, an ebony-skinned native of Madagascar, stayed in Dumas's service for some eight years, and then decided to join the army. 'Be a good soldier,' said his master by way of valediction, 'rise to be a field-marshal and then, black as you are, everyone will swear you are white.'[3] Finally there was Rusconi, an Italian who had never learned to speak French properly. He had been, in his time, an architect, police commissioner at Elba during Napoleon's brief rule of that island, and secretary to General Dermoncourt, the one-time aide-de-camp to Dumas's father. When Dermoncourt was implicated in the Carlist rising of 1832 and cashiered in consequence, he asked his former patron's son to give Rusconi employment, and so, discharging a variety of ill-defined functions, he remained on Dumas's payroll for at least twenty years.

The break-up of his marriage meant that the rôle of lady of the house devolved on his daughter, Marie, still in her teens. She would have immensely preferred to live with her stepmother in Florence where, it would seem, her moral susceptibilities would have been less bruised by contact with Ida's aristocratic lover than they were by the succession of plebeian girl-friends whom Dumas imported on a temporary basis and who set up house, sometimes inviting their relatives to join them, until as a result of some violent quarrel they decamped, the light-fingered among them pocketing whatever portable property they happened to covet. They were all theatrical ladies, mostly of slender talent, for whom Dumas conceived a sudden passion dying away as quickly as it had flared up. In 1848 the reigning divinity was a singer from Rouen, Céleste Scrivaneck; a letter she wrote to Alexandre Dumas *fils* indicates the kind of footing she was on. 'Your father is making me work hard; I am writing under his dictation. I am so proud and happy to act as secretary to *him*, the *universal man*.' She also refers to plans being mooted by the 'universal man' for all three to set off on a tour of Europe, herself in masculine attire: 'the tailor has already measured me for a suit of clothes.'[4] Nothing came of this project; perhaps Alexandre put his foot down; at all events she was replaced, around 1850, by an actress named Isabelle Constans,[5] some thirty years younger than Dumas, who was consumed by a violent passion for her that hovered between the paternal and the sensual. 'There are two true loves in a man's life,' he told her, 'the first, which dies, and the last, of which he dies. Alas, it is with the second of these loves that I burn for you. . . . I cannot do without you, I need to caress you all the time and can no more forgo your caresses than I can live without air to breathe.' He was conscious, however, of middle age creeping up on him, and an ugly thickening of the body brought about by the long hours of sedentary labour at his desk; he could no longer count, as was possible ten or twenty years ago, on his virile appearance and heroic physique to sweep a young woman off her feet. There was only one rôle left for him now, the ungrateful one of sugar-daddy, promising to help her in her career in return for favours received. 'If it cannot be altogether for love that you do what I ask you to do, let it be at least for ambition's sake. You love your art; hold it dearer, if you like, than you hold me, I will tolerate that rival if no other. In that respect, your ambitions will be more fully satisfied than any queen's. No woman—not even Mlle Mars—will have such parts to play as I will write for you over the next three years.'[6]

Isabelle Constans was a fair-haired, gently mannered girl, doomed in all probability to an early death from some wasting disease. She was a pupil of Samson and had also taken lessons from the ageing Mlle George. Dumas kept his promise to secure her parts in the plays he wrote, which at this time were chiefly adaptations from his novels. The liaison lasted for five or six years at least, for Delacroix writes in his journal of an evening he spent with his friend on May 22nd, 1855, when after dinner they took a cab to pick her up and take her to the theatre. The diarist implies that, although Dumas was still seeing Isabelle regularly and making sure she lacked for nothing, he had to be content with her society: 'she had asked him to spare her, the demands he was making of her would bring about her death from pulmonary consumption.'[7] He wrote to her from Russia in 1858, but after that she seems to have dropped out of his life, perhaps out of life itself.

Delacroix was the recipient too of a strange confidence Dumas made him one evening about 'his love affair with a *virgin* who had buried one husband and acquired a second'.[8] Although Dumas's sex-life was so multifarious and labyrinthine that it is not always possible to be sure how one should interpret a veiled allusion of this kind, there is a strong likelihood that the reference here was to Anna Bauër whose husband, it appears, was impotent, and who turned to Dumas, as Dinah de La Baudraye to Lousteau in Balzac's *La Muse du Département*, to give her the child she would otherwise never have conceived. This child, who came into the world in 1851, was given the name Henri Bauër, but his resemblance to Dumas was so striking when he grew up that nobody could be in serious doubt as to his true paternity.[9]

A far less furtive liaison, but also a very brief one, was that with the celebrated dancer Lola Montes. She had been the mistress of Liszt and of a couple of English peers before falling in love with a brilliant young journalist on the staff of *La Presse*, Dujarrier. But on March 11th, 1845, Dujarrier was killed in a duel. His challenger was arrested on suspicion of foul play, and at the ensuing trial both Dumas and Lola Montes appeared as witnesses for the prosecution. In deep mourning, but darting furious glances at the prisoner through her veil, she made a profound impression on all those present, not excepting Dumas, though the evidence she gave was insignificant.

Born in Seville, Lola had been married very young to a British army officer who carried her off to Bengal. Bored with colonial life, she left her husband to drill his sepoys, took ship to England, then returned to Spain. Some instinct told her she would make her fortune if she came to Paris, which she did at the age of twenty, and drew crowds at the Théâtre de la Porte-Saint-Martin with a well-advertised performance of the cachucha; in private, and for an appropriate fee, she was prepared to do this dance unclothed. Lola had a number of other talents: she was a crack shot, a fearless fencer, and an expert horsewoman. With her pale skin, her hair falling in natural ringlets, and lips the colour of pomegranates, she had no difficulty in turning Dumas's head. But she was also notoriously fickle and after the briefest of romances she was off to wreak havoc at the court of the King of Bavaria, leaving her disconsolate lover to distract himself as best he could with the prosecution of his grandiose plans for his country seat at Marly-le-Roi.

The building of this house was only one of the ambitious projects seething in Dumas's brain when he set off for Madrid. Another involved nothing less than the founding of a new theatre in Paris, along the lines originally suggested by the Duc de Montpensier, a keen supporter of the dramatic art and, as we have seen, a great admirer of Dumas. Without this august backing the scheme could never have got off the ground, for to set up a new theatre under the July Monarchy required specific government authority which Montpensier, as one of the king's sons, was obviously well placed to obtain. A limited company was formed on March 24th, 1846, with an initial capital of 600,000 francs, and a site secured in the Faubourg du Temple. Naming the new theatre gave rise to some argument among the principals. Dumas would have liked it to be called the Théâtre Européen, which would have sounded like a direct challenge to the Théâtre Français and was judged altogether too irreverent; so the name Théâtre Historique was adopted instead. It was, perhaps, rather more appropriate since it was understood from the start that the repertoire would consist mainly of dramatizations of Dumas's historical romances.

The series was to begin with an adaptation of *La Reine Margot*, a novel set in the reign of Charles IX and centring on the figure of Marguerite de Valois, the daughter of Catherine de Medicis who instigated the Massacre of St. Bartholomew. It was announced in the press that the Théâtre Historique would open its doors for the first time on February 20th, 1847, and the news created a great surge of public interest; the building itself, immensely tall for the period and yet with an extremely narrow street façade, aroused considerable curiosity and it was known, besides, that the Duc de Montpensier would be present with his young Spanish bride. In the fortunately mild February weather, queueing started twenty-four hours in advance. Itinerant vendors drove a roaring trade in bowls of bouillon and, when the bakeries finished work at midnight, in buns fresh from the ovens. The street was gaily hung with lanterns, the crowd, from time to time, good-humouredly broke into song, and an enterprising ballad-monger, having improvised a set of verses entitled 'Le Théâtre Dumas', rushed off to a printing works and returned within the hour to sell the wet sheets to the waiting spectators.[10] After this vigil, they cheerfully sat through a performance of record length, starting at 6.30 p.m. and finishing at 3 a.m., but everyone was too enthralled to complain, even of hunger, though according to Gautier 'towards the end, during the short intervals, people began to feel rather as though they were stranded on the raft of the *Medusa* and the plumper members of the audience were not altogether easy in their minds.'[11]

In the course of the year several other plays, written wholly or in part by Dumas, were staged at the Théâtre Historique: *Intrigue et amour*, an adaptation of Schiller's *Kabale und Liebe* (June 11th); *Le Chevalier de Maison-Rouge*, drawn from his novel of the same title (August 3rd); and *Hamlet, prince de Danemark* (December 15th), based on Shakespeare's tragedy. This version, in spite of the considerable liberties Dumas took with the original, succeeded in establishing itself on the French stage, superseding all other adaptations until well towards the end of the century.

All in all 1847 represented a highly successful season for the Théâtre Historique; receipts totalled over 700,000 francs. The following year too began auspiciously, with a two-part adaptation of *Le Comte de Monte-Cristo* performed on successive evenings; this was an innovation in the French theatre, but one that worked surprisingly well. The play, however, had been running for only three weeks when the February Revolution broke out, and the rest of the year was disastrous for all Paris theatres. As usual in times of civil commotion, audiences dwindled; the timid citizens stayed indoors, the bolder spirits spent their time at political meetings. Balzac's play *La Marâtre* (*The Stepmother*) was so ill-attended that the manager of the Théâtre Historique, Hippolyte Hostein, closed the theatre and took the company over to London to put on *Monte-Cristo* at Drury Lane where the audiences, however, were so hostile that the actors could scarcely be heard above the shouts and cat-calls. For the rest of the year the Théâtre Historique had to struggle hard to keep going at all. The one new historical play Dumas wrote, *Catilina*, was a failure, and the experiment of reviving earlier romantic triumphs, including *Antony*, met with an uncertain reception. Box-office receipts for 1848 were only 40 per cent of what they had been in 1847.

The truth was that Dumas himself was losing interest in the enterprise, the revolution having diverted his energies into new channels. He felt no keen regret when Louis-Philippe was forced off the throne, for he had never been on particularly good terms with the monarch, however friendly he may have been with his sons, especially the eldest, the Duc d'Orléans, until he was killed in a carriage accident in 1842, and of course the Duc de Montpensier. Like a great many other Frenchmen, he disliked the timidly cautious foreign policy pursued by Louis-Philippe's ministers, and disapproved strongly of Guizot's *entente* with the hated British; but what he resented most bitterly was the clause in the Constitution of 1830 restricting the franchise to a mere 200,000 wealthy landowners and manufacturers. Viktor Balabin, a diplomat attached to the Russian embassy, records overhearing at one of Mme de Girardin's *soirées* a fierce argument between Dumas and the Duc de Morny (a half-brother of Louis-Napoleon) which took place on March 26th, 1847, less than a year before the revolution broke out. 'When you think,' Dumas stormed, 'that the government which has raked in hundreds of thousands of francs in theatre dues thanks to my plays, will not permit me to stand for election, while any Tom, Dick or Harry who builds himself a mud-and-wattle shanty and pays the property tax, he can be a deputy! . . .' 'But,' objected Morny sardonically, 'if your argument is that you ought to have a seat in the Chamber because your plays bring in more than anyone else's, then it follows that the smoker who consumes the greatest number of cigars ought to have one too, since cigar smoke resolves itself into pure profit for the government.'[12] Dumas, who loathed even the smell of cigar smoke, was for once reduced to silence.

However, on March 5th, 1848, the Provisional Government announced elections to a Constituent Assembly to be held on the basis of universal male suffrage, and Dumas—following the example of Hugo, Eugène Sue, and a number of other writers—decided to put forward his candidature. The difficulty was to select the constituency at which he stood most chance of adoption. In his native department of Aisne his reputation was still that of a firebrand among those who remembered his raid on the powder magazine at Soissons in 1830. In Seine-et-Oise, where the Château de Monte-Cristo was situated, he had tried to persuade the local battalion of the National Guard to march on Paris in support of the Provisional Government, and this misplaced zeal had dissipated what little respect the solid burghers of Saint-Germain-en-Laye retained for him. He thought, whimsically, of standing as candidate for the French West Indies though, not having the money to pay his passage, he would have had to content himself with sending the coloured voters a lock of his hair to prove he was really one of them.

Finally, it was suggested to him that he might stand as good a chance as any in the department of Yonne. He drafted an electoral address, in the form of a letter to the editor of the regional newspaper, in which he presented himself as an energetic, disinterested, and toughly independent prospective parliamentarian.

Conflict is a basic need of my constitution. *Je vis de la fièvre qui me brûle*—the fever that consumes me is the flame by which I live. I have no political ambition, since any office I obtained would be

6

more likely to cost me money than bring me any in. No, all I have is the private conviction that wherever I go I carry with me a certain inherent power of illumination. Then again, I am a man of initiative. As a legislator, I shall be as audacious as I have been in my plays and my books, risking what no one has risked before me.[13]

As a statement of political beliefs, this was, perhaps, a little imprecise, but as an enunciation of the man's sense of personal mission the document has its value.

He took his candidature seriously enough to pay at least one lightning visit to the constituency and address a public meeting. His local agent, a certain Du Chaffault, who accompanied him throughout, has left a vivid account of the occasion.[14] The hall in Joigny where he was to speak was packed by a predominantly hostile crowd, and as Dumas strode in one humourist shouted: 'Ah, here comes the half-caste! Hello, nigger boy!' Dumas, without a word, walked up to him and smacked him right across the face with the flat of his hand. This resolute reaction, far from cooling tempers, provoked a renewed hullabaloo and a storm of protests and insults from the body of the hall in the midst of which one gentleman, with stronger lungs than most, could be heard shouting: 'You call yourself a republican, yet you claim to be the Marquis de La Pailleterie, and you were the secretary of the Duke of Orleans!' The candidate, vaulting on to the platform, turned on this heckler and dealt with him intrepidly. 'I call myself Alexandre Dumas, nothing more, and the whole world knows me under that name, including you in the first instance, you, a nobody, who have come here to see me and be able to boast tomorrow, after insulting me, that you have met the great Dumas.'

The audience finally gave him a hearing, and indeed did not disperse until midnight. On leaving the hall, Du Chaffault and he took a walk along the banks of the Yonne and, as they were crossing a bridge, became aware that they were being followed by a group of dock labourers who were jeering and passing rude comments. Suddenly Dumas turned round, grabbed the nearest, lifted him off the ground and held him by his coat-collar over the parapet of the bridge. 'Ask my pardon or I'll drop you into the water!' The man, seeing his mates shrink back, stammered out an apology which Dumas accepted magnanimously. 'I wanted to show you that even if I don't work with my hands, I've got as good a grip as you. And now be off with you, you and those drunken sots who were with you!' The bystanders, marvelling at this display of muscular strength and presence of mind, cheered him all the way back to the hotel. Even so, the electors of the department of Yonne did not choose Dumas to represent them in the Assembly.

Wars and revolutions were never good times, in the nineteenth century, for those who normally made a living by the pen. During the first two troubled years of the Second Republic, political journalism was the only kind of writing that commanded a ready market and Dumas, ever adaptable, was prepared to try his hand at this; but, typically, instead of writing for somebody else's newspaper, he founded his own journal, *Le Mois*, and wrote each issue of 32 quarto pages entirely by himself. *Le Mois* sold for 4 francs and reached, in its heyday, 20,000 subscribers. It must have provided a useful supplement to his income at a time when receipts from other sources had fallen off calamitously. We have already seen what a poor year the Théâtre Historique had in 1848. 1849 was no better, in spite of an excellent start with a dramatized version of *Les Trois Mousquetaires* in which Mélingue, Dumas's favourite actor, strutted and ranted superbly in the part of D'Artagnan. At the end of the year Hostein, unable to cope with Dumas's incurably unbusinesslike methods, resigned; four other managers succeeded him, one after the other, over the next nine months, but on October 16th, 1850, the Théâtre Historique finally closed its doors, and Dumas, who had mortgaged his country-house and estate to the hilt to avert this catastrophe, was ruined. 'Monte-Cristo' and its contents passed under the auctioneer's hammer. The house and grounds were adjudicated to an American dentist called Fowler for a mere 30,000 francs. The landlord of his rented Paris apartment had the furnishings sold to pay arrears of rent. When Dumas was finally declared bankrupt, on January 20th, 1852, his debts totalled over 100,000 francs. The unsatisfied creditors included, sadly, a large proportion of artisans and small tradesmen, saddlers and shoemakers, carpenters, florists, and sempstresses, who had let their accounts run on too long, never imagining that a man whose books everyone read, whose plays everyone flocked to see, who had such a fine house and entertained on so lavish a scale, could ever fail to meet his obligations.

And, indeed, the suddenness with which this millionaire became a pauper—at least on paper—is almost inexplicable even today. To be sure, the untold riches that started pouring into his coffers when newspaper editors discovered how marketable his stories were, must have gone to his head. Instead of telling himself that this gold-rush might well be only a temporary phenomenon, like the Californian gold-rush of the same period, and that seven fat years could, as easily as not, be followed by seven lean ones, he behaved as though his annual income was certain to increase by leaps and bounds year after year. So he spent every franc he earned, and then anticipated his future revenues. Whereas a more cautious man, like Hugo or even Maquet, invested his surplus income wisely, Dumas saved nothing; as he later observed, ruefully enough, had he followed their example he might have had a handsome private income before he was fifty which would have relieved him of the necessity of working for his bread for the rest of his life.

Such an analysis suggests a certain childish irresponsibility in Dumas which is only one part of the picture. Looking more closely, one can see that his attitude to money was on a par with his attitude to authorship and literary property, so strangely at variance with current conceptions, for he could never quite understand why people got so heated over trifling quibbles about whether this or that novel should be attributed to him, to Maquet, to Meurice, or to any one of half a dozen others who might have had a hand in it. He was that rare type, the natural communist, as the word was understood before Marx appropriated it, a man totally devoid of a sense of property. If Rousseau was right in dating the establishment of civilized society from the moment when some man, 'having fenced off a plot of ground, declared "This is mine", and found other people simple enough to take him at his word,' then Dumas must be regarded as, in Rousseau's terms, a true primitive. When he was building 'Monte-Cristo' and laying out the grounds, it happened more than once that he calmly staked off as his own a portion of a field belonging to his neighbour, and was genuinely astonished when the man came along to complain, stuttering with rage. Similarly, if there were bills to pay, it seemed to him perfectly normal for someone else to settle them for him if he forgot to do so himself. If he had taken a cab and chanced to see a friend on foot he would tell the driver to stop, offer the friend a lift and, when he had reached his destination, tell him to keep the cab; the other was then obliged to pay for Dumas's ride as well as his own, when he was quite possibly walking in the first place because he could not afford to do otherwise.

The chances were that Dumas never had the fare on him in the first place, for he was always short of ready cash. Money was something to be got rid of, squandered or given away. Of Eugène Scribe, a successful but relatively tight-fisted fellow dramatist, he was once heard to say: 'Scribe is not really *comme il faut*, he's never without money.'[15] In an emergency, one can always call on friends, and his friends would always oblige, for never was there a more debonair borrower than he. He gave the impression not so much of needing the money as of wanting to give you the pleasure of lending it. Arriving in Paris from one of his trips abroad he found himself literally penniless and called on a sculptor, Cain, whom he knew slightly. In her husband's absence, it was Mme Cain who received him. Learning the purpose of his visit, she produced the only money she had, a gold napoleon, which Dumas pocketed with profuse thanks. As he was leaving the room, his eye fell on a bowl of pickled gherkins, and he exclaimed in admiration.

'We make them at home,' said Mme Cain proudly. 'Would you like a bottle? I'll get my maid to bring you one to your carriage.' Renewed thanks, and renewed farewells. The maid was summoned as soon as Dumas departed, and given her instructions. 'As for dinner, heaven knows what we shall do,' Mme Cain said to her, 'for he's gone off with all my housekeeping money.' But the girl was back within five minutes, beaming all over and holding the gold napoleon in her hand. To tip her for bringing the gherkins to his carriage window, Dumas had pressed on her the coin he had gone to such trouble to borrow from her mistress.[16]

This casualness worked both ways; anyone could help himself to Dumas's money without the slightest formality. Payments, as they came in from newspaper offices, were never locked away; they were piled up, notes and coin, on the nearest shelf. At Saint-Germain, in 1843, his son remembered calling on him while he was in bed, dictating to a secretary; one of his dogs had bitten him, his hand was bandaged and he was unable to write. 'In the course of the day he had received 650 francs, it was all there in the house; I was returning to Paris to stay overnight, and said to him: "Look, I'll take fifty francs, is that all right?" "Could you leave me a hundred?" he said. "A hundred? What do you mean? I said I'm taking fifty." "I'm sorry, I didn't hear, I thought you said you were leaving me fifty." He believed I was taking 600 francs out of the 650 and thought it quite natural I should do so.'[17]

Alexandre, of course, was his flesh and blood, but the same reckless generosity was shown by Dumas to anyone who applied to him for help, even if they were complete strangers. Arsène Houssaye tells how he was lunching with him one hot summer day out of doors on the lawn of 'Monte-Cristo' when they noticed a woman standing timidly a short distance away, afraid to approach them. Houssaye recognized her as the wife of an out-of-work actor; her pride forbade her to beg the assistance she had come to ask for. Once he had grasped the situation, Dumas beckoned her over and said: 'My poor girl, the sun is beating down, how can you go around without a sunshade?' Then, taking out his wallet, he handed her a 500-franc note—enough, no doubt, to buy her a dozen sunshades. She was too overcome to say a word, but just curtseyed and turned to leave, with tears in her eyes. Dumas called after her cheerfully: 'And listen, when you next come, choose a rainy day, and I'll let you have something for an umbrella.'[18]

Another incident of a similar kind was recorded by Edmond de Goncourt a little before he died. He heard the story from an old surgeon who had attended Dumas during a minor illness. While he was still writing out his prescription, another caller was introduced into the bedroom, a starveling journalist from Marseilles who hoped Dumas might be able to help him to a job on one of the Paris newspapers. 'He promised he would do what he could, as soon as he was up and about again. "But in the meantime, young man, you'll need something to keep the wolf from the door. You'll find thirty francs on the mantle-piece; take fifteen." '[19]

Since it was only after he returned from Naples in 1864 that Dumas's health started to deteriorate, the probability is that this particular incident took place long after the financial débâcle of 1850–51. Dumas was never to know again the affluence he had enjoyed before the 1848 Revolution; but his relative poverty made no difference at all to his natural generosity though it obviously set limits on the scale of his munificence. In the last five years of his life he was rarely without pressing financial worries of his own, and what he wrote barely served to pay for the necessities of life, let alone any luxuries. Finding him at his desk as usual, writing away furiously, his son could not help commenting on how tired he looked. 'You should take some rest,' said he. 'I can't,' answered the older man and, pulling open a drawer, he showed Alexandre two *louis d'or*. 'When I first came to Paris in 1822,' he explained, 'I had 53 francs. Now, as you see, I have only 40. So long as I haven't made up the missing 13 francs, I shall have to go on working.' Authors, one may say, never reach pensionable age.

XII After the Crash

Conveniently for Dumas, just about the time his long-suffering creditors decided to foreclose, the Prince-President Louis-Napoleon for his part decided to throttle the Second Republic and establish himself as autocratic ruler, taking the title Napoleon III. His political opponents, who had anticipated this development for some months, went into hiding or escaped abroad, to Switzerland, Belgium or England. Dumas, in danger of imprisonment for debt rather than for his republican views, was not averse to giving the contrary impression; so he joined the band of refugees, travelling sedately by train to Brussels, along with his diminutive black servant Alexis, on December 7th, 1851, just five days after the *coup d'état*.

In the Belgian capital, where there were publishers eager for his product, he was able to open a new line of credit and so continue to live in much the same opulent style as before. His first action was to sign the lease on a large town house in the Boulevard de Waterloo which he proceeded to furnish without regard to expense. Emile Deschanel, one of the genuine political refugees, left a minute description of the interior of this house as it appeared to the guests whom Dumas invited to a supper party in honour of a visiting troupe of Spanish dancers.[1] His Excellency the Count of Monte-Cristo's house in the Champs-Elysées could hardly have been more palatially appointed. The principal reception-room on the ground floor had a sky-blue ceiling dotted with golden stars; round its walls were ranged Algerian divans and side-tables bearing samples of Barye's animal sculpture; while on the floor, carpeted with Javanese matting, was stretched, in the guise of a rug, the skin of a huge polar bear. Apart from this large reception-room there were other, smaller rooms for those of a retiring disposition or couples seeking privacy: one softly decorated in white and lit only by candles, with a white divan and white curtains; another full of Persian rugs, in which glowed a solitary opal lamp, like a moonbeam imprisoned in a white porcelain vase, said the poetic Deschanel; while a third, with a green-and-gold colour scheme, contained little but a capacious, dark-red sofa which could have told many a secret if, like Crébillon's, it had been endowed with the power of speech. Many of the *objets d'art* in the house must have been smuggled out of the Château de Monte-Cristo before Dumas's creditors could distrain them; there was statuary by Pradier and Auguste Préault, and Delacroix would have recognized two of his romantic masterpieces, Hamlet discussing Yorick's skull with Horatio in the graveyard, and Tasso mumbling in his madhouse, watched by a jeering crowd of courtiers.

The house, when Dumas leased it, lacked a conservatory, a *sine qua non* in the nineteenth century, so he had one built over the courtyard and stocked it with exotic flowers, creepers and tropical plants amongst which humming-birds and nightingales trilled and fluttered, uncaged. It was here, in this crystal 'winter garden', that the table was laid, large enough for sixty guests; at the last moment, a second, smaller one had to be brought in, for the diners were found to number finally between eighty and a hundred, it being recognized that this host never objected to gate-crashers.

An entertainment on this scale was, of course, exceptional. More often, when some distinguished visitor came to stay, Dumas would hire a family coach and drive out to tour the battlefield of Waterloo; or else he would give a display of the hypnotic powers on which he prided himself. His favourite 'subject' was a buxom, ox-eyed matron whom most people knew as 'the beautiful pastrycook'; Nerval referred to her more scathingly as a 'hysterical baker's wife' whom he suspected Dumas of bundling into a bed before he roused her from her trance.

Casual callers never quite knew what to expect when they rang his doorbell. Mathilde Schoebel, though she was only eleven or twelve at the time, never forgot the occasion when her mother took her along to 73, boulevard de Waterloo some time in 1852. Mathilde was the daughter of a professor of oriental languages; she and Dumas had known one another for as long as she could remember. He used to call her teasingly 'little Briar', a nickname dating from when she was eight and he had caught her in the garden tearing out a magnificent bed of pink briars to make them into toy brooms. This vandalism had so roused his ire that he gave the child a sound spanking, which in no way diminished her affection for him.

It was probably at her daughter's insistence that Mme Schoebel took her along to see Dumas, for the good lady had always disapproved of him; a bigoted Catholic, she regarded all actresses as fallen women, and all men who, like Dumas, associated with them as votaries of the devil. She was unexpectedly confirmed in this belief when, having been informed of their visit by his housekeeper, Dumas entered the sitting-room wearing the costume of Mephistopheles complete with tail and horns. He excused himself by saying that he was expecting an actress who was to rehearse the part of Gretchen with him: an explanation that meant little or nothing to Mme Schoebel, who would certainly never have looked inside Goethe's *Faust*; but, realizing the danger she stood in of encountering a daughter of Belial if they stayed, she nervously pulled her little girl towards the door, declining Dumas's kindly invitation to stay for dinner and make the lady's acquaintance. The real reason for his eccentric garb was slightly more complicated, as he explained to Mathilde years later: the actress he was expecting had been trying to convince him that the central character in *Faust* was not Faustus but Mephistopheles; he had donned this disguise to surprise her and, as he hoped, seduce her.

His love-life continued as active and varied as ever, and he showed himself in consequence less than delighted when his son suggested that Marie should come and housekeep for him in Brussels. 'There would be grave difficulties. I keep pretty unsavoury company', a statement amply confirmed later in the same letter when he asked Alexandre: 'Have you enough money to buy and send me a summer hat costing between 50 and 70 francs, trying it first on some pretty brunette of between twenty and twenty-five whom I'm sure you have at your disposal? Don't worry, of course, if you have to overrun by ten francs or so. I spent last night with a particularly lovely girl who wants nothing in return but a summer hat, either white or a very pale straw.'[2] Marie did, nevertheless, override her father's objections and visit him from time to time but, as he had foreseen, there was always friction between her and his currently resident mistress. Isabelle Constans in particular she could not stand, from jealousy, perhaps, or else out of sheer envy of the actress's fragile blonde beauty, and whenever she announced a forthcoming visit at a time when Isabelle was also due, he grew nervous. 'There is nothing in the world that would distress me more than to see you sulky with me as you were the last time you came. I love you so much, my darling child, that your expression alone can make me happy or unhappy. So please be brave and don't give me cause to grieve during the three or four days she will be here. Only what are we to do about mealtimes? . . .'[3]

His relations with his son presented no such difficulties, since Alexandre got on extremely well with his father's girl-friends and with Isabelle in particular. He was actively concerned in arranging the Paris production, in which she had a leading part, of *Benvenuto Cellini*, a drama drawn from one of Dumas's early romances, *Ascanio*. Thus he was keeping his promise to write her parts in his plays though in fact *Benvenuto Cellini* was billed as being by Paul Meurice, not by Dumas, who went so far as to write to the papers denying he had a hand in it. This disclaimer was, however, no more than a device to ensure that his vigilant creditors should not take legal action to have the royalties assigned to them. Meurice was to collect all the dues, and remit Dumas's share to his son.

Alexandre was at this time living in much straitened circumstances.

6*

Having been largely dependent hitherto on an allowance paid him by his father, which stopped abruptly when the crash came, he found it necessary to retrench drastically. He gave up his bachelor quarters and went to live with his mother, who was now running a *cabinet de lecture* (subscription library) in the Rue Pigalle. Having been trained to no particular profession, he could see his future only in terms of a literary career. *La Dame aux camélias*, based on his affair with Marie Duplessis, had been published as a novel in 1848; hoping to cash in on its success, he turned it into a play. The prudish censorship bureau of the Second Republic refused to license it for public performance, but the author had a good friend in the Duc de Morny and the good luck to see him become a minister of the crown after the *coup d'état*. Morny lost no time in personally authorizing the production of *La Dame aux camélias* which accordingly had its première on February 2nd, 1852. Since at this time his father still did not dare show his face in Paris, he only learnt of its instantaneous and phenomenal success from a telegram Alexandre sent him. *La Dame aux camélias* proved to be one of the greatest theatrical draws of the Second Empire, and Dumas *fils* went on to establish his reputation as a fashionable dramatist with a series of other works, today rarely read and almost never performed. But he had achieved financial independence and indeed was well enough off to relieve his mother of all further need to earn her living; he set her up in a sunny apartment at Neuilly, overlooking the Bois de Boulogne, where she spent her declining days in relative comfort.

Meanwhile, in Brussels, the elder Dumas was writing as busily as ever. The work that occupied most of his time was one for which no collaborator was needed—his Memoirs. The period of the great historical novels was now over, having ended when he and Maquet fell out. Always a prudent man, Maquet had foreseen the coming financial collapse, and had tried to safeguard his position as 'co-author' by insisting on a legal contract. On the eve of the 1848 Revolution, still trusting blindly to his star, Dumas signed an agreement by which he bound himself to pay Maquet something like a hundred thousand francs a year over the next eleven years in return for his collaborator's pledge to renounce all claim on past and future royalties. In the event, this agreement could not be honoured and Maquet started court proceedings which dragged out over several years, driving Dumas into a fury and causing him to denounce Maquet as a rogue and a cheat. The other man professed to deplore these outbursts, declaring that he personally would always consider himself Dumas's friend and that he was only anxious to secure what was due to him. Of the two, it was certainly not Maquet who suffered; he ended his days living in great comfort as the proprietor of a handsome manor-house near Dourdan.

His place as Dumas's right-hand man was taken, temporarily, by one Noël Parfait, a committed republican who had served a two-year prison sentence for publishing a panegyric of the insurrectionists of 1832 and who, when the Orleans monarchy disappeared, stood—with more success than Dumas—for election to the new Chamber. Known as a radical and an ardent anti-Bonapartist, he was expelled from French territory when Napoleon III seized power, and in January 1852 found himself stranded, friendless and destitute, in Brussels. In desperation he applied to Dumas, whom he did not know, for help; Dumas took him in, with his wife and small son, and offered him employment as his secretary.

They made a curiously disparate couple, Dumas in his open-necked shirt and baggy trousers, Noël Parfait always wearing his severely cut black suit, as they sat at separate tables in an ill-heated room at the top of the house, the writer covering sheet after sheet with his usual practised ease, the secretary picking them up from the pile, reading them through, inserting the punctuation, correcting the grammar and spelling, and then making copies to send to the translators in England and Germany. After a while, shocked at Dumas's happy-go-lucky housekeeping, he made himself responsible for the financial management of the Brussels establishment; he took it on himself to write reminders to publishers who were slack in remitting royalties, conducted Dumas's business correspondence with his agent in Paris, and finally ventured to exercise some control over his employer's personal expenditure. Dumas had still not cured himself of his fatal habit of putting all moneys, as received, into a drawer and helping himself to the contents whenever he found himself short. Noël Parfait put the remittances in a safe place as soon as they came in and used them to pay the tradesmen's bills. 'It's very odd,' Dumas remarked, peering into his empty drawer and pulling a rueful face, 'but I've never been so badly off as I have been since I brought an honest man into the house.'[4]

He was doubly lucky, for he had an equally honest man working as his representative in Paris to sort out the tangled mess he had left there and make it possible for him eventually to return without risking arrest for debt. This was Hirschler, a cultured Jewish businessman who regarded Dumas as a sublime artistic genius manifestly out of his depth in dealing with sordid matters of profit and loss. Hirschler acted as Dumas's proxy in all negotiations with publishers, newspaper editors and theatre managers in Paris, and represented him in the bankruptcy courts where he defended his interests tooth and nail. After a series of meetings with the creditors he persuaded them to accept an arrangement whereby 45 per cent of Dumas's future earnings would be paid over to them until the debt was worked off. Thus, early in 1853, it became safe for the writer to set foot in France again; he continued, however, to keep a *pied-à-terre* in Brussels for at least a year longer, so as to have a bolt-hole in an emergency.

In contrast to the superior establishment in the Boulevard de Waterloo, the apartment he rented in Paris, 77 Rue d'Amsterdam, was poky and ill-furnished, without pictures on the walls or curtains at the windows; but Dumas gave some memorable dinners there notwithstanding, often cooking the *pièce de résistance* himself. There were not always enough chairs to go round, but the table-linen was snow-white and the silver- and glassware highly polished. As for the guests, they included some new satellites, Henry Murger, the author of the book on which Puccini based his popular opera *La Bohème*, and the cartoonist Henri Monnier, creator of the unforgettable M. Joseph Prudhomme, that prototype *petit bourgeois*, smug, squat-bodied and narrow-minded. The women one saw at these dinner-parties were a strange assortment of adventuresses on the make, decrepit actresses from the provinces, and society women in search of novelty.

Mostly, however, Dumas met his friends elsewhere, either backstage at the theatre, or on the terrace of Tortoni's where Frédérick Lemaître would join him for a drink, or else in the Café de Paris, the famous restaurant where Dr Véron, the newspaper magnate and former manager of the Paris Opera, had had a table reserved for his use from time immemorial and where Lord Palmerston insisted on dining every evening when he was in Paris. Another favourite haunt was the *salon* of Princess Mathilde, a cousin of Napoleon III whom Dumas had known since she was a child living with the rest of her family in exile at the Villa Quarto in Florence. A cultivated woman who preferred the company of men of letters to any other sort, she kept up a pretence of disdaining the new Emperor and his dull, philistine court, and blandly tolerated between the four walls of her drawing-room the kind of seditious talk that Dumas loved to engage in. Daringly, he derided Louis-Napoleon for his feebleness in getting himself arrested in 1836 when he tried to incite the garrison at Strasbourg to mutiny. He went further, repeating the rumours circulating in the underground to the effect that the Emperor was not, in reality, a nephew of the great Napoleon at all. 'There isn't a drop of the blood of the Bonapartes in his veins at all. All the chancelleries of Europe know he's the son of Hortense Beauharnais and Admiral Woerhul. We are doing obeisance to a Dutch bastard!'[5] On June 5th, 1853, the Princess asked him, after dinner, whether he had written any verses recently; he obliged by reciting a satirical quatrain which can be roughly rendered as follows:

> Napoleon First and Napoleon Third,
> The difference between 'em lies just in a word:
> The Uncle he captured capital cities,
> The Nephew's content with capital levies.[6]

The police spies of the Second Empire were everywhere, and it is likely that some of these incautious sallies were reported; as too were his open professions of admiration for Victor Hugo, regarded by the régime as one of their most dangerous opponents. Hugo's book of polemical verse, *Les Châtiments*, composed in Jersey, was strictly banned inside France; at every frontier post and seaport customs officers were on the alert to seize all illicit copies, and the penalties for trying to smuggle one in were severe. Nevertheless Dumas had his, acquired probably in Brussels, and took great delight in reading aloud his favourite pieces, 'Souvenir de la nuit du 4', 'Le Manteau impérial', to anyone who cared to listen. He finally presented it to Princess Mathilde, who knew of the book only by hearsay and was delighted to have a copy.

Wisely, the administration turned a blind eye on these on the whole harmless acts of defiance: there was no point in making a martyr of this buffoon who was, it had to be admitted, still the most popular writer in the land. When Queen Victoria paid her state visit to France it was one of Dumas's plays, *Les Demoiselles de Saint-Cyr*, that was selected to be performed before her in the small private theatre in the Palais de Saint-Cloud (August 20th, 1855). There may not be any truth in the story that the Queen asked specially for a performance of this play, though she had seen it done once before, at the St. James's Theatre, and had pronounced it then 'a very pretty and amusing piece'. But the choice of *Les Demoiselles de Saint-Cyr* for the entertainment of this particular visiting monarch constituted at least an indirect tribute to Dumas's good taste, for Victoria had stipulated in advance that any dramatic production she was to see in France would need to be '*very proper* and free from *équivoque*, which is a thing the Queen *abhors*'.[7]

Dumas was never so close to Hugo as at this period. He visited him at Hauteville House, Guernsey, where the poet was living in exile with his wife and family around him and with Juliette Drouet, his middle-aged mistress, tucked away in discreet lodgings down one of the steep side-streets of St. Peter's Port. When Marie-Alexandrine was married, in 1856, her father would have dearly liked Hugo to be one of the witnesses; but of course the great exile could not come to France, and Dumas had to be content with Boulanger, acting as Hugo's proxy. The letter he sent the poet on that occasion is altogether remarkable for its extravagant expressions of tender affection. Hugo, for his part, was ever gracious, and when Dumas started up his own newspaper, *Le Mousquetaire*, at the end of 1853, he wrote him a brief, lapidary letter of encouragement: 'Dear Dumas, I read your paper regularly. You are Voltaire come among us again. A supreme consolation for the suffering, humiliated French nation. *Vale et me ama*.'[8] Dumas considered communicating this message to his readers but decided he could not; to insert it would have been to invite police intervention and the immediate closure of the paper.

Le Mousquetaire was yet another attempt on Dumas's part to renew his image by presenting himself before his wide public in a fresh guise: first dramatist, then writer of travel-books, then novelist, and now newspaper editor. 'Scientists have long sought the principle of perpetual motion; you have gone one better,' Lamartine told him, 'you have invented perpetual astonishment.'[9] As a business proposition, the idea was basically sound, and had Hirschler's approval. The rigours of Second-Empire censorship had drastically reduced the number of periodicals in circulation; a new one would stand an excellent chance of attracting subscribers, particularly since anything Dumas signed was manna from heaven to his countless readers. He calculated that he would do far better publishing his own copy in his own newspaper than letting other editors have it to swell their shareholders' profits. In particular *Le Mousquetaire* would serve as a vehicle for the publication of the later part of his autobiography. Girardin had brought out the first 213 chapters of *Mes Mémoires* serially in *La Presse*, the equivalent of 22 volumes in the original edition as published by Cadot; but Dumas reckoned there were another 40 or 50 volumes to come, twice what he had written so far and, since these later volumes would treat of more recent events and deal extensively with persons still living, he preferred to take full editorial responsibility for their publication.[10]

Offices for the new journal were found in a building in the Rue Laffitte, called 'La Maison d'Or'. As usual, Dumas chose the top room in the house for his own office and, as usual, he furnished it with Spartan simplicity: just three wicker chairs and a deal table covered with a red cloth. On the table stood an ink-well, a stack of the famous azure writing-paper, and one small vase just big enough to contain a single rose or carnation, or a twig of lilac blossom. Here he would sit, steadily writing from early morning till late at night, with his sleeves rolled up, never wearing a jacket even in the depths of winter; an open-necked, coloured or check shirt, loose trousers, and red slippers constituted the work-a-day costume everyone saw him in.

Noël Parfait having been obliged to remain behind in Brussels, his place as secretary was taken by Edmond Viellot, a pale-faced, rangy, towsle-haired man whom Dumas had lighted on in a typically round-about way. Picking up a piece of wrapping paper in which the cook had brought home a parcel of spiced meat, he had noticed to his astonishment that it appeared to be a sheet from one of his own manuscripts. Inquiries made at the pork-butcher's shop put him on the track of Viellot, whose handwriting happened to be practically identical with his own. Whether or not, as was hinted, Dumas profited from this coincidental resemblance to get his new secretary to recopy books and articles written by hacks so that he could sell them for a good price as his own, it seems certain that collectors of autographs at auctions were more than once inveigled into paying handsomely for a specimen of Viellot's writing in the belief it had been penned by Dumas. Unfortunately Viellot had one vice: he could not keep away from the bottle; in the course of time his writing became unsteady and he had to be discharged.

On the ground floor of the 'Maison d'Or' were the editorial offices, for ever in an uproar, the rendezvous it seemed of all the talkative idlers in Paris. Dumas had recruited a quite remarkable team of collaborators. The four most assiduous, constituting as it were the regular staff, were his old friends Joseph Méry and Roger de Beauvoir, plus Philibert Audebrand who later wrote an entertaining account of the *Mousquetaire* years under the title *Alexandre Dumas à la Maison d'Or*, and finally a brilliant cub reporter, Aurélien Scholl, who has been credited with the invention of the gossip column; a remarkably handsome young man, ogled by all the pretty girls who received in return nothing but the blankest of blank stares, for Scholl was excessively short-sighted. The freelance irregulars included two front-rank poets, Théodore de Banville and Gérard de Nerval who first published his famous sonnet 'El Desdichado' in *Le Mousquetaire*. Henri Rochefort, one of the most implacable enemies of the Second Empire in its decline, contributed a series of pieces under the pseudonym Saint-Henri de Luçay. Society tittle-tattle was provided by Countess Dash, and there were translations of stories by Lermontov, Edgar Allan Poe, and the American frontier-romance writer Mayne Reid. Dumas himself did not confine his activities to the publication of his inexhaustible memoirs (which he grew tired of writing, in fact, long before he completed the additional 'forty or fifty volumes' he contemplated; he never took the story of his life beyond the year 1832). *Le Mousquetaire* saw the serialization of the first part of *Les Mohicans de Paris*, an interminable *roman-fleuve* set under the Restoration, and Dumas also published in its columns his charming reminiscences of the denizens, human and animal, of the Château de Monte-Cristo, under the general title *Histoire de mes bêtes*.

With all this talent, linked to the prestige of Dumas's name, it was not surprising that *Le Mousquetaire* enjoyed at the outset a sweeping success. Circulation figures rapidly climbed to 10,000, a very respectable achievement for the period, and there was even an attempt at a take-over. Henri de Villemessant, who founded *Le Figaro* in 1854, was approached by a financier, Polydore Millaud, with the suggestion they should jointly pay Dumas a visit at the Maison d'Or to see whether he would sell out. They knew the enterprise was undercapitalized; Dumas had launched it with a mere 3,000 francs, but Millaud was prepared to bid up to 100,000. There would have to be some changes in administrative procedures, of course, for Dumas's methods were hopelessly unbusinesslike. Anyone, it seemed, who applied for a job was found one; on the other hand nobody was ever paid. Dumas, sublimely self-confident, refused to listen to Millaud and Villemessant. He had a little gold-mine here, he said, and would not be prepared to let it go even for a million.

This was unwise, as the sequel showed, for before long Dumas was in deep financial trouble. His first accountant, an unhappy man called Martinet, resigned in despair after the first few weeks. He could never convince Dumas of the need to build up reserves. When he warned him that the cash-flow problem was becoming serious, Dumas would not believe him: what about all those subscriptions? all the copies sold in the streets?

'That's all very well, my dear sir, but only ten minutes ago you helped yourself to 300 francs for your private needs.'

'Well, after all, what's 300 francs, when I've provided a thousand francs' worth of copy over the past two days? In any other newspaper office I should have taken twice that and the cashier wouldn't even have noticed.'

Martinet smiled.

'My dear sir, these other newspapers, Le Siècle, La Presse for example, have been in existence for thirty years; Le Mousquetaire hasn't been going for thirty days. Wait until your acorn has grown into an oak-tree.'[11]

To replace Martinet, Dumas perversely decided on his gardener and animal curator, Michel, who when 'Monte-Cristo' was put in the hands of the receiver had followed him to Brussels where he had busied himself stocking and maintaining the famous winter garden in the Boulevard de Waterloo. After Dumas returned to Paris, Michel had to be found fresh employment, so he was put in charge of the financial fortunes of Le Mousquetaire; and to all objections Dumas answered with a snort that he was just the man for the job: 'Michel can't read, or write, or count.' But there were manifest drawbacks in putting an ignoramus in charge of this important department. Gustave Claudin, hearing Dumas complain one day that subscriptions were drying up, had the curiosity to examine the office waste-paper basket and was amazed to discover dozens of letters that had not even been opened, several of which contained postal orders from would-be subscribers.

In the circumstances, it is a little astonishing that Le Mousquetaire should have survived as long as it did—it ran regularly from November 12th, 1853, to February 7th, 1857. Brilliant, amateurish, full of juvenile brio, this venture might well be accounted the last crackling flare-up of the great festive bonfire of romanticism before it turned to cold grey ashes. Significantly, its disappearance coincided, almost to the day, with Flaubert's acquittal at the obscenity trial that the government had mounted against *Madame Bovary*, the novel that inaugurated realism in France by demolishing the shibboleths of the romantic ethos. It was the Belgian painter Alfred Stevens who later claimed to have brought the two Dumas a copy of Flaubert's maiden novel and urged them to read it. 'Dumas *fils* said to me: "That is a terrible book!" As for Dumas *père*, he flung it on the floor saying: "If that is good, then everything we have written since 1830 is worthless." '[12] With his uncanny sense of what the future held in store, a faculty we have commented on already, Dumas may have had at this moment of disillusion some premonition that whatever he wrote now would, in France at least, bear the stigma of obsolescence. But beyond the frontiers of his own country there was a faithful mass readership that still acclaimed him as the greatest of living French writers. That was where he had to turn now; 'posterity begins abroad'; and over the next few years, Dumas was to grasp at every opportunity that presented itself to seek out his faithful public in foreign lands.

XIII The Restless Years

To the continental European with a bent for travel, few countries were reckoned less appealing in the early nineteenth century than England, supposedly blanketed in fog from November to May, inhabited by arrogant aristocrats at one end of the social scale and, at the other, by the 'starving operatives and rick-burning peasants' of whom Trevelyan speaks. The suicide rate among these morose islanders was alleged to be significantly high, proof enough of how intolerable life was in their country, and if further evidence was needed, one had only to think of the droves of apparently homeless Britishers one encountered, like so many Wandering Jews, ceaselessly travelling in every part of the globe. Dumas first met the species, it will be remembered, in Switzerland; he had come across them again in Italy and Spain; and when crossing the Baltic from Stettin to Kronstadt in midsummer 1858 he fell into conversation with an Englishman who had arrived straight from the banks of the Blue Nile and was heading for Tornio, the most northerly port of the Gulf of Bothnia, expressly to view the midnight sun on June 23rd. He confessed to Dumas that this was his second attempt to witness the spectacle; three years previously he had arrived tired out at ten in the evening and had slept through the night.

If even the natives fled from their inhospitable homeland, propelled by an unquenchable wanderlust, it was not to be supposed that foreigners from more fortunate climes would be greatly tempted to cross the Channel for the pleasure of touring this abominable country. So it is hardly surprising, however regrettable, that Dumas never wrote one of his inimitable travelogues about the British Isles. He did, however, pay four separate visits to these shores; they were all very brief and only one of them, the last, is properly documented.

His first trip took place some time in 1833, a little after his return from Switzerland; presumably the itch to travel was still with him.[1] The only memory of this visit he records was the sight of the Duke of Wellington's London residence with its windows protected by iron shutters, the wooden ones having been smashed by radical mobs during the disturbances that attended the passing of the Reform Bill the previous year. He crossed the Channel again in August 1850 in order to pay his respects to the dead ex-King Louis-Philippe, whose remains were lying in state at Claremont Park in Surrey. Dumas no doubt performed this pious duty more out of regard for his friend the Duc de Montpensier than because of any lingering respect for the exiled monarch. His well-known republicanism meant, however, that he was greeted with cold stares in this house of mourning, so instead of attending the obsequies he left for London where he spent a night as the guest of Lord and Lady Holland, whose acquaintance he had made in Florence. The following day he boarded the train for Nottingham, where the sole attraction was Newstead Abbey, Byron's ancestral home. Having accomplished this literary pilgrimage, he travelled on to Liverpool to visit the trade fair. In the course of this week, he saw as much of the country as he was ever to, since on his remaining two visits he never moved out of London except to go down to Epsom on Derby Day.

The one piece of advice he had to offer his fellow countrymen was that they should never spend more than six days at a stretch in England, arriving on a Monday and leaving the following Saturday so as to avoid the exquisite torture of having to spend Sunday here. The horrors of a British sabbath were revealed to Dumas on his first visit, in 1833; but he had forgotten the lesson when he decided to slip over to London for a week-end twenty-four years later, drawn by curiosity to observe the election campaign which followed the dissolution of parliament on March 21st, 1857. Sabbath observance, if we are to believe Dumas, was taken to some quite extraordinary lengths in the mid-Victorian era. At one house he visited his attention was drawn to a number of disconsolate hens in the backyard and a depressed looking cock shut up in a cage all by himself. Even the poultry had to be kept from transgressing on the Lord's Day.

So when he returned to England later the same year, accompanied this time by his son, he was careful to schedule his departure so that the cliffs of Dover were receding in the distance on Saturday evening. He spent a busy five days, visiting Mme Tussaud's wax-works, the Crystal Palace (now re-erected at Sydenham after having served its original purpose of housing the Great Exhibition in Hyde Park in 1851), and, as already stated, the races on Epsom downs. Great Britain, at that time, made an impact on the French visitor in many ways analogous to that made by the United States a hundred years later. It was the dominant economic power, and everything seemed to be slightly larger than life. 'When you arrive at the island of Elba, you are warned that everything is a third smaller than anywhere else; if you go to London, you should be warned that you will find everything a third bigger—hams, joints of beef and steaks included.'[2] The omnibuses towered above the other traffic, drawn by huge shire horses; the reins were lightly held in the gloved hands of drivers perched fifteen feet above street level. The *Great Eastern*, the biggest steamship in the world, was then under construction, but its size failed to impress Dumas, his own seafaring experience having convinced him that small ships often ride storms better than large ones.

It was gratifying to find that, even in this materialistic society, his own contributions to the world of poetic fancy had not gone unnoticed. Starting with *The Three Musketeers*, all Dumas's great historical romances had been translated into English as soon as they appeared in French, and he had a sizeable public even in a country where Dickens, Thackeray, and Trollope offered formidable competition. When he visited Daniel's porcelain emporium, at the corner of New Bond Street and Grosvenor Street, the manager recognized him, and to mark his gratification at being patronized by such a man as Alexandre Dumas, insisted on his paying no more than the cost price for the pieces he bought. A nation of shopkeepers, maybe, but very gentlemanly shopkeepers! Having completed his purchase, Dumas walked down Oxford Street and wandered into Hyde Park, to admire the riders in Rotten Row, particularly the women. In the Bois de Boulogne, one hardly ever saw a lady on horseback without her husband or some other male escort at her side; here they trotted along unaccompanied, save for a groom following behind, or else in groups like a detachment of Amazons on patrol. The spectacle inspired him to a flight of unaccustomed lyricism about the peerless beauty of these fresh-complexioned upper-class Englishwomen, the descendants, doubtless, of the Elizabethan damsels on whom Shakespeare modelled Miranda, Rosalind, Cordelia and so many other enchanting heroines.

The same scene also provoked a curious reflection about the 'aristocratic pride of this nation which has achieved liberty by trampling equality underfoot'.[3] To understand what he meant by this remark, one has to remember that for a republican like Dumas, France in 1857 was a country which had seen its liberties filched from it by a usurping autocrat, whereas England, with its House of Commons elected on the basis of a broader franchise than ever before, its press subject to no political censorship, its judicial system functioning independently of the executive power, was in comparison the land of the free; and yet there was no country where the gap between the rich and the poor, the privileged and the underprivileged, yawned more widely. In Hyde Park, by day, there were these elegant horsewomen riding splendid mounts each one of which must have cost a small fortune, while after nightfall, a walk down Haymarket was enough to open one's eyes to the very different lot of their poorer sisters. Here the footpaths swarmed with painted prostitutes, soliciting the passers-by in French as well as English, jostling, shrieking and quarrelling without any kind of policing or attempt at control such as had been introduced, in an effort to prevent the spread of venereal disease, in Paris and other large French towns. 'The reason given by British puritanism is admirable,' Dumas commented drily. 'Vice must not be encouraged by the hope of impunity.'[4] The English remained a baffling enigma; their vaunted freedom took so many forms, some fair, some as ugly as sin itself.

Less than a year after his return from London, Dumas was off again, this time to Marseilles. A new play, *Les Gardes forestiers*, drawn from an earlier novel of his about the verderers and poachers of the woods around Villers-Cotterêts, was being staged in the southern city and his presence in the theatre on the first night was thought imperative. The audience was in raptures. After the performance Dumas was called on stage to receive a golden crown from the hands of the leading actress. Subsequently, the theatre orchestra stationed itself in the street outside his hotel to serenade him; Dumas appeared on the balcony, thanked the musicians and harangued the enthusiastic crowd; after which he was taken off by his admirers to a supper-party at one of the most renowned restaurants in the city, where toasts and speeches went on till three in the morning.

The novelist Edmond About had been the almost involuntary witness of this extraordinary popular triumph. He had been passing through Marseilles on his way to Civitavecchia when Dumas, recognizing him on the railway platform, gave him a bear-hug and bore him off to his own hotel, insisting that he should come and see the play and join him in the celebratory supper. As they drove back to the hotel in the early hours About could hardly keep his eyes open. Dumas told him pityingly to go to bed. 'Old men need their sleep.' (About was thirty at the time, Dumas fifty-five.) 'I've got three articles to write which must go off by first post tomorrow—today I mean.' About, thinking this to be no more than a typical piece of Dumasian rodomontade, fell asleep straight away and was woken the following morning by the sound of his companion singing cheerfully if not tunefully as he wielded his razor. The three articles, each in its envelope addressed to three different newspaper editors, were lying on the table, sealed and ready for posting.[5]

Southern exuberance was no doubt partly responsible for the uproarious welcome extended to Dumas by the citizens of Marseilles; but they had sound reasons for taking him to their hearts. The early chapters of *Le Comte de Monte-Cristo* had, if not put their city on the map (for it had been 'on the map', as they were never tired of pointing out, centuries before Paris), at any rate made its handsome streets and quaint old quarters familiar by name to readers the world over, and encouraged many of them to spend time and—more importantly— money on coming to Marseilles so as to identify the scenes of various episodes in the novel. The resultant influx of tourists had been of particular benefit to the poorer sections of the population, as Dumas discovered to his delight when he had himself rowed over to the Château d'If. The boatman recognized him and refused to take his money, adding that none of his comrades either would have charged him. Rather, he went on, 'we ought all to club together and serve you a pension; you are the father of us all; it is you who put the bread into our mouths by writing the romance of *Monte-Cristo*; it's thanks to you that we have three times as much custom as we used to. Everyone wants to go to the Château d'If, and in all weathers. Why, when there's a heavy swell, and we pretend we would rather not risk it, the English give us anything up to two *louis-d'or* to row them over.'

His guide at the Château d'If, an old Catalan woman, either failed to recognize him or was clever enough to pretend not to have done so. She launched forth on her usual patter, claiming she had known Mercédès, Dantès's betrothed, in her youth, and when Dumas asked her whether she could give him any tidings of the Count of Monte-Cristo—hoping, as he said, that 'she was going to help me write the sequel to my romance for which everyone is pressing me'—she looked him straight in the face and said: 'There's only one man who is in touch with him and could give you the information.' 'And who might that be?' 'Why, M. Alexandre Dumas.'[6]

After this brief holiday in Marseilles Dumas was back in Paris, assiduously turning out copy for *Le Constitutionnel*, *Le Journal pour tous*, *L'Echo des feuilletons*, and his own weekly paper *Le Monte-Cristo* which had been started up on April 23rd, 1857. Pressure of work obliged him to decline all but a small proportion of the numerous invitations he was constantly receiving, a circumstance he greatly regretted, since it deprived him of the opportunity to meet a number of interesting foreigners temporarily resident in Paris. One of these was the Scottish medium, David Dunglas Home, whom some, like Robert Browning, judged to be an imposter, but who none the less had a considerable following even among the sceptical French; he was invited on two occasions to demonstrate his occult powers before the Imperial court. Home, who may have heard of Dumas's experiments with hypnotism, more than once expressed a wish to meet him; and he was finally enabled to do so when two mutual friends, one of them Henry Delaage, the author of several treatises on paranormal phenomena, brought Home to Dumas's chambers and effected an introduction.

Home had recently become engaged to the eighteen-year-old daughter of a Russian general, Alexandrine de Kroll, whom he had met in Italy where she was travelling with her married sister, Countess Kushelev-Bezborodko. The entire family had now moved to Paris and were living in great style in a suite in the Hôtel des Trois Empereurs, and nothing would satisfy Home but that Dumas should accompany him back to the hotel that very evening. The novelist demurred; it was already midnight, rather late for a social call. But this was no objection, it appeared, for the Kushelevs rarely went to bed before six in the morning.

Dumas had had until then very little contact with Russians, though his son had successfully courted two high-born ladies in the Russian colony in Paris, one of whom he eventually married. He probably knew something of the popularity his early plays, from *Henri III et sa cour* to *Richard Darlington*, had enjoyed in Russia during the romantic period; though Gogol had attacked them, they had found defenders in two of the most eminent literary critics of the period, Belinsky and Herzen. In 1839, encouraged by what he had heard of the warm welcome extended by the Muscovites to Horace Vernet, the painter, when he visited their country and was received in audience by the Tsar, Dumas had the idea of presenting the manuscript of one of his plays, *L'Alchimiste*, to Nicholas I, hoping at least for the same decoration, the Order of St. Stanislas, as had been bestowed on Vernet. However, the only token of appreciation he received was a diamond ring, so, possibly to revenge himself for this snub, he published, under the innocent seeming title *Mémoires d'un Maître d'armes*, a pathetic story based on actual incidents in the Decembrist rising of 1825–6 which came near to costing Nicholas I his throne. Not unnaturally, Dumas's novel was banned in Russia as soon as it appeared, which did not prevent it having a wide undercover circulation. According to one story, when the Tsar entered his wife's apartments one day he noticed that her lady-in-waiting not only stopped reading, as etiquette demanded, but hid the book under a cushion. 'I can guess what you've been listening to,' said the Tsar, 'it's M. Dumas's novel *Le Maître d'armes*, isn't it?' 'How did you know, sire?' 'Not very difficult,' grumbled the Tsar; 'it's the last book that I've had banned.'

By 1858, however, Nicholas I had been gathered to his fathers. Alexander II, who succeeded him, was a more liberally minded monarch who, shortly after the conclusion of the Crimean War, set up a commission to study ways and means of effecting the abolition of serfdom throughout the Russian Empire, as a first step in the slow process of modernizing the country's institutions. It was in every respect a propitious moment for embarking on an exploration of those remote and semi-legendary regions, though if the Kushelevs had not put the idea to Dumas, and indeed pressed him warmly to accompany them and Home back to St. Petersburg for the wedding ceremony, it is doubtful whether he would have given it serious consideration. An expedition to such distant parts would entail a massive financial outlay, and he was no longer a rich man. The count dismissed these scruples:

he would come as their guest. But Petersburg, Dumas objected, was after all only the gateway to Russia; having gone that far, he would want to continue to Moscow, to Nizhny-Novgorod, Kazan, Astrakhan, the Crimean peninsula . . . No difficulty there, exclaimed the countess. I have my estate at Koralovo, near Moscow; my husband has another at Nizhny, we own steppes in Kazan province, a fishery on the Caspian, we'll be able to offer you hospitality wherever you go, we or our friends. Confounded by this display of generosity and impressed by the lady's casual inventory of territorial wealth, Dumas allowed himself to be persuaded.

It was the longest journey he ever accomplished, starting on June 15th, 1858, when the party entrained for Berlin, and finishing nine months later when the steamship *Le Sully*, on which he embarked at Trebizond, conveyed him back to France. He travelled by rail from Petersburg (Leningrad) to Moscow, by river boat down the Volga, and in a variety of exotic conveyances—troikas, tarantasses, droshkies, and heaven knows what else—along the ill-made roads of the Tsarist Empire. The food was usually execrable, unless Dumas himself took a hand in the cooking, and between leaving Moscow and embarking on the French liner in the Black Sea, he never knew the comfort of sleeping in a bed. Yet it seems probable that, of all the journeys he ever made, that which he accomplished through Russia gave Dumas most pleasure, not just because of the strangeness of the country and the wildness of the sights, but above all because of the unfailing kindness of the inhabitants.

He had only to express a wish to have it granted with almost embarrassing promptitude. At Nizhny-Novgorod (the city now called Gorky) he happened to mention how much he appreciated Russian tea; everyone within hearing hastened to present him with a chest of the finest leaf they had. At Kazan he was observed to be fingering admiringly the skins offered for sale in the market and, on returning to his lodgings later that day, he found an assortment of magnificent hides which he was implored to take away with him. Any merchant of standing or high-ranking officer with whom he fell into conversation on the way immediately pressed him to come and stay at his house for as long as he chose to remain in the neighbourhood. When he crossed into Georgia, he found the inhabitants not merely hospitable but extravagantly open-handed, so that it was necessary to keep a guard on one's tongue so as to avoid being betrayed into expressing, lightly or in jest, some desire which one's host would consider himself in honour bound to fulfil on the spot. After seeing them installed for the night, the head servant of a local prince with whom Dumas's party was staying asked them if they had all they needed, and Jean-Pierre Moynet, the artist who accompanied Dumas throughout the journey, replied jokingly that the only thing they lacked was a dancing-girl. The majordomo bowed, and within a quarter of an hour was back . . . with a dancing-girl. Their Russian interpreter, seeing his employers' embarrassment, took her into his own room. Elsewhere, Dumas incautiously mentioned in company that he needed to acquire a pair of Georgian trousers to serve as a pattern for a pair he proposed to have made up for his own use from a length of cloth he had bought locally. One of the other guests immediately divested himself of the trousers he was wearing and handed them over. Knowing that to have refused the gift would have mortally offended the donor, Dumas had no option but to accept though, as he acknowledged ruefully when recording the incident, the garment was all but useless to him, being six inches too tight in the waist.

Considering that he was traversing a country which only three years previously had been at war with his, it is remarkable how little hostility Dumas met with on the way. He had the good fortune to be visiting Russia at a time when a strong Westernizing current was flowing through the sluggish national consciousness, and found himself everywhere greeted as ambassador-extraordinary of the far-flung French cultural empire. As a patriot he could not help feeling his spirits lift when he saw how complete this ascendancy was. Down at Astrakhan he was entertained to dinner by the chief civil administrator, a man in his thirties who spoke French like a Parisian. The meal, prepared by a French cook, was served to a dozen guests all of whom conversed fluently in Dumas's native tongue, and who,

once the doors were closed, caused me to forget completely that France lay a thousand leagues away. It is unbelievable how powerful an influence our civilization, our literature, arts and fashions have on the rest of the world. In what they had to say about the latest styles in dress, about contemporary fiction, plays and music, the women were not more than six weeks behind the times. The talk was of poetry, novels, the opera: Meyerbeer, Hugo, Balzac, Alfred de Musset; and what was said was perhaps not quite what one might have heard in a gathering of artists, but certainly no different from what one might expect to hear in a drawing-room in the Faubourg de Roule or on the Chaussée-d'Antin . . . And to think that one had but to open a window and stretch out one's hand and there was the Caspian Sea, which the Romans never discovered, and Turkestan, a country unexplored even today.[7]

However gratifying to hear Balzac's novels discussed on the shores of the Caspian, it was even more satisfactory to find that his own books were known and loved throughout the length and breadth of the Russian Empire. On the remote island of Valaam in the middle of

Lake Ladoga, at 61° latitude north, he visited a monastery where he had the honour of being received by the abbot who 'talked to me of the *Musketeers* and of *Monte-Cristo*, not as one who had read them, but as one who had heard them highly spoken of by people who had read them,'[8] while at Derbent in Dagestan, at 42° latitude, he was waited on by a deputation of Persians, one of whose number had read his novels in Russian translation and had retold them subsequently to his spellbound compatriots in the Iranian tongue, sitting with his back against a fig-tree in accordance with the immemorial fashion of story-tellers in the east.

Dumas's journey fell roughly into three parts. The first lasted from June 22nd, when he arrived in St. Petersburg, until October 21st, when he left Moscow and embarked at Kalyazin on the river boat that was to take him all the way down the Volga to its mouth. While at Petersburg he was the guest, naturally, of Count Kushelev and lodged at his summer residence, Bezborodko, on the right bank of the Neva; the palace still stands in modern Leningrad and has not changed its name, even though the city has. On their first night there, in spite of their tiredness, both he and Moynet sat out on the balcony, too ravished by the pearl-grey opalescent shimmer of the Petersburg summer night to think of going to bed. But by day, the city was a disappointment, with its badly paved roads and the ugly green of the roofs; and the crowds he saw moving along the sidewalks astonished him. They were more silent than ghosts drifting down the avenues of a necropolis on All Souls' Day. Even the little children walked gravely, neither chattering nor laughing, and the parks resembled the sad Elysian Fields as the Greeks imagined them, peopled by mournful shades.

So he was the more delighted to discover an old Paris friend in this lugubrious northern city with whom he could joke and flirt; this was Jenny Falcon, the younger sister of the much more famous Cornélie Falcon, the leading soprano of the Paris Opera, whom Dumas had known ever since Véron 'discovered' her in 1832. At that time, Jenny was a little girl of seven, looked after tenderly by her elder sister who made sure she was given as good an education as money could buy. At the age of sixteen, Jenny went on to the stage, and almost immediately received a handsome offer of employment in one of the big Petersburg theatres. She had stayed in Russia ever since, though she had now given up acting and was leading the life of a lady of leisure under the protection of a wealthy patron, Dmitri Naryshkin, whom Dumas refers to disrespectfully as 'an old Russian boyar'. The couple had delayed their departure from Petersburg long enough to make sure of seeing Dumas and persuading him to stay with them in their town house in Petrovsky Park when he came to Moscow.

He could not move on, of course, until after the wedding of Home and Alexandrine de Kroll which had been fixed for August 1st, and it was to fill in the time that he decided on an excursion into what was then the Russian province of Finland, a remote region rarely visited even by the most intrepid tourist; but, as Dumas said, 'when I am on my travels I prefer, even though I am gifted with the faculty of seeing differently from everyone else, to see what no one else has seen; it constitutes an additional guarantee of originality.'⁹ Acting on this principle, he decided against visiting Abo or Helsinki, since his friend Xavier Marmier had already been to these places and described them; instead, he headed for the eastern part of Finland (now absorbed into the U.S.S.R.), which is how it came about that this tireless lover of life celebrated his fifty-sixth birthday on the shores of Lake Ladoga, a vast and lonely stretch of water surrounded by impenetrable pine forests, where he feasted joyously with his companions on fat perch, black bread, and salad, all washed down with copious draughts of kvass.

The journey from Petersburg to Moscow was accomplished by rail. It was a shorter distance than from Paris to Marseilles but took eight hours longer; still, at least they had toilets at the ends of the carriages, a refinement as yet unknown on French railways. The only time the train speeded up a little was when they had to traverse a forest fire. The spectacle was magnificent—the sun was setting at the time—but it became unpleasantly hot in the unventilated compartment. He witnessed another fire in Moscow itself, one evening when by good luck Naryshkin had invited the chief of police to dinner. This official was obliged to interrupt his meal when word was brought him of the fire and rush down to the scene; Dumas begged a seat in his droshky, and so was able to watch everything at close quarters. What astonished him most was that the ordinary Muscovites made no effort whatsoever to help the firemen; in Paris, when a fire broke out, everyone formed a chain from the nearest fountain or the river itself, passing buckets of water from hand to hand. The police chief agreed that it might be a good idea to pass a law obliging the people to perform this service. 'We have no such law,' Dumas protested, 'but everybody joins in. When the Théâtre-Italien caught fire, I saw princes working on the chain.' 'My dear M. Dumas,' replied the official, 'that's what's called fraternity, and here in Russia we haven't yet reached the stage of fraternity.'¹⁰

Without liberty and equality, no fraternity. Dumas did not need to spend more than a few weeks in Russia before realizing that the long history of serfdom, which might account for the dead-and-alive appearance of the Petersburg townsfolk, meant that the country was totally different from any other, and almost impossible for a Westerner to understand. Superficially it was like any other European state, with at least a rudimentary railway system, a modern army, a French-speaking upper class—but all this was just the façade. 'Whoever tries to look behind the façade is like a cat, seeing itself in a mirror for the first time, and walking round the mirror expecting to find another cat on the other side.'[11] The French cat can only see its own reflection, while behind the façade the Russians live their own alien lives and think their own inconceivable thoughts.

The second part of his journey comprised a thousand-mile trip down the Volga to the delta on which Astrakhan is built. The first city of interest on the way was Nizhny-Novgorod, with its world-famous fair. It was here, in the governor's residence, that he met Annenkov and his French wife Louise, the hero and heroine of his novel *Le Maître d'armes*. The story he had related in that book was far from being pure invention; it had been told him by a certain fencing-master, Grisier, who had lived many years in Moscow and had known the unfortunate Annenkov before he was arrested, tried, and sentenced to hard labour in Siberia for his part in the Decembrist conspiracy. His mistress, a Parisian dressmaker who had opened a boutique in the Russian capital, had undertaken the dangerous winter journey across the Urals to join her lover, and it was this adventure that had provided Dumas with the bare bones of his plot, fleshed out by the colourful details of Russian life supplied by Grisier. For a novelist to meet and talk to the real-life people he had depicted as imaginary characters in a story written eighteen years earlier must count as an occurrence quite without parallel in the history of literature.

At Kazan the Volga broadens and starts flowing due south towards the Caspian. His host in the city, a former aide-de-camp of the Tsar, suggested he should interrupt his progress down the river at Kamyshin and strike across country to visit the curious salt lake of Elton. So Dumas had his first sight of the South Russian steppes, particularly melancholy under the biting autumn winds. They rejoined their river steamer at the town called in those days Tsaritsyn, destined to be known the world over, under its new name Stalingrad, as the scene of one of the truly decisive battles in the Second World War, and now renamed, yet again, Volgograd. It was a relatively short, three-day journey from here to Astrakhan.

Dumas was now in Asia, among strange tribes, Tartars and Kalmucks, whom the Russians had conquered but not yet christianized. He spent an extraordinary two days as the guest of a Buddhist prince, feasting on raw fillet of horse, camel steak and roast bustard, hunting swans with falcons, and attending a wild horse rodeo.

The third and final part of his journey involved crossing from Baku, on the Caspian, to Poti on the Black Sea, following for the most part the southern slopes of the Caucasian mountains, with a six-week halt at Tiflis (Tbilis) where the French consul turned out to be an old friend whom Dumas had not seen since 1848. It was wild country, inhabited by nations only recently subjugated, and they had to be perpetually on their guard against brigands who specialized in kidnapping for ransom. There were deep rivers where, in the absence of fords or bridges, the horses had to be coaxed into swimming across, and it was sometimes hard to make out the road. Almost at the last stage of their journey, after leaving Kutaisi where, according to tradition, Jason finally located the Golden Fleece, Dumas got separated from the rest of the caravan. Without realizing it, he had attached himself to another party travelling in the opposite direction. By the time he discovered his mistake, night had fallen, he was lost in a trackless forest, with no firearms, and the howls of hungry wolves distinctly audible in the distance. He judged his best policy was to let the reins hang on his horse's neck, trusting to its instinct to lead them both to safety, and this is what, fortunately, the sagacious animal was able to do.

Having been persuaded to stay on at Tiflis in order to see the ceremonies marking the beginning of the Russian New Year (January 12th–13th), he not only had to renounce his original plan of making a detour to climb Mount Ararat, but arrived too late at Poti to catch the steamer on which he and his party had booked a passage back to France. There was nothing to do but wait there until another vessel called at the tiny port; the only accommodation was a room in one of the miserable huts that made up this primitive coastal settlement. But it was at Poti that he made the acquaintance of Vasili, a serving-man in his early twenties, who so impressed him by his alacrity, sobriety, and resourcefulness that Dumas finally asked him, through his interpreter, whether he would like to come to France and enter his employment. Vasili was overjoyed at the prospect, but explained that in order to leave the confines of the Russian Empire he would need a passport which could be delivered him only at his home-town of Gori, some two hundred miles distant; by the time he got back, some ship or other would have arrived and taken the travellers away. So Dumas wrote out a chit in which he stated that Vasili was attached to his service but that he had been forced to leave without him; he called on 'everyone whom he asks in my name—if my name inspires the wish to assist—to help him by all means possible to perform his journey.'[12]

Several weeks after his return to Paris, his cook-housekeeper woke him at six in the morning in a state of agitation, wanting to know what to do about a young man who could speak no Christian tongue but kept asking for 'Moossoo Doomah'. It was, of course, Vasili. With the help of the written recommendation Dumas had given him, he had travelled the whole two thousand miles from Poti to Paris, via Trebizond, Istanbul (where he had been holed up sick for a month),

Smyrna, Athens, and Messina, without ever needing money for his passage until he got to Marseilles, where the Turkish consul advanced him 61 francs 50 centimes for his third-class fare to Paris. Otherwise the entire journey had been paid for, it seems, solely by the prestige of Dumas's signature on a piece of paper.

XIV With the Redshirts

Journeying home from the Black Sea in February 1859, Dumas took advantage of a brief stop-over at the island of Siros in the Cyclades in order to commission a Greek shipwright to build him a schooner, to be called the *Monte-Cristo*. He had remembered reading in one of About's books—About being regarded as an expert on all matters connected with the Near East—that one could get a small vessel built at Siros for half what it would cost in France. Moreover the craftsmen there, being direct descendants of the men who fitted out the fleet that took the Achaeans to Ilium, could be expected to know their business. True, it had taken Odysseus ten years in one of those ships to reach Ithaca from Troy, but he had had a few mishaps on the way, and in any case Dumas did not want a racing yacht; the *Monte-Cristo* needed to be tough, manoeuvrable, and to have a shallow enough draught to thread its way through the shoal-dotted waters of the Eastern Mediterranean.

It was natural enough, perhaps, that after the longest land-journey he had ever accomplished, Dumas should be yearning—his wanderlust still unassuaged—for a long sea-voyage. The sea always held a special fascination for him; not the sea viewed from a rocky shore or some high cliff on Guernsey, as Hugo was content to view it, but as seen from the deck of a small sailing vessel cradled in its bosom. It was only when far from the sight of land, on a gently creaking, gently dipping craft, with the topsails fluttering merrily in the breeze and the bright sea sparkling on the waves, that Dumas could ever take a complete rest from his endless round of work and amusement.

I who, whether in Paris or in the country, reproach myself for spending an hour away from my dear writing-paper, from my own good table, from my ink which flows so easily from the nib of my pen, at first I remain idle on board not for an hour, but for hours, not for a day, but for days. And without a second of lassitude, of weariness, or ennui. As soon as my sight is lost in immensity, my thought gives place to a dream; I dream of what? God knows—of the infinite, of the worlds rolling above me, of the sea sparkling below me. Then there falls on my senses a delightful twilight, different from but as sweet as the dawn of day or the evening light, something that smokers of opium and eaters of hashish can alone understand—that voluptuous absence of the will.[1]

Even when contemplating an inland sea, the Caspian, the memory of his voyage in Captain Arena's diminutive lugger, back in 1835–6 when they circumnavigated Sicily, visiting Pantelleria in the south and the Aeolian Islands in the north, returned to haunt him and inspire him with renewed nostalgia. He had no love for Ralph Hodgson's 'mighty ships ten thousand ton'. He liked to feel the heaving sea under his feet, 'and it has seldom happened that, leaning over the gunwale of the vessel that held me between the vast, swaying skyline of the ocean, I have not been able to stretch out my hand and stroke the foamy tresses of the waves . . .'[2]

The most hazardous of all these remembered voyages was the one he undertook in 1842 with the young Prince Napoleon, the son of Napoleon I's brother Jérôme, to visit Elba. They used the prince's travelling coach to reach Leghorn from Florence, but could find no ship in port that was sailing to Portoferraio, the chief town in Elba. So they hired one of the small fishing boats in the harbour and had themselves rowed over, encountering on the way a thunderstorm that tossed their frail bark mercilessly for three hours. Finding nothing of interest to detain them in the island over which Prince Napoleon's uncle had briefly ruled, they decided to row on to Pianosa for the shooting; but they found only partridges and rabbits. One of the boatmen suggested they should sail on further, to another island said to be overrun by wild goats. Its name? The Island of Monte-Cristo. 'It was the first time, and in this fashion, that the name of Monte-Cristo sounded in my ears.'[3] The distance, though twice as great as from Elba to Pianosa, took them only a few hours, for it was a fine morning and there was a favouring breeze. In contrast to the flat surface of Pianosa, Monte-Cristo rose menacingly out of the sea in the form of a single, conical shaped mountain surrounded by a rocky foreshore; and it proved to be uninhabited except, possibly, by the goats, who were left undisturbed however, for in the end Dumas and his companion decided not to land but simply circle round the island before returning to Leghorn.

A dream he had cherished for almost half his life was to acquire a trim yacht and, with a few chosen companions, all witty and some fair, explore the whole of the Mediterranean of which he knew, properly speaking, only the Tyrrhenian Sea. The idea had first taken shape back in 1834. Encouraged by the success of his travel-book on Switzerland, he had consulted a couple of experts, Amédée Jaubert and Alexandre de Laborde, and with their help drawn up an itinerary for a long voyage to include Corsica, Sardinia, Sicily, Greece, Turkey, Palestine,

Egypt, the North African coast and Spain. He issued a 'prospectus' and petitioned the Ministry of Public Instruction for financial support on the grounds that it was a mission of outstanding cultural importance. On August 4th, 1834, he discussed the project with an old friend of his father's, Baron Thiébault, at a social gathering in the *salon* of the Duchesse d'Abrantès. His intention was, he said, to recruit five like-minded young men, explorers, artists and scientists; he hoped to have a sailing vessel put at his disposal by the government, who would also undertake to subscribe to 800 copies of the handsomely illustrated book that he would write on his return; this should enable them to meet the costs of the expedition. What struck the baron most in all this was less Dumas's enterprising spirit than his insufferable cocksureness, especially when he ended the conversation with the words: 'In any case, I need to get out of Paris; the women here don't leave me any time for my work.'[4]

This grandiose scheme failed in the end to obtain government backing, and Dumas was reduced to undertaking, out of his own resources, and with Jadin as his sole companion, the journey through the Two Sicilies subsequently related in the three travelbooks *Le Speronare*, *Le Capitaine Aréna*, and *Le Corricolo*. But he never quite gave up the idea of a long-term expedition, taking in Greece, Turkey, Palestine, and Egypt, and in 1859, while he was still in Russia, an unexpected windfall made it appear that, at long last, he might have sufficient funds to carry out the whole of the voyage originally planned. Michel Lévy agreed to advance him the sum of 120,000 francs in exchange for the right to republish his complete works; and the first step Dumas took was to commission the construction of the schooner *Monte-Cristo* at Siros.

After some unlucky delays, the vessel was completed and brought to Marseilles in ballast. Dumas was less than enchanted when he saw her, judging her lines to be rather more those of a sturdy old tub than the elegant craft he had mentally pictured. Moreover, she still needed fitting out, and he could foresee breakers ahead when it came to getting her properly registered so that he could sail under the French flag. On a visit to Rome, he mentioned these difficulties and disappointments to his old friend the Duc de Gramont, French ambassador to the Vatican, who told him immediately that he—or rather, a friend of his—had just the ship he wanted, 'an entrancing little yacht, 78 tons, built at Liverpool, made of mahogany and maple, copper-bottomed—in short a marvel.'[5] It was registered under the name *Emma* and was lying at anchor in Marseilles harbour. The present owner, who could not use it, would probably part with it at a considerable sacrifice.

Dumas went straight from Rome to Marseilles, viewed the *Emma*, and fell in love with her. 'A most charming *goélette* [schooner], graceful

7

in her slim lines—elegance and an aristocratic appearance everywhere, a true sea-bird . . . Everywhere she revealed the talent of the English builder, who had succeeded in every detail—comfort above all.'[6] The owner accepted his offer of 13,000 francs and at 9,000 francs he found a buyer for the unwanted *Monte-Cristo* which had cost him, all told, about 30,000; so rather more than a quarter of Michel Lévy's advance was gone already, but at least he had the right ship.

He signed on a skipper, an experienced Breton sailor called Beau-grand, and left it to him to engage the crew. Then he started to look round for congenial fellow travellers. He found an interpreter, a Greek called Théodore Canape who spoke Turkish and French beside his native language; a doctor to act as ship's surgeon; and a photographer, Legray, of whose work Dumas thought highly. By now, of course, photography had displaced sketching as a means of providing visual record of a voyage of exploration.

He decided further to take Vasili with him as his valet. After his almost miraculous arrival from Poti, Dumas had made him dress up in his gorgeous native Georgian costume instead of the usual sober clothes worn by manservants, with the result that Vasili was generally regarded by the Parisians as, at the very least, a high-ranking Russian officer to whom Dumas was extending temporary hospitality. Des-patched ahead of the others to Marseilles to make preliminary arrange-ments for the journey, Vasili, thanks to his dignified bearing and a trick he had of giving slightly ambiguous answers to the questions put to him, conveyed the rough impression that he was a Georgian prince who had graciously offered to take Dumas on a cruise with him.

The complement was made up of three other young people. Edouard Lockroy, whose father, an actor-playwright, had been known to Dumas in his youth, was travelling for his education—the young man was studying for a career in the fine arts. Next there was Paul Parfait, the grown-up son of the secretary who had rendered him such devoted service in Brussels. And finally there was Emilie Cordier, the only woman on board, referred to by the others, whether affectionately or mockingly is not certain, as 'the Admiral'.

She was a girl of twenty and like most of Dumas's mistresses had contrived an introduction to him in the hope of obtaining, through his patronage, a part in one of his plays. Her origins were of the humblest —her father had earned his living making the wooden pails used by water-carriers in those days when drinking water was still hawked through the streets of big cities. A delicate child, she was not sent out to work at as early an age as was customary among the class of poor artisans to which she belonged; as a result, she had time to read, and had devoured Dumas's novels. A friend of her mother's had taken her to see the great man in the weeks immediately before he left for Russia;

with her slight figure, fresh complexion and soft, fair hair she made a strong enough impression for him to remember to write to her on his return and suggest a further meeting. In appearance, she was not unlike Isabelle Constans when she was of the same age; but on closer acquaintance he discovered her to be quite different from her predecessor in at least two respects. She had nothing of Isabelle's acting talent; on the other hand, she was far more uninhibited in her love-making and cheerful company at all times. Dumas found her quite irresistible and decided, regardless of convention, to take her with him. Entering into the spirit of the adventure, she said she would join the ship's company as a midshipman, and designed her own uniform—for she had been apprenticed previously as a dressmaker—a fetching affair of mauve velvet with a blue and gold lanyard worn over the shoulder.

The *Emma* weighed anchor from Marseilles on May 9th, 1860, heading east along the French Riviera. Venice was the first city at which they were to make a prolonged stay, both Rome and Naples being barred them since Dumas was listed as an undesirable alien by the authorities in control of central and south Italy. After the stop at Venice, the plan was to cruise down the Dalmatian coast, visit Corfu and all the historical sites in the Peloponnesian peninsula and the isles of Greece, and then sail through the Sea of Marmara to reach Constantinople. After that, rounding the shores of Asia Minor, they would land in the Lebanon and make the obligatory pilgrimage to the hallowed places in the Holy Land. In Egypt they would sail up the Nile as far south as was feasible, after which these latter-day Argonauts would set their helm for the Pillars of Hercules along the barren coastline of Cyrenaica and Tripolitania.

How long the journey would take was left undetermined, but in 1849–51 Flaubert and Maxime Du Camp, who visited many of the same spots though they did not follow the same itinerary, had been away for twenty months, and it seems unlikely that Dumas and his friends could have accomplished their voyage in less time, especially since they were dependent on a small craft which, however good of its kind, was at the mercy of the winds and, especially in the Mediterranean, risked being becalmed for days on end as well as being blown miles off course in a storm.

It took them all of six days to reach Nice, where Dumas had arranged to spend a night with Alphonse Karr, an old friend who, some four years previously, had retired from the literary scene in Paris and was now engaged, like Candide, in cultivating his garden; there was a growing market for fresh fruit and vegetables among the increasing number of wealthy visitors who were now building villas on the Riviera. It was only six weeks earlier that Nice, together with Savoy, had been ceded to France as a result of some shrewd bargaining between

Victor Emmanuel II and Napoleon III; the talk between the two friends naturally embraced this topic, and Karr was able to show Dumas the text of the speech of protest against this transfer of territory made in the Turin parliament by Nice's most celebrated son, Giuseppe Garibaldi.

Garibaldi's name already meant a great deal to Dumas. His interest in the colourful career of the inventor of guerilla warfare can be traced back to 1849, when the story of Garibaldi's prodigious feats in rendering assistance to the Montevideans in their struggle against Argentinian overlordship was related to him by one of the leader's South American lieutenants, Colonel Pacheco y Obes. Dumas retold part of this story in his journal *Le Mois*, and the whole of it in a volume, *Montevideo ou Une Nouvelle Troie*, issued in 1850 and now a great rarity, since it was not included by Michel Lévy in his edition of Dumas's complete works.

Early in 1860, while he was still waiting for the *Monte-Cristo* to be fitted out for sea, he travelled to Turin expressly to meet Garibaldi, and his admiration for the man was if anything enhanced by personal contact. Garibaldi, at fifty-two, was an impressive figure, tall, broad-faced, with thin, fair hair touched with grey and a full red beard. Over his shirt he wore the poncho, a novelty imported from the land of the pampas. This first colloquy, which took place in a modest hotel room, was brief, but sufficed to fire Dumas with the ambition to write Garibaldi's life-story. He paid him a second visit in Milan, and persuaded the freedom fighter to lend him his manuscript diaries which he busied himself translating once he was back in Paris.[7]

It was while he was staying with Alphonse Karr at Nice that the electrifying news came through of Garibaldi's armed invasion of Sicily at the head of a small band of volunteer troops. Dumas weighed anchor immediately and made as fast time as he could to Genoa, where he hoped to get fuller information from the officers Garibaldi had left in charge of his headquarters at the Villa Spinola.

Prospects for the unification of Italy had never looked brighter than they did in 1860; the great question at issue was, under whose auspices this unification should take place. Count Camillo Cavour, the statesmanlike minister of the King of Piedmont, was manoeuvring to have his master assume control; at the same time he wanted to avoid a direct military confrontation with the Neapolitan king, Francis II, whose writ ran in Sicily as well as in that part of the peninsula that lay south of the Papal States. What would have suited Cavour best would be a spontaneous rising of Francis II's subjects against his rule, and it seemed that Garibaldi, who had worn the Piedmontese uniform but, having resigned his commission, could be regarded as a private citizen, might well be just the man to shake down the fruits of victory without putting Victor Emmanuel to the necessity of risking a large-scale war for the sake of Italian unity.

On the other hand there were those who, like Dumas, hoped to see the Bourbon monarchy in Naples, which Gladstone had in a famous phrase referred to as 'the negation of God erected into a system of government', replaced not by a constitutional monarchy administered in the first place from Turin, but by a federal republic on the American model. Republicanism had deep historic roots in Italy; in 1849 Garibaldi himself had defended the short-lived Roman Republic against a French expeditionary force, heroically though unavailingly, and in 1860 Mazzini and Crispi, the two principal proponents of Italian republicanism, saw him as the obvious instrument for the achievement of their aims.

There were a number of reasons why Sicily should have commended itself equally to Mazzini and Cavour as the ideal starting-point for a revolt against the Bourbon monarchy in Naples. It was an extremely backward country, divided up into large estates run along feudal lines by wealthy landowners; the peasantry, as Dumas had seen for himself when he traversed the island in 1834, lived in a state of chronic and desperate poverty,[8] while the working-class population of Palermo and Messina was seething with revolt. Disaffection had been smouldering in Sicily for at least a generation. During his first visit there, Dumas had been contacted by a group of *carbonari* in Palermo who had entrusted him with written plans for an insurrection to be headed by Leopold, Count of Syracuse, a brother of Francis II's predecessor, Ferdinand II, who occupied the throne of Naples at that time. Dumas took the document, stitched into the lining of his hat, to Naples and had a secret meeting there with the Count of Syracuse on the promenade of Chiaia. He showed him his lugger, standing out to sea, and offered to take him straight to Sicily. But in spite of his well-known liberal views, the Count was horrified at the idea of leading a revolt against his own brother, so that particular conspiracy was still-born. Dumas's life-long republican convictions partly account for the risks he was prepared to run in assisting the plotters, but in addition he had a particular, personal reason for wanting to do all he could to encompass the downfall of the Bourbons of Naples, for it had been Ferdinand I, the grandfather of Francis II, who had, he believed, been responsible for ruining his own father's health by the administration of slow poison while he was a prisoner of war between 1799 and 1801.

Dumas may have been none too clear about Garibaldi's real intentions in those fateful weeks of April and May 1860, and indeed the situation was confused. It was Mazzini's representatives, Crispi and Bertani, who were fomenting revolution in Sicily and urging Garibaldi to take charge of an expeditionary force and lead the liberation movement; yet Garibaldi regarded himself as a servant of Victor Emmanuel rather than a republican tribune. But for Dumas these were political niceties; the cause was the freedom of Italy, and Garibaldi was a man whom he would follow, as he said, to the moon, if it occurred to Garibaldi to launch an expedition in that direction. The leader had promised to let him know when he might join him, and Dumas settled down in Genoa to await the summons, working sixteen hours a day to complete his translation of Garibaldi's memoirs.

At first, there were wild and contradictory rumours. Garibaldi had sailed to Sicily with his famous thousand volunteers on May 5th. On May 23rd, five days after Dumas's arrival, Genoa was decked with flags when the story got about that Palermo had fallen to the revolutionaries. The report was premature; it was not until May 28th that Dumas heard from Bertani that the British consul at Palermo had telegraphed the news that the redshirts were inside the city. On the same day Dumas received the impatiently awaited telegram from Garibaldi: 'Ralliez-vous au canon! (Join me where the cannon roars!)'

With his ill-equipped force, short of rifles but above all of ammunition, Garibaldi had landed at Marsala where, miraculously, he encountered no serious opposition. Summoned by Crispi, the town council met and declared that the rule of the Bourbons was now abrogated in Sicily; they further invited Garibaldi to assume provisionally the office of Dictator. Four days later, at Calatafimi on the road to Palermo, Garibaldi's men, using their bayonets, won a victory over a superior force of Neapolitans and then, helped by an insurrection inside Palermo, succeeded in entering the city despite the fact that it was defended by 20,000 troops with heavy artillery. The Neapolitans retired to a nearby fort from which they carried out a sporadic bombardment of the city until, on June 6th, they finally capitulated.

Dumas and his friends did not arrive until June 10th, having had a difficult crossing to Palermo. A violent storm had swept the *Emma* round the west coast of Corsica; they were forced to make landfall in Sardinia, not far from the isle of Caprera which Garibaldi had acquired as a private estate. When finally he set foot on Sicilian soil, and saw the barricades in the streets of Palermo, Dumas was vividly reminded of Paris as it had looked in the aftermath of the 1830 revolution. Apart from the visual similarities, there were political analogies too, for once again it was a Bourbon monarch whose throne was tottering as the result of a popular rising, and Garibaldi's position was akin to that of La Fayette—another soldier who had won his spurs on the American continent fighting for the cause of freedom.

The first acquaintance he met was Garibaldi's son Menotti, who offered to take him to his father. It was a joyous reunion. 'My dear Dumas, how I have longed for your coming!' exclaimed the general and, putting his arm round his neck, set off with him to the Pretorian Palace where he had established his headquarters, with Dumas's two companions, Paul Parfait and Edouard Lockroy, bringing up the rear. Dumas introduced them once they were indoors and Garibaldi invited all three men to join him and his staff for lunch—a frugal collation consisting of roast veal and Dumas's least favourite vegetable dish, sauerkraut.

According to one of Garibaldi's officers, Giuseppe Bandi, who left his own account of this reunion,[9] Emilie Cordier was also present at this lunch, wearing her midshipman's uniform. Apart from Dumas's own statement that 'twelve of us sat down to table' of whom only three, himself, Lockroy, and Parfait, were guests,[10] it does seem inherently unlikely, given the code of male protectiveness current at the period, that he would have taken her ashore immediately on arrival in Palermo and before making sure that street fighting had ceased. Possibly Bandi was confusing the occasion with a slightly later one, when Garibaldi held a banquet to celebrate the series of victories that had culminated in the capture of the principal city in Sicily. Henri Rochefort, the journalist who, as we have seen, started his career as a member of the staff of Le Mousquetaire, describes this banquet in his memoirs, relying on the account given by a friend of Nino Bixio, one of Garibaldi's senior officers. The general placed Dumas on his left and Emilie on his right, next to Bixio. If we are to believe Rochefort, whose account is of course third-hand rather than second-hand, Emilie appeared this time in woman's dress and was introduced by Dumas as his daughter. Bixio, who had spent much more of his life in France than had Garibaldi, realized at once from her speech that Dumas's companion, daughter or not, was no lady, and had a hard time of it throughout the meal covering up for her incongruous solecisms.[11]

One imagines that Garibaldi's officers may have been more than a little jealous of the marks of esteem and affection their leader showered on this foreign civilian, with his loud voice and expansive gestures, who suddenly appeared on the scene after the victory was won, trailing a pert little camp-follower behind him. The 'Thousand' included no more than a handful of non-Italians, among them Paul de Flotte whom Dumas had got to know during the 1848 revolution and whom he met again, not at this time but a few weeks later, at Messina. Paul de Flotte had much to complain of in the way his fellow volunteers were treating him. 'The General had been kindness itself to him; but the fact that he was a Frenchman was sufficient to arouse the antipathy of ignorant people towards him.' 'Italy,' concluded Dumas, 'in respect of fraternal feelings for other nations, has a long way to go.'[12] Tragically, De Flotte was killed, only a week after this meeting, in one of the engagements on the heights of Aspromonte.

Dumas spent in all ten days at Palermo, comfortably lodged in the suite of the former governor of the province. Then, hearing that Turr was to lead an expedition into the hinterland to ascertain that no Neapolitan troops were lurking there, he asked for permission to accompany them; Beaugrand would take the *Emma* round the island and await their arrival at Agrigento. Before leaving, he presented Garibaldi with a photographic portrait, one of the many executed by Legray, with an inscription that tells us much about Dumas's rose-tinted view of the future of Italy and of the role that he imagined Garibaldi playing: 'Avoid Neapolitan daggers; become the head of a republic; die as poor as you have lived; and you will be greater even than Washington or Cincinnatus.'[13] Garibaldi made no comment at the time; but, privately, he must have known how remote were the chances of his ever becoming first President of the United States of Italy, even supposing such an ambition had ever stirred him.

In the journey across Sicily from north to south, they followed roughly the same route as Dumas had taken, in the reverse direction, in 1834. It was as uncomfortable a march as it had been then, with the mosquitos biting by day and the fleas by night. In all the towns and villages they passed through—Misilmeri, Alia, Caltanissetta, Canicatti —the enthusiasm of the inhabitants was evident, but the temperature was in the hundreds. It was possibly at this point that Emilie, wilting in the heat, confided to Dumas that she was pregnant—a fact she may have suspected even before they embarked at Marseilles. The news caused him to wonder seriously about his future plans. Should he continue his journey to the Near East, risking the possibility of having her confined in some God-forsaken spot in Greece or Turkey? Besides, he felt more and more reluctant to leave the theatre of operations. Garibaldi, he knew, was intent on overrunning the garrison at Messina, where the last remnants of Neapolitan troops were holed up; and after that, he would no doubt cross the water again and storm Naples itself in order to drive Francis II finally out of his dominions. Dumas knew that, however many recruits were now flocking to the banners of the redshirts, they were badly short of weapons, firearms in particular. Finally he made up his mind and, having joined up with Menotti in Agrigento, gave him a letter for his father in which he reported what he had seen in his journey through the interior of Sicily: 'enthusiasm and good-will for the struggle everywhere, but no arms. Shall I leave for France and bring some back? Just a word from you to the *poste restante* at Catania, and I shall give up my voyage to the East . . .'[14]

Not all his party, however, shared his eagerness to see Garibaldi's campaign through to its triumphant conclusion. Legray had had enough of taking pictures of shelled streets and bearded redshirts. The doctor, Albanel, similarly intimated his unwillingness to continue, which made it all the more urgent to get Emilie back to France where she could have proper care. Finally Lockroy, bitterly disappointed at being robbed of the chance to see the Orient, decided to join Ernest Renan who was heading a government sponsored archaeological expedition to Phoenicia and Palestine.

Dumas left the malcontents at Malta, where they would have no difficulty in finding transport to their respective destinations, and then turned back to Sicily. At Catania, his first port of call, the citizens gave him a great welcome, serenading him from a flotilla of small boats bobbing up and down round the *Emma*. After the concert was over, Dumas put on his own show—a firework display, one of his well-wishers having presented him, before he left France, with a large case of Roman candles, catherine wheels and Bengal lights.

They sailed out of Catania harbour on July 17th, passed through the Straits of Messina on the 18th, and on entering the Bay of Milazzo were in time to watch the only action Dumas witnessed during the whole of the campaign: Garibaldi landing from a steamship with a small body of redshirts to capture the town, as a first step towards the final onslaught on Messina. Afterwards, Garibaldi consented to come aboard the *Emma*; they drank a toast to the liberation of Italy and talked of the newspaper Dumas hoped to found at Naples once the city was taken. He asked Garibaldi to suggest a name for this newspaper. 'Call it *L'Indipendente*,' he answered. 'It will deserve that fair name all the more if, for a start, it does not fear to attack me if ever I swerve from my duty as a son of the people or from my humanitarian principles.'[15] Garibaldi then boarded the British paddle-steamer that was to take him to Messina, while Dumas transferred to one of the regular French passenger ships plying between Italy and France.

He needed to go no farther than Marseilles to purchase the arms he had promised Garibaldi: 500 carbines and 950 rifles, with their ammunition. To settle the bill Dumas had to discount the three drafts on Constantinople, Smyrna and Alexandria that he had taken with him to finance his journey; but this considerable financial sacrifice, in so great a cause, cost him hardly a pang. The exploits of the 'Thousand', thanks partly to the dispatches Dumas had been sending to *La Presse*, were now ringing all round Europe, and cash contributions were flowing in; as he sat in a Marseilles café that evening, eating an ice, he was recognized by one of the other customers who immediately made a collection and emptied the contents of his hat on to Dumas's table; counting up the money, he was amazed to find that the sum came to no less than 620 francs.

By the time he was back in Messina with his shipment of arms Garibaldi had already left and no one seemed sure where he was nor where, exactly, he proposed to begin his assault on the mainland. Thinking it might be somewhere in the vicinity of Naples, Dumas instructed Captain Beaugrand to sail up the coast and on the morning

7*

of August 20th he dropped anchor off Salerno, a small fishing port about thirty miles south-east of Naples as the crow flies. The people there were overjoyed to see him, and celebrated his arrival much as they had in Catania; the shore buildings were illuminated, the town council came aboard, and Dumas treated the inhabitants to a firework display from the deck of his yacht. A regiment of royalist troops— chiefly Bavarians and Croats—was quartered on the town and their commander, General Scotti, drew them up in a wide semi-circle to block access between the harbour and the inland roads. These dispositions may have been intended to catch any agents Dumas might try to land, but more probably Scotti had been taken in by the rumour that Garibaldi himself was on board the *Emma*. The result was that his troops, instead of marching on Potenza to deal with an insurrection there, were tied up for two crucial days in Salerno.[16]

On the night of August 21st firm news came at last of Garibaldi's landing near Reggio di Calabre, at the toe of Italy, twenty-four hours earlier. Rather than sail back down the coast to link up with him, Dumas decided to moor the *Emma* in the Bay of Naples and await his arrival there. The ten days that followed, between August 24th and September 3rd, constitute perhaps the most extravagant episode of all in the history of Dumas's participation in the freedom fight. He did not dare risk going ashore, but equally the Neapolitan authorities, seeing he was flying the French flag, felt powerless to board the *Emma*. In any case, even among the King's closest advisers there was little real hostility towards Garibaldi. Liborio Romano, the Minister of the Interior, came aboard secretly one night and had a private conference with Dumas, as the result of which he was able to write to Garibaldi informing him that Romano was ready to go over to his side whenever the time should be judged ripe.[17] As a safeguard, should the minister's double game be discovered and necessitate sudden flight, Dumas visited Admiral Parkings on board H.M.S. *Hannibal* and got him to agree to give Romano asylum in case of need.

Beyond that, Dumas did everything in his power to foster pro-Garibaldian sentiments within the city and undermine the morale of those who still remained faithful to Francis II. He opened a fund among the townsfolk for the purchase of lengths of red cotton to make the shirts that were the uniform of Garibaldi's adherents, and at one point he had fourteen tailors sitting on deck busily cutting and stitching up the material. When the first hundred were ready, he got them distributed on the mainland by the ingenious device of finding four volunteers each of whom put on twenty-five shirts, one on top of the other. 'The thinnest of them looked enormous,' he commented happily; 'the others had lost all human resemblance; fortunately it was nighttime.'[18] He also used up the last of his fireworks, shooting off rockets and lighting up Roman candles to sustain the spirits of his supporters in the city. And all this time he was anchored close enough to the royal palace to see the King standing at his window with his telescope trained on the *Emma*.

Eventually Francis II decided he had had enough of this impertinence, and signed an order requiring the French vessel to leave the harbour without delay. Dumas was forced to stand out to sea and made his way south down the coast, hoping to have news of Garibaldi's exact whereabouts; then, failing to do so, he decided his best hope was to return to Messina to ship more arms and obtain precise information. Having reached his destination on September 8th he learned to his disappointment that he had missed the final act of the drama. On the 5th, as Garibaldi entered Salerno, the King had left Naples and taken refuge in the fortress of Gaeta. On receipt of a telegram from Romano, Garibaldi took the train from Salerno to Naples, making his entry the day before Dumas had stepped ashore at Messina.

There was nothing to do but to make what haste he could back to Naples. Unfortunately the *Emma* first ran into a storm, then into a dead calm, so that it took him four days to complete the return journey. He was met by Liborio Romano who took him immediately to the Palazzo d'Angri where Garibaldi had set up his headquarters. 'Here you are at last, God be thanked,' cried the victorious champion of liberty. 'You have made me wait long enough!'[19] Dumas was speechless; for the first time in his life, Garibaldi had used the familiar *tutoiement* in speaking to him, and he threw himself into his arms, weeping for joy.

xv The Last Fling

As recompense for the services he had rendered the cause of Italian unity, Dumas had, almost playfully, made two requests of Garibaldi: that when Naples was taken, he should be issued with a licence to shoot game in the Capo-di-Monti reservation; and that excavations at Pompeii should be started up again under his personal supervision.

Systematic digging to uncover the remains of this imperial Roman city, buried under ash and lava in the great eruption of Vesuvius in A.D. 79, had begun in 1763 and had continued in a leisurely and sporadic fashion ever since. Dumas had visited the site in 1835 and devoted six chapters of his travel-book, *Le Corricolo*, to a detailed account of everything that could be seen at the time both at Pompeii and at the neighbouring town of Herculaneum. But the Bourbon kings had seldom shown much interest in the work of excavation, and above all had rarely permitted foreign archaeologists to co-operate. Dumas intended to change all that. When Maxime Du Camp visited him in the Palazzo Chiatamone, the ex-King's summer residence which Garibaldi had assigned to him, he found him quite oblivious to the war still raging outside. With a large street-plan of Pompeii spread over the table, he would talk only of the amazing discoveries that could still be made if he could persuade a properly qualified team of French archaeologists and art-historians to join him, and if Victor Emmanuel would agree to place a company of sappers at his disposal to dig the trenches.

The official title conferred on Dumas was that of Director of Excavations and Museums of the City of Naples; Garibaldi had signed the order confirming him in this office on September 14th, 1860, just two days after Dumas's arrival in Naples.[1] It was understood that he would draw no salary, but he very soon discovered that the city council were disinclined even to make him a budgetary allocation, so that he found himself occupying a honorific post without the means of discharging the duties attached to it. The Neapolitans were none too pleased that a foreigner with no obvious qualifications should have been chosen for the job, and Du Camp witnessed a painful scene when some three hundred brawlers staged a demonstration one evening outside the palace, shouting for Dumas to be 'thrown into the sea'. Although Du Camp tried to make light of the incident, it was clear that Dumas was badly affected by it. 'I was accustomed to the ingratitude of France; I never expected the same thing of Italy,' he said, his cheeks wet with tears. 'All that labour lost and money thrown away—really they must have very warped characters if they want to kick me out now.'[2]

Another source of bitter disappointment was Garibaldi's prompt retirement from public affairs as soon as King Victor Emmanuel had taken possession of the former domains of Francis II. The romantically bearded guerilla-fighter and his royal master, personifying, some would say, the monkey and the cat that had pulled the roast chestnuts out of the fire for him, drove into Naples in a heavy rainstorm, sitting side by side in an open carriage, on November 7th. The following day Garibaldi ceremonially relinquished his dictatorship and before dawn on November 9th he took ship for his island home of Caprera, empty-handed save for a bag of seed-corn. Dumas had tried to dissuade him from taking this course: he was imitating Cincinnatus too closely. Far better to deny the Piedmontese monarch the fruits of victory and establish a federal republic in Italy. 'I am a republican and I believe you are too,' he declared in one of his letters to Garibaldi written during the short period between the capture of Naples and its cession to Victor Emmanuel. 'In public, we may talk about a constitutional monarchy, but our consciences urge us in the direction of a universal republic.' And in a letter written a few days later, after telling Garibaldi how high his credit stood in the city, he asked him wickedly: 'Do you want to be King of Naples? You have almost as good a chance as M. Murat [Joachim Murat, whom Napoleon placed on the throne of Naples in 1808], and a better one than King Victor Emmanuel.'[3] Even Dumas could never have seriously imagined that Garibaldi would accept a crown, but the sequel must, even so, have come as a blow to his hopes as it probably was to his pocket too; for whether Dumas ever recovered the 75,000 francs he spent on procuring arms for Garibaldi is open to doubt.

The year ended, however, with cheering news: on December 24th Emilie Cordier gave birth to a daughter, christened Micaella. The young mother rejoined him in Naples in February 1861, followed shortly by the wet-nurse and the baby. Dumas was delighted to dandle this diminutive child of his old age and talked of acknowledging his paternity in law; this would have put Micaella, when it came to dividing up his inheritance at his death, on an equal footing with Alexandre and Marie. However, he would not go so far as to regularize the situation completely by making an honest woman of Emilie, as it was open to him to do since Ida had died of cancer of the womb on March 11th, 1859, shortly after his return from Russia. Angrily, Emilie confronted him with the alternatives: either he married her, or she would refuse to certify the child was his, thus nullifying any legal steps he might take to have Micaella recognized as one of his rightful heirs. But whatever reasons Dumas might have had for contracting a first marriage, he would not commit the folly of contracting a second with 'the Admiral'. So she left Naples, taking the child with her, and found another lover with whom she settled down at Le Havre, presenting him in the course of time with twins. Dumas had no further dealings with her, though he continued to see Micaella as frequently as possible after his return to Paris.

This did not happen for another three years, however. What chiefly kept Dumas in Naples, after the collapse of his high hopes of major archaeological discoveries in Pompeii, was the editorship of the daily newspaper *L'Indipendente* which started publication on October 11th, 1860. It was printed partly in French and partly in Italian, but as far as can be ascertained every issue was written entirely by Dumas. Having free access to the royal archives, he was able to compose, and serialize in *L'Indipendente*, a history of Naples between 1804 and 1815 under the title *I Borboni di Napoli*—a complete misnomer, of course, since the throne was occupied at that period by nominees of Napoleon. His rummaging in state papers was also useful in bringing to light some surprising documentation concerning Nelson and the Hamiltons. The general outline of the story was known to him already, and he had re-told it in a chapter of *Le Corricolo*, written fifteen years earlier. But this new material enabled him to paint a much more detailed and picturesque canvas, which he began publishing on his return to Paris under the title *La San-Felice*. Never as well thought of in this country as in France, no doubt because of its critical presentation of a great national hero,[4] the novel, in spite of its inordinate length, made a big impact on the French reading public, and helped to reassure his admirers that his prolonged absence from the cultural capital of the world had in no way robbed the old magician of his spell-binding powers of literary invention.

Nor, apparently, had the passage of years diminished other powers for which he was famous among a more restricted circle. For Dumas did not return to Paris unaccompanied. Callers at his new address, 70, Rue Saint-Lazare, were introduced to a raven-haired, olive-skinned lady, no longer in her first youth, called Signora Gordosa, whom he had brought back with him to France in order, he said, to help her make her *début* as a singer at the Théâtre-Italien. At least he did not have it on his conscience that he had wrested her from her husband, whom she had in fact abandoned some time before. Finding himself unable to cope with her constant demands for proofs of his love, this gentleman—an Austrian baron, no less—tried to damp her ardour by compelling her to wear wet towels round her waist. One day she threw the towels away, changed her name, and joined the opera company at Naples, which was where Dumas first saw her. A closer acquaintance convinced her that with him for a lover, she would never need to moderate her transports.

All these intimate, not to say scabrous details, were confided by Dumas to his old friend Mathilde Schoebel, 'Little Briar', to whom much had happened since he last set eyes on her, that morning in Brussels when he received her and her mother dressed up as Mephistopheles. She had spent her girlhood in New Zealand, then returned to Belgium, finally moving with her mother to Naples, where she had married. Her husband had gone off to Russia, abandoning her and her child; at present she was in Paris, still with her mother, both of them hard up. Mathilde's first encounter with Fanny Gordosa had been, to say the least, disconcerting. A friend living in Marseilles had sent her a letter for Dumas, asking for it to be delivered directly into his hands. Overriding her mother's protests, she made her way to his place of residence where she had some difficulty in persuading the maid to carry word to Dumas that she needed to see him personally. Suddenly the door was flung open and what she describes as 'a white ball from which a smaller black ball emerged, with smouldering eyes', bounced in and, addressing her in a fine fury and with a pronounced Italian accent, asked her what she wanted with 'Dooma'. 'What do you want with me?' asked the astonished visitor, 'and who are you?' 'I am La Gordosa, and since you ask, I want you to leave Monsoo Dooma in peace. The poor man is sick, he don't need to see any other woman.'[5]

Dumas admitted she was a little eccentric but, he added with an indulgent smile, she had a heart of gold. Mathilde was to learn, as she got to know him better, that almost everyone in his wide circle of acquaintances, however outrageous their behaviour, had a heart of gold. In order to promote Fanny's professional interests, he had started giving musical *soirées* every Thursday evening, to which he invited Nestor Roqueplan, the director of the Paris Opera, and all the music critics and composers he knew. At a given moment the violins would be tuned, the concert would start, and Fanny's powerful soprano would be raised in a duet with some moustachioed tenor; without waiting for this to begin, Dumas took Mathilde by the arm and hastened upstairs with her to his study, leaving the others to 'caterwaul', as he said, in the drawing-room. He had absolutely no feeling for music at the best of times; 'noise substituting for thought', he called it.

The summer of 1864 was spent in a rented villa at Saint-Gratien, near Enghien, where he was able to renew his old friendship with Princess Mathilde Bonaparte whose country seat was within walking distance. The house he had taken was set in extensive grounds sloping down to the lakeside and, as years ago at Saint-Germain-en-Laye, Sundays normally brought their contingent of visitors, invited or

uninvited. 'Impossible, my dear fellow,' he was heard to say in answer
to one guest's request to be introduced to another. 'I haven't been
introduced to him myself!'[6] Fanny's uncertain temper did nothing to
contribute to the smooth running of the establishment. One Sunday
morning, when some twenty guests were expected for lunch, it was
discovered that she had dismissed the cook and indeed every servant
in the house, and only Dumas's culinary expertise saved the situation.
The cupboard was not quite bare; although no provisions had been
laid in, there were a few sacks of rice and two or three pounds of cooking butter left in the larder and, luckily, in one drawer, a plateful of
beautifully ripe tomatoes. With the light of genius kindling in his eye,
and putting to good use the parcel of ham and Bologna sausage that
one of the more thoughtful guests had brought along as an offering,
Dumas set to and within the hour had 'invented' the *risotto*, a dish
which, our informant tells us,[7] though widely known in America, had
never before made its appearance on a French bill of fare.

    Fanny Gordosa was not only irascible by nature but intensely
jealous, casting suspicious eyes—no doubt with good reason—on the
numerous young women who flocked to the house to flirt with her
lover: Eugénie Doche, starring in a revival of his son's *Lady of the
Camellias*; Aimée Desclée, whom he had admired at Naples where he
saw her acting in other, later plays by Alexandre; Blanche Pierson, a
blue-eyed, fair-haired picture of innocence whom Claudin thought
worthy of Greuze's brush and Banville of Leonardo da Vinci's;
Léonide Charvin, a gifted tragic actress who had followed the fashion,
instituted by Rachel, of borrowing stage-names from the Bible, and
was known on the playbills as Agar; tawny-haired Esther Guimont,
nicknamed 'the Lioness' for her boldness as much as for her appearance
—when asked her profession, in a police case where she had been called
as a witness, she replied: 'Courtesan', spelling the word out letter by
letter for the benefit of the scandalized clerk of the court. There were
even a few society ladies in the running, including one who had told
Dumas she would spend a night with him on condition he first presented her with a mongoose and an ant-eater. (The mongoose was not
too difficult, but where was he to get hold of an ant-eater, short of
burgling the Paris zoo?) Constantly on tenterhooks, her nerves frayed
by incessant alarms, La Gordosa finally made a scene in public when
she discovered Dumas in amorous dalliance at the back of a theatre
box. He gave her enough money to pay her fare back to her native
land and hoped he had seen the last of her.

    In the social history of France the late Second Empire counts as one
of those periods when, as under the Regency at the beginning of the
eighteenth century and the Directory at the end, the balance normally
maintained between the extremes of puritanism and licence was danger-

ously tilted towards the latter, at any rate in the capital. It was a time
of hectic gaiety, culminating in the carnival of Exhibition Year, 1867,
whose best-advertised products were the can-can, Offenbach's operettas,
and the expensive ladies of pleasure, Hortense Schneider, Cora Pearl,
Blanche d'Antigny and others scarcely less notorious, who could be
seen every day driving along the boulevards in their luxurious *huit-
ressorts*. Dumas was certainly not the only grizzled sexagenarian to be
swept up by this wave of sensual indulgence, so soon to break against
the humiliation of national defeat and to be replaced by the 'Ordre
moral' of the 1870s. Perhaps he was a little more open in the pursuit of
pleasure than most, being a man to whom cant and affectation had
always been foreign. 'Shame on you!' exclaimed the manager of
the Théâtre de la Gaîté, coming upon Dumas during an interval in the
dress-rehearsal of *Les Mohicans de Paris* and seeing him sitting with the
youngest actress in the company on his lap and two others on either
side of him rumpling his hair. 'Shame on you! You're past sixty, you're
too old even to marry.' As usual, Dumas was equal to the occasion.
'You're wrong, my dear fellow,' he retorted. 'Sixty is twenty times
three, which makes me twenty years old for each of these three young
ladies.'[8] The stereotype pen-picture of the ageing reprobate, for
circulation in Victorian Britain, was provided by the theatre critic
Clement Scott in his account of a visit he paid Dumas in 1868. Instead
of being received in the writer's study he found himself, to his horror,
taken down to the kitchen, there to behold 'the hero of hundreds of
dramatic successes, in his shirt sleeves, his negro skin beaded with
perspiration, his hair like an iron-grey scrubbing-brush reversed,
sitting before the fire with a pretty girl on each knee, pretending to
cook an omelet or preside over a vol-au-vent. . . . . The girls pinched
him, kissed him, chaffed him and called him "Papa". He returned the
compliment.'[9] As between the beaming Silenus with his frying-pan and
the tight-buttoned English gentleman amazedly eyeing him, each will
judge according to his principles and prejudices.

If there was one man thoroughly disconcerted by Dumas's embarrass-
ingly persistent vitality, it was his son, now one of the pillars of the
literary establishment and self-appointed guardian of public morality.
He would undoubtedly have preferred his harum-scarum father to
remain in Naples for the rest of his life, as his stepmother had
stayed in Florence. When he first reappeared the younger man used to
turn up at his parties with a little notebook in which he could be
observed jotting down all the most amusing remarks or interesting
observations that were made at table. Nothing, one imagines, could
have been more freezingly inhibiting. However, he stopped coming
when he got married, a step he had long wanted to take so as to put
an end to an irregular situation which had lasted for years and was oddly

similar to that existing formerly between Balzac and Eve Hanska. He had had a long-standing liaison with a Russian princess, Nadezhda Knorring; they had a child, a pretty girl called Colette who at the age of five could prattle charmingly in French, German and Russian. The bridegroom had, of course, invited both his father and his mother to the wedding, and this was how, on December 31st, 1864, Dumas and Catherine Labay met for the last time. The old lady was still living in the house at Neuilly that her son had secured for her with some of the proceeds of *La Dame aux Camélias*, and he would probably have regarded it as eminently fitting if, even at this late stage, his parents could agree to marry. But it was Catherine who proved recalcitrant. 'I am over seventy,' she wrote to one of her few remaining friends. 'I am not strong and I live very quietly, with just one maid. M. Dumas would be too much for my little house. The suggestion comes forty years too late.'[10] Not that she bore him any ill-will. She still set aside for him a few jars of jam, made every year from the fruit-trees in her garden, hoping as she said that the spongers would not eat it all.

Once settled into respectable domesticity, Alexandre avoided seeing his father as much as possible. They met, naturally, at Catherine's funeral (she died on October 22nd, 1868), and it may have been on his return from this inhumation that Dumas observed with grim humour to his secretary: 'I only ever meet Alexandre at burials and now, I dare say, I shan't see him again until my own.'[11] Disapproval of his father's dissolute way of life was only one reason for his coldness; another— never avowed—was professional jealously. Even now, he still found himself standing in his father's shadow; too many people thought of him not as the author of *La Dame aux Camélias* but as the son of the man who wrote *Les Trois Mousquetaires*. Félix Duquesnel, calling on him one day at the seaside villa in Puys that he had bought as a holiday home for his growing family, arrived just as a tall, bearded man, speaking French with a slight English accent, was taking his leave. Duquesnel, having noticed that Alexandre addressed him as 'Your Excellency', wanted to know who he was. 'The Marquess of Salisbury,' was the answer.[12] 'He just dropped in like that, paying me the first visit. "No one can expect Alexandre Dumas to wait to be introduced," said he, "so let me introduce myself. In any case I am your debtor. Your father's novels have always been my favourite reading matter and my principal relaxation . . . " '[13]

In contrast with the strained relations between father and son, those between father and daughter were much easier than they had been when Marie was trying to run the house for him in Brussels. Her marriage had not lasted long and, once Fanny Gordosa had left, she joined Dumas in his new establishment at 107, Boulevard Malesherbes, near the Parc Monceau, a very fashionable district at that period. She had left her husband, Pierre-Olinde Petel, on the grounds of his insanity; but Marie had her own eccentricities, which led the more uncharitable to wonder whether she herself was quite right in the head. The first room into which visitors were ushered resembled an oratory, with crucifixes and sacred pictures hung round the walls. The lady of the house, however, seemed to imagine herself the priestess of some pre-Christian religion. She dressed for dinner, when Dumas had company, in a long white woollen tunic, held at the shoulder by a gilded sickle; a great bunch of mistletoe was fastened at her breast and she wore a crown of mistletoe on her head.

Poor Marie had inherited little of her mother's graceful beauty; she was a dumpy woman with a swarthy complexion, mannish features and thick lips. She spent her leisure hours composing poetry of an ethereal and mystical nature which she was apt to recite at social gatherings. In 1867 she even got a novel published. Dumas was inordinately proud of this achievement, though ordinarily he despised woman novelists, even talented ones like George Sand. Shortly after its publication date he chanced to run into Emile Littré, the lexicographer, in one of the galleries of the World Exhibition, and started an animated conversation with him. After a while he suddenly exclaimed, reddening: 'But you haven't said a word, my dear sir, about the one literary event the whole of Paris is buzzing with.' Littré looked at him in puzzlement, whereupon Dumas flew into one of his rare, but terrible rages. 'You're insulting my daughter, pretending not to know of her first book, *Madame Benoît*,' he shouted and, turning on his heel, walked away, leaving the mild-mannered scholar dumbfounded.[14]

He was just as fond in a different way of his younger daughter, Micaella. She was a wan, frail, and waif-like creature, not at all pretty—unlike Dumas's granddaughter Colette—but she was passionately attached to her old father and the two of them presented a touching spectacle as he carried her proudly round the room on one of her rare visits, introducing her to all his guests; she clutching him tightly round the neck with one of her thin arms while pressing to her chest with the other the two new dolls that Marie had dressed for her.

The first few months back in Paris were enough to convince Dumas that everything was much as it had been and very boring; so he started casting around for ways and means of escaping abroad again. His hopes of ever seeing the East had now been abandoned, though there had been a brief period, during the succession crisis that followed Otto I's dethronement, when he thought of sailing to Greece and lending a hand in the establishment of a free democratic republic in the land that had seen the birth of democracy; but he missed his opportunity and the Greeks retained their monarchical institutions. The outbreak of the American Civil War, while he was in Italy, made him wonder about crossing the Atlantic, and he was still mulling over this possibility when, in the autumn of 1864, the tide of war started to flow strongly against the Confederates. Some of his friends who had contacts in the United States urged him to think seriously of touring the country and writing up his impressions; there could be no question, he was told, but that his views would command respect and attention on both sides of the Atlantic.

As a preliminary step, he got in touch with the head of the American consular service in Paris, John Bigelow, inviting him to come and discuss plans over lunch. Dumas was thinking in terms of a four months' stay which, Bigelow warned him, would be really too short if he wanted to see the country from coast to coast. Thinking of Thackeray's success as a speaker when he came to the United States in 1852, he suggested Dumas might consider a lecture tour rather than a simple sight-seeing visit. The following day (October 5th) he wrote pressing Dumas very strongly to carry out his plan, and with the minimum of delay; it was essential he should be in New York by November so as to witness the presidential election, and he ought to stay at least until the following March to attend the inauguration ceremony. Bigelow finished his letter with a little well-directed flattery:

> Your name is more universally known in the United States, I venture to say, than it is in France, for the proportion who read there is larger than here; and you would be sure of such a welcome from my country people as they have given to no Frenchman certainly except Lafayette. Nor can I conceive of anything better calculated to preserve the traditional friendship of our two countries, which has been subjected to some severe trials during the past three years, than a report from such a witness of the memorable events occurring on the other side of the Atlantic.[15]

Bigelow also wrote to his superiors at home, stressing the advantages that might accrue from Dumas's presence in America at that particular juncture, but not concealing, either, the difficulties that might arise. On the credit side, one had to take into consideration that 'there is no living writer sure of a larger audience in France than Dumas; he reaches a class who do not read political journals much. He is a republican in all his sympathies, as he has shown in his writings and recently in his Italian experiences. He is universally beloved by all who know him and has not an enemy in the world. He will make the most readable book about America that was ever written . . .'. But on the debit side, there was firstly the question of his black ancestry. 'He has been in doubt, I judge from a remark he made to me, whether we had sufficiently conquered our negrophobia to receive a person of mixed blood as he is accustomed to be received in France, for here and throughout Europe Dumas is one of the great powers.' And in the second place, 'he is a man whose domestic arrangements are—to put it modestly—extremely French. To illustrate—when I asked him if he spoke English, "No," he replied, "I read it and translate it, but I can't speak it; but my mistress is English and I shall pick it up very soon." '[16] That Dumas had an English mistress at this time—or at any other time —is a circumstance unrecorded anywhere else.

William Seward, at that time Secretary of State in Lincoln's administration, replied to this letter on October 22nd, intimating that he would be 'glad to receive M. Dumas, and to contribute all in my power to make his sojourn here profitable and pleasant to him'.[17] But in spite of the very considerable interest the Americans displayed, the proposed visit never took place, probably because Dumas found it difficult to lay his hands on the necessary cash to pay his travelling expenses, while the economic strains of the Civil War precluded all possibility of a subvention from the United States Treasury.

His last journey abroad was made two years later, immediately after, and largely in consequence of, the brief war between Prussia and Austria fought in 1866. One of the many territorial gains made by Prussia in the ensuing peace settlement was Hanover, the original home of the British royal dynasty. The exiled ruler of Hanover founded a newspaper in Paris the same year, primarily as a propaganda sheet to urge his claims to repossession of his kingdom. The editor of this paper decided to enlist Dumas's help and asked him to undertake a tour of the battlefields, including that of Langensalza, where the Hanoverian army was forced to surrender to the Prussians, and Sadowa, where the Austrians sustained so crushing a defeat. However, he did not want a simple account of this journey but rather, having in mind Dumas's unfailing success as a writer of fiction, a novel based on the recent events, for which he even furnished the title: *La Terreur prussienne*. Dumas accepted the commission and constructed his plot round the adventures of a patriotic young Frenchman who has a series of encounters, in all of which of course he emerges victorious, with Francophobe German bullies. Though obviously written to order, the book provides one further instance of Dumas's political perspicacity, for at a time when very few of the French were inclined to take Prussian sabre-rattling very seriously, he did his best in these pages to warn them of the rampant and almost pathological hatred of France widespread beyond the Rhine and to alert them to the imminent danger of a German war of aggression. As usual, he proved a Cassandra, and when the invasion did take place in 1870 he was already too ill to realize how accurate his predictions had been.

La Terreur prussienne was the last piece of fiction and almost the last work of any kind Dumas published, apart from volumes made up of articles written many years previously. His inventive genius was flagging and, as his fluency as a writer began to fail, so his income shrank. As early as July 25th, 1866, Mme Letellier (i.e. his sister Alexandrine-Aimée, widowed since 1857) registered a complaint that the allowance her brother had been making her was no longer coming through. By the beginning of the following year, it was obvious that Dumas was finding the greatest difficulty in meeting his own household expenses; the rent on the apartment was overdue, the servants had had no wages for several weeks, and tradesmen's bills were mounting up. His account with Michel Lévy was overdrawn, and the few valuables he still possessed were finding their way to the pawnshop. Finally, he was reduced to asking his secretary, Victor Leclerc, to call on his son and beg the occasional small loan—never refused, but never gladly given.

It was at this point of deep crisis that whatever providence it was looked after this feckless but amiable hedonist sent him one final consolation, in the shape of a high-spirited, warm-hearted, radiantly immodest daughter of New Orleans whom the world knew as Adah Menken, the 'Naked Lady'.

Having started life as a ballet-dancer, a bit-part actress, a sculptor's model, and a bare-back rider in a circus, she owed this flashy sobriquet, at once tantalizing and misleading, to a chance engagement in 1861 at a theatre in Albany, the capital of the State of New York. The management was staging a revival of an old play based on Byron's narrative poem *Mazeppa*, which tells of the fearful punishment visited on a young Polish nobleman discovered in adultery with the wife of a local magnate; he was stripped and tied with ropes to the back of a wild horse which was then allowed to gallop off into the forest. The actor who normally took this part had fallen ill, and the impresario, realizing the excitement that would be caused if a beautiful woman was shown bound naked to the horse's back, persuaded Adah to stand in for him. Although she was not actually naked, but covered from thighs to neck in a pink silk leotard, the effect none the less was sufficiently striking to arouse a powerful thrill of suppressed sadistic interest in the audience.

It may seem extraordinary that, on the strength of this one stunt act, Adah Menken should have reached the pinnacle of fame not just in the eastern United States but subsequently in California too. In San Francisco her nightly performances in the Opera House drew far bigger crowds than ever the works of Verdi or even Offenbach had done. She was feted by the intellectual élite—including Bret Harte and Mark Twain—no less than she was damned by the spokesmen for conservative morality. For Charles Warren Stoddard, she represented

'the embodiment of physical grace' with 'the lithe sinuosity of body
that fascinates us in the panther and the leopard when in motion'.
There was nothing lewd or even suggestive in her performance, he
claimed. 'She was a vision of celestial harmony made manifest in the
flesh—a lovely and breathing poem that set the heart to music and
throbbed rhythmically to a passion that was as splendid as it was pure.'
Against this view must be set the strictures of the newspaper editor
who wrote that 'her exhibitions are immodest and overdrawn carica-
tures, unfit for the public eye; degrading to the drama whose temples
they defile; a libel upon women whose sex is hereby depraved and
whose chastity is corrupted'.[18]

Her decision to come to Europe was dictated only in a minor degree
by the desire to add good English sovereigns and French napoleons
to the store already amassed of eagles minted from new-mined Californian gold. Adah was anything but mercenary; she was a woman of
courage and charm, who also possessed a genuine, if minor literary
talent and had written quantities of impassioned, melancholy verse,
strongly influenced by the work of Walt Whitman to whom she had
been introduced in New York. Her primary purpose in coming to
England in the summer of 1864 was to persuade one or other of the
literary pundits over here to sponsor an edition of her poetry. She
met, and cast her spell over, Dickens and Charles Reade, and embarked
on a somewhat unsatisfactory love-affair with Swinburne. Then at the
end of the year she paid a hurried visit to Paris, hoping above all to
see Dumas. He was out of town, however, and she had to content herself with Théophile Gautier, with whom she conferred over possible
plays in which she could make her début in France. One was eventually
concocted for her by Anicet Bourgeois and Ferdinand Dugué: *Les
Pirates de la savane*, a worthless melodrama devised simply to give her
an excuse to appear on stage in her customary scant garb riding a
mettlesome horse. The opening performance, on December 31st, 1866,
was a stunning success. No American artiste had ever produced such an
electrifying effect on the Parisian stage. There was a short-lived
'Mazeppa craze': men wore hats in imitation of hers and young
women had their hair cut short and frizzed, Menken-style. The excitement eventually drew Dumas to the theatre; Adah, advised that he
would be there, recognized him by his ample silhouette looming in
the wings and went up to greet him. Her French was halting, his
English non-existent, but they held some kind of a conversation after
which he gave her the ritual kiss on the cheek that he never failed to
bestow on every good-looking actress he met.

She had, however, made a far stronger impression on him than any
woman had for some years, and he soon found that she filled all his
waking thoughts. Flattered, she gave him what time she could spare

from her professional obligations; they were to be seen walking arm in arm through those parts of old Paris spared by Haussmann's demolition workers, with Dumas eloquently holding forth on the history and legend of the various buildings, squares and monuments past which their wanderings took them. On Adah's side, satisfied vanity and a genuine interest in what he had to tell her probably counted for more than any passion her corpulent adorer can have aroused in her. Be that as it may, she was too honest a woman to have refused to respond to his. Alexandre, paying one of his rare visits to his father, was scandalized to find the pair of them locked in a close embrace, with Adah wearing even less than she was accustomed to on the stage of the Gaîté. He stormed out, after expressing his indignation in a few biting words, and when, some days later, a mutual friend asked Dumas whether he had seen anything of his son recently, he replied with lordly disdain: 'No. I prefer not to. He misses no opportunity to be disrespectful to me.'[19]

One of Adah Menken's weaknesses was to have herself photographed alongside the literary celebrities whose conquest she had made. Dumas readily consented to oblige her in this and, along with formal groupings of a kind no one could take exception to, he permitted the photographer to take a number of much more intimate studies where he and Adah were shown together in various languorous and suggestive poses. These were intended, of course, for his own album; but the photographer, doubtful whether the impecunious author would ever settle his bill, decided to recover his costs by printing a quantity of these more improper portraits and selling them to the boulevard art shops for public display. The scandal was enormous, and was prolonged by a suit for damages—which he won—entered by Dumas against the offending photographer. For a few weeks, there was talk of little else in Paris. Young Verlaine wrote a clever but highly offensive triolet about 'Uncle Tom and Miss Adah' and *La Vogue parisienne* was so outspoken in one of its articles that Dumas sent his seconds round to the newspaper office and Alexandre had to intervene to prevent a duel.

Public ridicule, though it had no effect on the continuing popularity of Adah's performances at the Théâtre de la Gaîté, destroyed the charm of her relationship with Dumas. She continued, however, to treasure the memory of the few weeks of passionate friendship they had enjoyed, as witness the fulsome words she used in a letter she wrote from Vienna to her old friend Stoddard, enclosing an autographed postcard from Dumas: 'Value it for his sake, as well as for the sake of the poor girl he honours with his love. Oh! I wish you could know him. You could understand his great soul so well—the King of Romance, the child of Gentleness and Love.'[20]

After this last, wild adventure, so miserably ended, Dumas fell into a kind of listless lethargy, painful to witness for those who had known him formerly, when his store of physical energy and his fund of brilliant conversation seemed inexhaustible. Arsène Houssaye, who in 1868 inaugurated his celebrated 'Venetian nights'—supper parties at which the women, but not the men, were allowed to wear masks to preserve their anonymity—recalls how sad it was to see Dumas moving silently among the laughing guests, smiling at the women but no longer able to compliment them or tease them as he used to. At home he would lapse into moods of black melancholy, and Pifteau, one evening, distressed to see him so dejected, asked him what had happened to bring on this depression. 'Why,' answered Dumas heavily, closing his eyes and uttering one of the two aphorisms with which he permanently enriched the French language: 'The trouble is, *tout passe, tout lasse, tout casse*.'[21] The time had arrived when, in the words of his favourite English poet, 'the sword outwears its sheath, And the soul wears out the breast'. He would still sit in his study, hour after hour, but no longer engaged in writing; all he could do now was to reread the works he had written in his prime. 'Each book,' he would say, 'calls back to my memory a day long fled. I am like one of those leafy trees full of birds which are silent at noon but wake up towards the end of the day; when the evening comes they will fill my old age with the rustling of wings and with song.'[22]

His health, which had triumphantly withstood all the hardships of travel and the strains of overwork, now showed unmistakable signs of rapid deterioration. The distension of his abdomen led the doctors to suspect incipient dropsy. He was shaky on his legs, but the most disturbing symptom of all was the uncharacteristic torpor that caused him to sit for hours in his armchair, inertly dozing. About the last contract his secretary, Victor Leclerc, managed to secure for him was for a dramatization of one of his late novels, *Les Bleus et les Blancs*, a tale of the revolutionary wars. He drafted the play with something of his old speed and skill, but when one of the members of the cast paid him a visit to discuss certain production details, he saw Dumas close his eyes in the middle of a sentence and drift off to sleep. The actor waited respectfully till he woke up again and was able to resume the conversation.

In June 1869 Marie grew so alarmed at the gravity of the symptoms that she called her brother in for consultations. The doctor, uncertain how to treat his patient, suggested a change of air, and Dumas was accordingly put on the train to Roscoff along with his cook, one of the few servants still in his employ. Unfortunately she was so disgusted at the poor quality of the vegetables obtainable in Brittany that she abandoned her master and returned to Paris almost immediately. Learning of his plight, the good-hearted citizens of Roscoff organized a series of dinners and every evening he was invited to a different house. Whether thanks to the country air or to the touching hospitality of the Bretons, his health improved noticeably and he was even able to complete his *Grand Dictionnaire de cuisine*, commissioned by Lemerre but planned by Dumas years previously. In the second of his two travel-books about Russia he had noted: 'Since I travel to inform myself, . . . whenever I come across a tasty dish I immediately ask for the recipe in order to add it to the cookery book which I intend to publish one of these days'[23]—a remark serving to introduce the description of a method of preparing mutton which turns out to be nothing other than the shish kebab so familiar to us today, but evidently unknown in the West in 1859.

His recovery of health and spirits was, unfortunately, purely temporary. As soon as he was back in his apartment in the Boulevard Malesherbes he relapsed into the same torpor as before and it now became bitterly apparent to him that the flame of inspiration which had burned so brightly for years and which he had thought would prove eternal, had flickered down to a pinpoint of light and would shortly be extinguished for ever. The thought plunged him into a deeper distress than any he had experienced, and Marie was appalled to hear him, in the small hours, weeping and groaning in his room.

In the spring of 1870, having begged Alexandre for a little money, he travelled down to Marseilles to take one last look round the city that held so many and such happy associations for him. He was still there when, on July 19th, France declared war on Prussia. The news of the disastrous defeats in the opening battles of the campaign brought on a mild stroke. Recovering, he struggled back to Paris, where Alexandre, fearing the city might be besieged or sacked, insisted he should join the rest of his family in the house at Puys, just outside Dieppe. Here, in a room overlooking the sea, he sat quietly waiting for the end, incapable of anything but an occasional game of dominoes with his two grandchildren, Colette and Jeannine. Incredibly, their father declined to allow a farewell visit from the ten-year-old Micaella, his half-sister. He coldly refused even to admit that she had any right to expect this, as the letter he wrote her at the time of his father's terminal illness proves (among other things):

Mademoiselle,
It is I who opened the three letters you have addressed to my father and which I felt I could not let him see, since you refer in them to his illness and we are trying to hide from him, as far as possible, the fact that he is ill. The affectionate name you give him proves that you love him as much as one can love anyone at your age, and that he used to feel affection for you. Indeed, I seem to

remember occasionally seeing you at his house when you were quite
small. I have decided to let you have news of him, since he cannot
do so himself. . . . It is natural, Mademoiselle, since you are fond of
my father, that I should do what I can to oblige you.[24]

Micaella learned of her father's death through a chance remark overheard at table in the Marseilles boarding-house where she was staying.
She burst into tears, to the astonishment and alarm of the other
residents.

One would like to think that the old man himself, as he sat in his
chair with a rug over his lap listening to the distant breakers, remembered her, and her mother too, whom he always associated with
the salt taste of the sea spray on her cheeks, and all the other women
whose lips he had pressed and whose bodies he had caressed, from
little Adèle Dalvin in Villers-Cotterêts to the athletic Adah Menken
from distant New Orleans; not forgetting, in particular, Mélanie
Waldor, who had certainly not forgotten him. Reading of his death,
some months after it had occurred, she wrote a dignified letter of
condolence to Alexandre in which she said, among other things: 'If
there was one man who was always kind and charitable, it was quite
certainly your father. Only his genius equalled his great goodness and
his constant desire to render service to others.'[25] This was perhaps
true, but it was none the less astonishing that it should have been
Mélanie Waldor who said it; the lady was, however, in her late
seventies, and time is a great healer.

Did his fading memory present him, too, pictures of the distant
lands he had visited, the Russian steppes, the Tunisian deserts, showing
him images of the Alhambra, the castles of the Rhine, the Jungfrau
glittering under its eternal snows, and the shimmering Mediterranean
he loved so dearly, with all the islands scattered over its blue expanse,
Stromboli, Pantelleria, Pianosa, Monte-Cristo? Monte-Cristo . . . and
there, perhaps, his wandering thoughts shifted again. He had lived in
two worlds, and lived as intensely in both of them as any man: the
world created by God for some immortal and incomprehensible
purpose, and the world he had created himself for his own pleasure
and that of his millions of readers. The first would endure after him;
but what of the other? One night he had a dream which troubled him
greatly and about which he spoke to Alexandre. He was standing on
the peak of a pyramid or mountain made up of all his books, piled like
blocks of masonry one on top of the other. Little by little, the ground
shifted, slithered, gave way beneath his feet, and what he had been
standing on revealed itself as nothing but a heap of pumice stones, the
grey ashes of a volcanic lava that had long cooled. 'Alexandre,' he
asked, 'on your soul and conscience, do you think anything of mine

will survive?'[26] Greatly moved, Alexandre reassured him, vehemently and, it must be said, with complete conviction. They embraced, and neither of them ever reverted to the subject.

Only a few days later, he had a further stroke and died at ten in the evening of December 5th, 1870. Paris had been under siege since September; the German armies were sweeping across France. On the very day Dumas was provisionally interred in the cemetery at Dieppe, Prussian troops entered the town. The streets were empty, the shutters were up at all the windows; hardly anyone other than members of the family attended the funeral. After the war, a reburial was arranged at Villers-Cotterêts, and on this occasion the mourners included a few representatives of the literary, dramatic, and artistic worlds, notably the veteran Baron Taylor, who had rendered Dumas such stalwart assistance forty years earlier when he was trying to get his first play accepted by the Comédie-Française. No doubt Hugo would have come, had he not been prevented. He sent a letter instead, famous for one phrase as grandiloquent as any Hugo ever penned, but rigorously true at the same time. 'The name of Alexandre Dumas is more than French, it is European; and it is more than European, it is universal.' By this he meant, perhaps, no more than that Dumas's following was world-wide. But the saying can be given another interpretation. Outside France there are thousands, perhaps millions, who on first reading one of Dumas's novels, translated into their own language, no more think of it as French than Dumas himself, when as a boy he first read *The Thousand and One Nights*, thought of it as Arabian or Persian. These books belong to world literature, in a way that none of the works of the great galaxy of French novelists in the nineteenth century, from Stendhal to Zola, can be said to, universally admired though they are. In his later years Francisque Sarcey, the theatre critic, liked to tell the story of the Spanish boy he was at boarding-school with in Paris and who started losing sleep and appetite, out of homesickness, as Sarcey thought. So he questioned him: did he miss his mother? No, she was dead. His brothers or sisters? No, he had none. Why was he pining, then, to return to Spain? Well, there was a book that he had started in the holidays but had to leave behind. 'And you can't wait to get back home to finish it, is that it? And what's the book called?' 'It's called *Los Tres Mosqueteros*.'

Notes

Except where otherwise indicated, references to Dumas's works are to the standard Calmann-Lévy edition in 301 volumes.

Chapter I. Roots

1 See William J. Eccles, *France in America* (New York, 1972), pp. 157–8.
2 Details given by Gilles Henry, *Monte-Cristo ou l'extraordinaire aventure des ancêtres d'Alexandre Dumas* (Paris, 1976), p. 27. This recently published work has greatly extended our knowledge of the Davy-Dumas family, for which earlier biographers have had to depend almost entirely on the sketchy and unreliable information provided by Dumas himself, who had only family tradition to go on.
3 Ibid., p. 90.
4 Though the units of measurement (feet and inches) were the same in pre-revolutionary France and England, they were not equivalent, a French foot equalling 324 millimetres, while the English foot measures only 304.8 millimetres. Thus Dumas's father must have been well over 6 feet tall.
5 Alexandre Dumas, *Mes Mémoires*, ed. Pierre Josserand (Paris, 1954–68), vol. I, p. 38. The writer was rather proud of having inherited these small feet which he passed on, it seems, to his own son.
6 Thomas's account of the affair, given in the written declaration he made to the police, is reproduced in Henry, *op. cit.*, pp. 105–6. The version he gave his son or wife years later, which can be read in Alexandre Dumas's memoirs, is much embellished: the incident is said to have occurred at the more fashionable Théâtre Montansier; Thomas said he flung his insulter bodily out of the box into the stalls and subsequently wounded him in a duel.
7 Letter originally published by Ernest Roch in the *Bulletin de la Société historique régionale de Villers-Cotterêts* (1906), pp. 91–2.
8 Paul Dermoncourt, whom Dumas attached to his staff in April 1796, had taken part in the capture and destruction of the Bastille. After that he had seen service in Dumas's native island of San-Domingo and, while attempting to reach the United States, had been captured by pirates operating from Bermuda. Set free, he sailed back to Europe to rejoin the army of the Republic. The stories he later related to Alexandre Dumas must be considered a main source of the chapters in *Mes Mémoires* dealing with his father's campaigns.
9 Dumas, *Mes Mémoires*, vol. I, p. 111.

Chapter II. Mother and Son

1 Dumas, *Mes Mémoires*, ed. P. Josserand, vol. I, p. 160.
2 A. V. Arnault, *Souvenirs d'un sexagénaire*, ed. Auguste Dietrich (Paris, 1908), vol. III, pp. 30–31. See also ibid., p. 305.

3 Stendhal, *Vie de Henry Brulard*, chapter IV.
4 Clearly Mme Dumas can only have been an agent in this plot. Henri
  Clouard (*Alexandre Dumas*, Paris, 1955, p. 25) speculates that the man
  who gave her the pistols and the money may have been the notary
  Mennesson, a notorious Bonapartist, who a little later became Alexandre
  Dumas's first employer.
5 Dumas introduced the story of his two brief encounters with Napoleon
  into at least three of his published works; each version differs from the
  others in a few details. The account given here is based on the earliest
  of the three redactions, which occurs in *Excursions sur les bords du Rhin*,
  vol. I, pp. 38–43. The other versions are to be found in *La Villa Palmiéri*,
  pp. 220–1 and 228–9, and *Mes Mémoires*, vol. I, pp. 301–4.

Chapter III. Buds of May

1 Dumas, *Mes Mémoires*, ed. P. Josserand, vol. I, p. 376.
2 Ibid., vol. II, p. 424.
3 Ibid., vol. I, p. 420.
4 Though Dumas says nothing about this play in his memoirs, the text has
  survived and is printed in the first volume of Fernande Bassan's edition of
  Dumas's *Théâtre complet* (Paris, 1974).
5 *Mes Mémoires*, vol. II, pp. 49–50.

Chapter IV. Bureaucracy versus the Theatre

1 Dumas narrated this scene in an article, 'Comment je devins auteur
  dramatique', published first in the *Revue des Deux Mondes*, December 20th,
  1833, then reprinted as the preface to his *Théâtre complet* (Paris, Charpentier,
  1834). With minor variants, the passage can also be found in *Mes Mémoires*,
  ed. P. Josserand, vol. II, p. 94.
2 £50 at the rate of exchange in 1823; equivalent to, say, £1,200 or £1,500
  today.
3 Dumas, *Mes Mémoires*, vol. II, p. 96.
4 Balzac, in his novel *Les Employés* (1837), paints a vivid and credible
  picture of the way of life of clerks in government administration in the
  first half of the nineteenth century. Whatever the hours they were
  required to put in, none of them regarded their job at the ministry as more
  than a part-time occupation.
5 *Mes Mémoires*, vol. II, pp. 147–8.
6 Dumas gets the date wrong in his memoirs (he writes that his eldest was
  born on July 29th) and, what is perhaps even more significant, he fails
  even to mention the mother; more probably out of shame than discretion.
7 *Mes Mémoires*, vol. II, p. 420.
8 Cf. *Mes Mémoires*, vol. III, p. 18: 'J'avais vu *Hamlet, Roméo, Shylock,
  Othello, Richard III, Macbeth*.'
9 Thus, Fernande Bassan cannot be right in dating Dumas's first viewing
  of this bas-relief by Mlle de Fauveau as 'vers le milieu de septembre 1827'
  (Dumas, *Théâtre complet*, Paris, 1975, vol. II, p. 11).
10 See Marie Mennessier-Nodier, *Charles Nodier: épisodes et souvenirs de sa vie*
  (Paris, 1867), pp. 291–7, for Marie's account of the confusion arising
  from this case of mistaken identity. When he came to write his memoirs,
  Dumas omitted all reference to these two visits, saying merely that he
  wrote Nodier a letter that remained unanswered.

11 *Mes Mémoires*, vol. III, p. 30.
12 This according to Samson himself: 'il n'y eut à cette lecture que Firmin et moi' (*Mémoires de Samson, de la Comédie-Française*, Paris, 1882, p. 260). In his own memoirs Dumas asserts that other members of the company, Michelot, Mlle Mars, and Mlle Leverd, were also present, besides his mother and Béranger.
13 Dumas, *Souvenirs dramatiques*, p. 236.
14 Charles Maurice, *Histoire anecdotique du théâtre* . . . (Paris, 1856), vol. I, p. 428. Maurice tells the story without stating directly that Dumas was the visitor Mlle Mars objected to, but the context and above all the date (1829) make the inference fairly clear.
15 Dumas, *Mes Mémoires*, vol. III, pp. 67–8.
16 See Charles Séchan, *Souvenirs d'un homme de théâtre* (Paris, 1883), p. 102.
17 *Mes Mémoires*, vol. III, p. 81.

Chapter V.   Don Juan on the Barricades

 1 Dumas's letters to Mélanie Waldor were originally bought back by his son from the lady's heirs (see H. Parigot, *Le Drame d'Alexandre Dumas*, Paris, 1898, p. 288, n. 4). They are now held in the manuscript department of the Bibliothèque Nationale (catalogued Nouvelles acquisitions françaises 24641).
 2 Dumas, *Mes Mémoires*, ed. P. Josserand, vol. III, p. 106.
 3 Arsène Houssaye, *Les Confessions: souvenirs d'un demi-siècle* (Paris, 1885), vol. IV, pp. 329–30.
 4 Théodore de Banville, *Les Camées parisiens, 2e série* (Paris, 1868), pp. 67–8.
 5 *Mes Mémoires*, vol. III, p. 228.
 6 Ibid., p. 276.
 7 Etienne Arago was an active member of the *carbonari*, a secret society pledged to social revolution; as proprietor of the Théâtre du Vaudeville, he distributed the firearms in its property store to the insurgents in July 1830. Today he is perhaps chiefly remembered for his initiative in introducing (in 1848) the French equivalent of the penny post.
 8 *Mes Mémoires*, vol. IV, pp. 113–14.
 9 B. N. Ms. Nouvelles acquisitions françaises 24641, fol. 313; quoted in F. Bassan & S. Chevalley, *Alexandre Dumas père et la Comédie-Française* (Paris, 1972), p. 48.
10 Girardin finally married Delphine Gay on June 1st, 1831, four weeks after the première of *Antony*.
11 'La salle était vraiment en délire; on applaudissait, on sanglotait, on pleurait, on criait' (Théophile Gautier, 'La reprise d'*Antony*', in *Histoire du romantisme*).
12 *Mes Mémoires*, vol. IV, p. 300. Gabriel Ferry records being shown the coat by Catherine Labay in her declining years; mistakenly, he supposes that it was at the première of *Henri III* that the garment was ripped to pieces. See his *Dernières années d'Alexandre Dumas* (Paris, 1883), p. 261.

Chapter VI.   Melodrama on and off the Stage

 1 Paul Huet (1803–1869), a landscape painter, had just recently come into prominence with his exhibits at the Salon of 1831.
 2 Dumas, *Mes Mémoires*, ed. P. Josserand, vol. IV, p. 346.
 3 Stendhal, *Correspondance*, ed. H. Martineau & V. Del Litto (Paris, 1967), vol. II, p. 881.

4 Alexandre Dumas *fils* related the incident in the preface to his play *Le Fils naturel* (*Théâtre complet*, Paris, 1868–98), vol. III, p. 19.

5 Quoted by Maurice Descotes, *Le Drame romantique et ses grands créateurs* (Paris, 1955), p. 230.

6 Beudin's collaborator, Prosper Goubaux, founded a private school using progressive educational methods, to which Dumas later sent his son (see below, pp. 108–9). Beudin and Goubaux normally used the composite pseudonym Dinaux to sign their plays.

7 'Je la fous par la fenêtre': Ernest Legouvé, *Soixante ans de souvenirs* (Paris, 1888), vol. III, p. 44.

8 Paul Foucher, *Les Coulisses du passé* (Paris, 1873), p. 453.

9 Musset had, at Harel's request, written a one-act play, *La Nuit vénitienne*, which was put on at the Odéon on December 1st, 1830. It was given only two performances, after which, nettled by the hostility of the critics and the unsympathetic reaction of the audience, Musset resolved in future to publish his plays but not to have them staged.

10 *Französische Zustände, Artikel VI* (Heine, *Sämtliche Werke*, Munich, 1972, vol. III, p. 147).

11 Fontaney, *Journal intime*, ed. R. Jasinski (Paris, 1925), p. 128.

12 Dumas, *Mes Mémoires*, vol. III, p. 21. Henri Blaze de Bury recalls seeing Dumas writing his plays in bed with one elbow propped on the pillow; see *Mes études et mes souvenirs* (Paris, 1885), p. 199.

13 Details given in Fernande Bassan, 'Histoire de *la Tour de Nesle* de Dumas père et Gaillardet', *Nineteenth-Century French Studies*, vol. III, nos. 1–2 (1974–5), pp. 40–57. The play is still occasionally seen; Mme Bassan notes a French television production broadcast on July 22nd, 1969.

14 Dumas, *Mes Mémoires*, vol. V, p. 259, and *Impressions de voyage en Suisse*, vol. I, p. 4.

Chapter VII. The Tourist

1 *A Hand-Book for Travellers in Switzerland and the Alps of Savoy and Piedmont* (London, 1838), p. xix.

2 See below, pp. 204–5.

3 Dumas, *Impressions de voyage en Suisse*, vol. II, p. 24.

4 Ibid., p. 179.

5 A case in point is his account, in chapter 38, of the destructive landslide at Rossberg in 1806. Dumas states he translated the story from a manuscript lent him by the daughter of an old peasant who had offered him hospitality. But Dumas knew no German. In fact, what he prints in the *Impressions de voyage en Suisse* is a slightly arranged version of an eye-witness account by Dr. Zay, of Arth, which he lifted from an earlier travel-book, Louis Simond's *Voyage en Suisse fait dans les années 1817, 1818 et 1819.*

6 Letter to Dumas (March 28th, 1854) quoted by Philibert Audebrand, *Petits mémoires du XIXe siècle*, Paris, 1892, p. 81.

7 Philibert Audebrand, *Romanciers et viveurs du XIXe siècle* (Paris, 1904), p. 269.

8 Dumas, *Mes Mémoires*, ed. P. Josserand, vol. V, pp. 266–7.

9 Dumas, *Le Speronare*, vol. II, p. 126.

10 Dumas, *Impressions de voyage en Suisse*, vol. III, p. 7.

11 Dumas spells the name Lesly. The Leslies (listed in John Bateman's

Great Landowners of Great Britain and Ireland) had their seat at Glaslough, co. Monaghan.

12 Dumas, *Impressions de voyage en Suisse*, vol. II, p. 232. 'Fifty years' is an exaggeration; thirty would have been more accurate. Chateaubriand's *René*, which was to influence so profoundly the development of French romanticism, was published in 1802.

13 See the notes made by Rigaud (first syndic of Geneva) of a conversation he had with Chateaubriand in 1831; quoted in M. J. Durry, *La Vieillesse de Chateaubriand* (Paris, 1933), vol. I, p. 66.

14 Dumas, *Impressions de voyage en Suisse*, vol. III, p. 146.

Chapter VIII.   Father and Husband

1 Anicet Bourgeois (1806–71), by his real name Auguste Anicet, a prolific writer of melodramas all of whose works were written in collaboration, sometimes with quite prominent dramatists like Labiche and Théodore Barrière. His greatest hit was *Latude ou Trente-cinq ans de captivité* (1834), done with the help of Pixerécourt.

2 Gautier, *Portraits contemporains. Littérateurs, peintres, sculpteurs, artistes dramatiques* (Paris, 1874), pp. 403–5.

3 *Angèle*, act I, sc. vi.

4 The story was told by Alexandre Dumas junior to Henry Blaze de Bury, who records it in *Mes études et mes souvenirs* (Paris, 1885), p. 12.

5 Marcel Thomas, 'Lettres inédites d'Alexandre Dumas père à son fils', *La Table Ronde*, May 1951, p. 85.

6 Countess Dash, *Mémoires des autres. Souvenirs anecdotiques sur mes contemporains* (Paris, 1897), p. 203.

7 Ibid., p. 205.

8 Dumas, *Le Corricolo*, vol. II, p. 299.

9 Gautier, *Histoire de l'art dramatique depuis vingt-cinq ans* (Paris, 1858), vol. I, p. 86.

10 *Mémoires de Samson, de la Comédie-Française* (Paris, 1882), p. 296. Viennet, recording his impression of the production, referred even more impolitely to 'a fat ball of grease called Ida who took the part of Stella' (*Journal de Viennet*, Paris, 1955, p. 217).

11 *Œuvres complètes de Mme Emile de Girardin, née Delphine Gay* (Paris, 1860), vol. IV, p. 235.

12 Félix Duquesnel, *Souvenirs littéraires* (Paris, 1922), p. 83.

13 The name was adopted not, as one might suppose, with reference to the meaning of the English word (Countess ——), but at the suggestion of a Russian princess who had a lapdog so called; see Henri de Villemessant, *Mémoires d'un journaliste*, vol. I, *Souvenirs de jeunesse* (Paris, 1867), p. 109. On the friendship between her and Alexandre Dumas *fils* while he was still a schoolboy, see Philibert Audebrand, *Alexandre Dumas à la Maison d'Or. Souvenirs de la vie littéraire* (Paris, 1888), p. 313.

14 Marcel Thomas, *loc. cit.*, p. 87.

15 This had occurred on August 1st, 1836.

16 Marcel Thomas, *loc. cit.*, p. 86.

17 Dumas *père* himself tells this story (*Causeries*, vol. I, p. 38).

18 Gustave Claudin, *Mes souvenirs. Les boulevards de 1840 à 1870* (Paris, 1884), p. 29.

19 *Lettres de Marceline Desbordes à Prosper Valmore*, ed. Boyer d'Agen (Paris 1924), vol. I, p. 280.

20 Horace de Viel-Castel, *Mémoires sur le règne de Napoléon III*, ed. P. Josserand (Paris, 1942), vol. I, pp. 194–5. However improbable this story, there is reason to suppose that Domange was one of Dumas's major creditors at this period; the arrangement, however, was that he should be reimbursed from Dumas's theatre royalties. Fiorentino tells how, attending the dress-rehearsal of *Mademoiselle de Belle-Isle*, Domange had the temerity to interrupt and suggest a different ending for one of the acts. Dumas rounded on him furiously, shouting: 'M. Domange, I don't touch your wares, don't you touch mine!' (*Comédies et comédiens*, Paris, 1866, vol. II, p. 357). The outburst, seeing that Domange's main business was the disposal of night-soil, provoked no little merriment.

21 Charles Glinel, *Alexandre Dumas et son oeuvre. Notes biographiques et bibliographiques* (Rheims, 1884), p. 366.

22 Xavier Marmier, *Journal (1848–1890)*, ed. Eldon Kaye (Geneva, 1968), vol. I, p. 365.

23 Dumas, *Mes Mémoires*, ed. P. Josserand, vol. IV, p. 134.

24 Roger de Beauvoir, *Profils et charges à la plume. Les soupeurs de mon temps* (Paris, 1868), p. xxv.

Chapter IX. The Novelist

1 There were two later ones, both produced by the Comédie-Française: *Un mariage sous Louis XV* (1841) and *Les Demoiselles de Saint-Cyr* (1843).

2 Dumas, *Le Capitaine Paul*, p. xli.

3 René Guise, 'Le Roman-feuilleton et la vulgarisation des idées politiques et sociales sous la Monarchie de Juillet', pp. 316–328 in *Romantisme et politique, 1815–1851: Colloque de l'Ecole Normale Supérieure de Saint-Cloud* (Paris, 1969).

4 Houssaye, *Les Comédiens sans le savoir* (Paris, 1886), p. 316.

5 P. A. Fiorentino, *Comédies et comédiens* (Paris, 1866), vol. II, p. 358.

6 Dumas, *En Caucase*, vol. III, pp. 134–5.

7 Dumas, *Mes Mémoires*, ed. P. Josserand, vol. II, p. 186.

8 'Il n'y a que des *tirets* qui puissent nous *tirer* de là': Benjamin Pifteau, *Alexandre Dumas en manches de chemises* (Paris, 1884), p. 61. Puns are, of course, untranslatable; I have done my best.

9 Nerval and Dumas shared in the composition of three dramatic works: *Piquillo*, a light opera with music by Hippolyte Monpou, produced at the Opéra-Comique in 1837; *L'Alchimiste*, a five-act drama based on Milman's *Fazio*, which the two men wrote when they were holidaying on the Rhine together (it was produced, rather unsuccessfully, at the Théâtre de la Renaissance in 1839); and *Léo Burckart*, first performed at the Porte-Saint-Martin, with Nerval alone being credited with its authorship, in 1839. On Nerval's probable share in the writing of the first two of these plays, see Alfred DuBruck, 'Nerval, collaborator of Dumas *père*', *Neuphilologische Mitteilungen*, vol. LXV (1964), pp. 481–93.

10 Henri de Villemessant, *Mémoires d'un journaliste*, vol. II. *Les Hommes de mon temps* (Paris, 1872), p. 239.

11 Dumas, *Mes Mémoires*, vol. IV, p. 360.

12 The most remarkable being, for an English (or Australian) reader, Lord de Winter's threat to have Milady transported to Botany Bay (chap. LII), which Captain Cook was not to discover for another 150 years.

13 *Le Comte de Monte-Cristo*, chap. XXXV.

14 *Mémoires tirés des archives de la police de Paris* . . . *depuis Louis XIV jusqu'à nos jours*, 6 vols., Paris, 1838.
15 *Le Comte de Monte-Cristo*, chap. XLVIII ('Idéologie').
16 Ibid., chap. CXI ('Expiation').
17 Ibid., chap. CXII ('Le Départ').

Chapter X.   The Triumphant Years

1   Henri de Villemessant, *Mémoires d'un journaliste*, vol. II. *Les Hommes de mon temps* (Paris, 1872), pp. 233–4.
2   Vicomtesse de Poillöüe de Saint-Mars, *Mémoires des autres par la Comtesse Dash. Souvenirs anecdotiques sur mes contemporains* (Paris, 1897), p. 191.
3   Villemessant, *op. cit.*, p. 235.
4   Houssaye, *Les Confessions. Souvenirs d'un demi-siècle* (Paris, 1885), vol. I, p. 268.
5   Dumas, *Mes Mémoires*, ed. P. Josserand, vol. III, p. 89.
6   'Sur ce carnet, Dumas écrit
                     Chaque jour, tout ce qu'il dépense;
                     Mais il n'y mettra pas, je pense,
                     Tout ce qu'il dépense d'esprit.'
    Beauvoir, *Profils et charges à la plume* (Paris, 1868), p. vii.
7   Perhaps the worst pun ever attributed to Dumas took the form of a comment he is alleged to have made after hearing the story of a young man surprised *in flagrante delicto* by his mistress's husband, who thrashed him so severely that he had to take to his bed. 'Comprend-on cela!' exclaimed the unfortunate young man's friend, who was relating the incident. 'Le mari revenir ainsi quand on le croyait si loin! C'est une fatalité!'—'Vous vous trompez de genre,' Dumas retorted; 'c'est simplement *un fat alité*.' (Benjamin Pifteau, *Alexandre Dumas en manches de chemise*, Paris, 1884, p. 64).
8   Dumas, *Mes Mémoires*, vol. II, p. 74.
9   Ibid., vol. III, p. 224.
10 Villemessant, *op. cit.*, p. 252.
11 Philibert Audebrand, *Alexandre Dumas à la Maison d'Or* (Paris, 1888), p. 46.
12 Villemessant, *op. cit.*, p. 253.
13 Anaïs de Bassanville, *Les Salons d'autrefois. Souvenirs intimes* (Paris, 1862–6), vol. III, p. 65.
14 Hugo, *Journal 1830–1848*, ed. Henri Guillemin (Paris, 1954), p. 243 (May 23rd, 1847).
15 Bassanville, *op. cit.*, p. 66.
16 Audebrand, *op. cit.*, p. 49.
17 Alphonse Karr, *Les Guêpes* (Paris, 1853), vol. I, p. 92.
18 Louis de Loménie, *Galerie des contemporains illustres* (Paris, 1842), vol. V, p. 34.
19 Charles Hugo, *Les Hommes de l'exil* (Paris, 1875), p. 99.
20 Charles Robin, *Galerie des Gens de lettres au XIXe siècle* (Paris, 1848), p. 257.
21 Dumas, *Causeries*, vol. I, p. 213.
22 E. &. J. de Goncourt, *Journal. Mémoires de la vie littéraire* ed. Robert Ricatte (Monaco, 1956), vol. I, p. 62.
23 Foucher, *Les Coulisses du passé* (Paris, 1873), p. 442.
24 Quoted in André Maurois, *Les Trois Dumas* (Paris, 1957), p. 166. The

writer's memory of the Old Testament story is at fault, of course: Abraham's barren wife was Sarah; Hagar, his handmaid, whom Sarah drove into the desert, had borne him Ishmael.

25 Horace de Viel-Castel, *Mémoires sur le règne de Napoléon III, 1851–1864*, ed. Pierre Josserand (Paris, 1942), vol. I, p. 131. The same anecdote, less the crudities, was related by W. A. Sollohub in his memoirs; see 'Mon Ami Dumas', *Revue des Deux Mondes*, 1 June 1953, pp. 512–13.

26 The story is told (no source given) in Hervé de Peslouan, *Mesdames Dumas père* (Paris, 1933), p. 224.

27 Dumas, *Causeries*, vol. I, pp. 37–8.

28 Ibid., pp. 192–3.

29 Dumas, *De Paris à Cadix*, vol. I, p. 20.

30 Hugo, *Journal 1830–1848*, ed. Henri Guillemin (Paris, 1954), p. 186.

31 Dumas, *De Paris à Cadix*, vol. I, pp. 36–7.

32 Ibid., vol. II, p. 110.

33 Ibid., vol. I, pp. 173–4.

34 Alfred-Auguste Cuvillier-Fleury, *Journal et correspondance intimes*, ed. Ernest Bertin (Paris, 1903), vol. II, p. 432.

35 Jules Janin, *Alexandre Dumas, mars 1871* (Paris, 1871), p. 23.

36 He may well have been the same 'négociant germano-anglo-indien fort aventureux, fort aimable, fort millionaire', Mr. Young, who hosted Dumas and his son on their visit to London in May 1857.

37 Dumas, *Le Véloce*, vol. I, p. 107.

38 Ibid., p. 290.

39 Ibid., vol. II, p. 294.

Chapter XI.   The Turbulent Years

1 Gozlan's article, 'Le Château de Monte-Cristo', was published in *L'Almanach comique* for 1848 and has been partially reproduced in Charles Glinel, *Alexandre Dumas et son oeuvre* (Rheims, 1884), pp. 407–12.

2 *Lettres à Madame Hanska*, ed. Roger Pierrot (Paris, 1967–71), vol. IV, p. 478. Balzac was, as so often, exaggerating. Dumas himself never admitted to spending more than 200,000 francs on 'Monte-Cristo'.

3 Philibert Audebrand, *Alexandre Dumas à la Maison d'Or* (Paris, 1888), p. 50.

4 Letter quoted in André Maurois, *Les Trois Dumas* (Paris, 1957), p. 231.

5 Dumas's biographers commonly give her surname as Constant; the spelling has been rectified by Josserand in his edition of Dumas's *Mes Mémoires*, vol. I, p. 11, n. 2.

6 B. N. Ms. Nouvelles acquisitions françaises 24641, fols. 16–17.

7 *Journal de Eugène Delacroix*, ed. André Joubin (Paris, 1932), vol. II, p. 328.

8 Ibid., p. 425.

9 He became a left-wing journalist, was active in the Commune and paid for this by being deported to New Caledonia. Repatriated in 1880, he developed an interest in the symbolist movement and devoted himself to popularizing the works of Wagner, Ibsen, and Henry Becque. His own son, Gérard Bauër (1888–1967), was also a writer (author of *Le Recensement de l'amour à Paris*) and was elected to membership of the Académie Goncourt in 1948.

10 Hippolyte Hostein, *Historiettes et souvenirs d'un homme de théâtre* (Paris, 1878), pp. 17–18.

11 Gautier, *Histoire de l'art dramatique* (Paris, 1858–9), vol. V, p. 41. Although

Géricault's famous picture does not show this, it was well known that the survivors of the wrecked *Medusa* resorted to cannibalism to stay alive.

12 *Journal de Victor de Balabine*, ed. Ernest Daudet (Paris, 1914), p. 288. Then as now, all tobacco products were a state monopoly in France.

13 This electoral manifesto, together with a number of others written by Dumas in 1848, has been reprinted in L. Henry Lecomte, *Alexandre Dumas, sa vie intime, ses oeuvres* (Paris, 1902), pp. 191–7.

14 Published originally in *Le Figaro*, it was reproduced by H. Blaze de Bury in *Mes études et mes souvenirs. Alexandre Dumas, sa vie, son temps, son oeuvre* (Paris, 1885), pp. 235–40.

15 Xavier Marmier, *Journal (1848–1890)*, ed. Eldon Kaye (Geneva, 1968), vol. I, p. 280.

16 This anecdote, related by Ernest d'Hauterive in an article in *Le Gaulois*, July 6th, 1902, has been reproduced in Henri Clouard, *Alexandre Dumas* (Paris, 1955), pp. 321–2. Another version, in which it was Porcher who had his loan so swiftly and unexpectedly returned to him, will be found in H. de Villemessant, *Mémoires d'un journaliste* (Paris, 1872), vol. II, p. 247.

17 Blaze de Bury, *op. cit.*, p. 111.

18 Houssaye, *Les Confessions. Souvenirs d'un demi-siècle* (Paris, 1885), vol. I, p. 267.

19 E. &. J. de Goncourt, *Journal. Mémoires de la vie littéraire* (Monaco, 1956), vol. XVIII, p. 15.

Chapter XII.   After the Crash

1 'Une soirée chez Alexandre Dumas à Bruxelles', pp. 217–33 in Deschanel, *A pied et en wagon*, Paris, 1862.

2 Letter quoted in H. Clouard, *Alexandre Dumas* (Paris, 1955), p. 383.

3 Letter quoted in A. Maurois, *Les Trois Dumas* (Paris, 1957), p. 268.

4 Charles Hugo, *Les Hommes de l'exil* (Paris, 1875), p. 85.

5 Philibert Audebrand, *Alexandre Dumas à la Maison d'Or* (Paris, 1888), p. 176.

6   'Dans leurs fastes impériales
                          L'Oncle et le Neveu sont égaux;
                          L'Oncle prenait des capitales,
                          Le Neveu prend nos capitaux.'

Quoted in Horace de Viel-Castel, *Mémoires sur le règne de Napoléon III*, ed. P. Josserand (Paris, 1942), vol. I, p. 176.

7 From a letter to Lord Clarendon (Foreign Secretary), quoted by gracious permission of Her Majesty The Queen: Royal Archives, Windsor Castle, Add. A29/2.

8 Quoted in John Charpentier, *Alexandre Dumas* (Paris, 1947), p. 177.

9 Ibid., p. 176.

10 See Dumas's 'prospectus' for *Le Mousquetaire*, quoted in Pierre Josserand's introduction to his edition of *Mes Mémoires*. In a letter dated December 23rd, 1851, printed in the first volume of the Belgian edition of *Mes Mémoires* (Brussels: Méline, Cans, 1852–6), Dumas complained that *La Presse* had made a number of unauthorized cuts in their *feuilleton* publication of his autobiography.

11 Audebrand, *op. cit.*, pp. 19–20.

12 E. &. J. de Goncourt, *Journal. Mémoires de la vie littéraire* (Monaco, 1956), vol. XVIII, p. 229.

Chapter XIII. The Restless Years

1 None of Dumas's biographers mentions this journey. The evidence for its dating is a reference in a text written in 1857 to 'mon premier voyage en Angleterre [qui] remonte à quelque chose comme vingt-quatre ans' (*Causeries*, vol. II, p. 187).

2 *Causeries*, vol. II, pp. 117–18.

3 Ibid., p. 197.

4 Ibid., p. 211.

5 Edmond About told this story in the course of the address he delivered at the unveiling of Gustave Doré's statue of Dumas in 1883; see Robert Gaillard, *Alexandre Dumas* (Paris, 1953), pp. 174–5.

6 'In Search of a Sequel to *Monte-Cristo*', in *On Board the 'Emma'* (London, 1929), pp. 55–6. (On the contents of this work, see below, chap. XIV, note 1.)

7 Dumas, *Voyage en Russie*, ed. Jacques Suffel (Paris, 1960), p. 613. This volume comprises an annotated reprint of *De Paris à Astrakhan*, the first of the two travel-books Dumas wrote about Russia, the second being entitled *Le Caucase*.

8 *Voyage en Russie*, p. 454.

9 Ibid., p. 414.

10 Ibid., p. 473.

11 Ibid., p. 239.

12 Dumas, *On Board the 'Emma'*, p. 68. A slightly different version of Dumas's engagement of Vasili and the journey the young man undertook to rejoin him can be found in *Le Caucase*, vol. III, pp. 253–90.

Chapter XIV. With the Redshirts

1 Dumas, *On Board the 'Emma'. Adventures with Garibaldi's 'Thousand' in Sicily* (London, 1929), p. 96. The book Dumas published in 1861 under the title *Les Garibaldiens: révolution de Sicile et de Naples* contained little more than half the material actually written on the subject of his involvement with Garibaldi's campaign of May–September 1860. *On Board the 'Emma'* is a translation made by R. S. Garnett from the manuscript of the complete work, which has not, so far, been published in the original French.

2 Dumas, *Le Caucase*, vol. II, p. 75.

3 Dumas, *Causeries*, vol. I, p. 267.

4 *Mémoires du Général Baron Thiébault*, ed. Fernand Calmettes (Paris, 1897), vol. II, p. 33.

5 *On Board the 'Emma'*, p. 36. Dumas's French biographers, with one accord, inform us that the *Emma* (which Dumas elsewhere calls 'this dream-bird, this swan from Liverpool') was built in Marseilles.

6 *On Board the 'Emma'*, pp. 37–8.

7 The work was serialized in *Le Siècle* and a first edition, bringing Garibaldi's life-story down to the year 1849, was issued by Michel Lévy later in 1860. In 1861 Méline, Dumas's Belgian publisher, brought out a fuller edition, amplified by the material written by Dumas at Genoa, which took the story down to present time. The authenticity of Dumas's *Mémoires de Garibaldi* has been convincingly established by Ferdinand Boyer who checked the text against that of Garibaldi's own *Memorie autobiografiche* (1888); see 'Alexandre Dumas historien de Garibaldi', *Rivista di Letterature Moderne e Comparate*, vol. XII (1959), pp. 279–86.

8 See above, p. 94.

9 Giuseppe Bandi, *I Mille. Da Genova a Capua* (Florence, 1903), pp. 201–2.

10 *On Board the 'Emma'*, p. 164.

11 Henri Rochefort, *Les Aventures de ma vie* (Paris, 1896–8), vol. I, pp. 211–12.

12 *On Board the 'Emma'*, p. 319.

13 Ibid., p. 232.

14 Ibid., p. 274.

15 This message, written in French, is reproduced in facsimile opposite p. 293 of *On Board the 'Emma'*.

16 See F. Boyer, 'Les Garibaldiens d'Alexandre Dumas: roman ou choses vues?', *Studi Francesi*, fasc. 10 (1960), p. 31.

17 On the circumstances in which Garibaldi received this letter and on his reactions to it, see G. M. Trevelyan, *Garibaldi and the Making of Italy* (London, 1911), pp. 149–50.

18 *On Board the 'Emma'*, p. 357.

19 Ibid., p. 377.

Chapter XV. The Last Fling

1 His tenure was limited to one year; see Artine Artinian, 'Alexandre Dumas, director of excavations and museums', *Romanic Review*, vol. XXVIII (1937), pp. 342–5.

2 Du Camp, *Souvenirs littéraires* (Paris, 1883), vol. II, pp. 183–4.

3 Letters quoted by F. Boyer, 'Alexandre Dumas à Naples avec Garibaldi en 1860', *Revue des Etudes Italiennes*, vol. VII (1960), pp. 318, 320.

4 Dumas's English-speaking readers had to wait until 1903 before a translation—cruelly abridged—was issued, under the title *The Lovely Lady Hamilton; or, The Beauty and the Glory*.

5 Mathilde Shaw, *Illustres et inconnus: souvenirs de ma vie* (Paris, 1906), p. 179.

6 Benjamin Pifteau, *Alexandre Dumas en manches de chemise* (Paris, 1884), p. 21.

7 Gabriel Ferry, *Les Dernières Années d'Alexandre Dumas, 1864–1870* (Paris, 1883), pp. 19–21.

8 Henri Clouard, *Alexandre Dumas* (Paris, 1955), p. 425.

9 Clement Scott, *The Drama of Yesterday and Today* (London, 1899), vol. I, p. 467.

10 Letter in a private collection, quoted by A. Maurois, *Les Trois Dumas* (Paris, 1957), p. 364.

11 Pifteau, *op. cit.*, pp. 62–3.

12 No doubt the third Marquess, secretary for India under the Derby administration of 1860, who inherited the title on his father's death in April 1868.

13 Félix Duquesnel, 'Alexandre Dumas intime. Le Cottage de Puys', *Le Temps*, September 20th, 1913; quoted in Maurois, *op. cit.*, p. 342.

14 Mathilde Shaw, *op. cit.*, p. 205.

15 John Bigelow, *Retrospections of an active life* (New York, 1909), vol. II, p. 215. The strains in Franco–American relations referred to here arose from Napoleon III's support of Maximilian, archduke of Austria, who had himself crowned Emperor of Mexico in 1862. This was regarded in Washington as a breach of the Monroe doctrine.

16 Bigelow, *op. cit.*, pp. 216–17.

17 Ibid., p. 227.

18 Quoted in Bernard Falk, *The Naked Lady. A biography of Adah Isaacs Menken* (London, 1952), pp. 64, 66.
19 Clouard, *op. cit.*, p. 427.
20 Quoted in Falk, *op. cit.*, p. 194.
21 Pifteau, *op. cit.*, p. 60. The other saying which has now become proverbial was 'Cherchez la femme' (in his drama *Les Mohicans de Paris*, act II, sc. iii).
22 Henri Blaze de Bury, *Mes études et mes souvenirs* (Paris, 1885), p. 205.
23 Dumas, *Le Caucase*, vol. I, p. 57.
24 B. N. Ms. Nouvelles acquisitions francaises 24642, fol. 66.
25 Quoted in Maurois, *op. cit.*, p. 370.
26 Blaze de Bury, *op. cit.*, p. 328.

Index

230 INDEX

PACHECO y Obes, Col. Melchor, 188
Palmerston, Henry John Temple, Viscount, 164
Parfait, Noël, 163, 166
Parfait, Paul, 186, 191
Parkings, Admiral, 194
Paul Jones, 115
Pearl, Cora (Eliza Crouch), 201
Petel, Pierre-Olinde, 203
Peuchet, Jacques, 126
Pichat, Amédée, 37
Pierson, Blanche, 200
Pifteau, Benjamin, 209
Pixerécourt, René-Charles Guilbert de, 38
Poe, Edgar Allen, 167
Poirson, Auguste, 48
Ponsard, François, 133-4
Porcher (theatre agent), 48, 115-16
Pradier, James, 160
Préault, Auguste, 160
Proust, Marcel, 17
Puccini, Giacomo, 164

Les Quarante-Cinq, 117

RACHEL, (Elisabeth Félix), 132, 200
Racine, Jean, 78, 135
Reade, Charles, 207
Récamier, Mme Jeanne-Françoise, 98
Reichstadt, duc de (Napoleon II), 98
Reid, Mayne, 167
La Reine Margot, 117, 151
Rémusat, Charles de, 49
Renan, Ernest, 193
Retou, Marie-Françoise-Elisabeth, 7
Retz, Cardinal de, 46
Richard Darlington, 79-81, 100, 103, 109, 175
Robespierre, Maximilien de, 10
Rochefort, Henri, 167, 191
Romano, Liborio, 194-5
Roqueplan, Nestor, 199
Rosny, J. H., 122
Rousseau, Jean-Jacques, 89, 156
Rousseau, Pierre-Joseph, 47-8, 122
Rowe, Nicholas, 50
Rusconi, (Dumas's factotum), 148-9

SAINT-MARS, Anne-Gabrielle de Poilloue de ('Countess Dash'), 109, 167
Saint-Simon, Louis de Rouvray, duc de, 8, 46
Sainte-Beuve, Charles-Augustin, 49, 124
Salisbury, Robert Arthur Gascoyne-Cecil, Marquess of, 202
Salvandy, Narcisse-Achille de, 141, 143
Samson, Joseph-Isidore, 54, 108, 150
Sand, George (Aurore Dudevant), 203
La San-Felice, 198
Sarcey, Francisque, 85, 212
Saussure, Horace de, 89
Schiller, Friedrich, 37, 40, 45, 55, 85, 89, 152
Schneider, Hortense, 201
Schoebel, Mathilde, 160-1, 199
Scholl, Aurélien, 167
Scott, Clement, 201
Scott, Walter, 38, 45, 79, 103, 122, 146
Scotti, Gen., 194
Scribe, Eugène, 38, 72, 73, 156
Scrivaneck, Céleste, 149
Sébastiani, Horace, 42
Seveste, Jules, 102
Seward, William, 205
Shakespeare, William, 37, 40, 45, 50-51, 114, 152, 172
Sheridan, Richard Brinsley, 50
Smithson, Harriet, 50
Soumet, Alexandre, 37, 45, 49, 134
Le Speronare, 185
Staël, Mme de (Germaine Necker), 36
Stendhal (Henri Beyle), 22, 49, 78, 90, 103
Sterne, Laurence, 90-91
Stevens, Alfred, 169
Stoddard, Charles Warren, 206, 208
Strindberg, August, 72
Sue, Eugène, 116, 153
Swinburne, Algernon Charles, 207
Syracuse, Leopold, Count of, 189